Doing Honest Work in College

Chicago Guides to Academic Life

The Chicago Guide to Your Career in Science
  Victor A. Bloomfield and Esam E. El-Fakahany

The Chicago Handbook for Teachers
  Alan Brinkley, Betty Dessants, Michael Flamm, and Cynthia Fleming

The Chicago Guide to Landing a Job in Academic Biology
  C. Ray Chandler, Lorne M. Wolfe, and Daniel E. L. Promislow

The Chicago Guide to Your Academic Career
  John A. Goldsmith, John Komlos, and Penny Schine Gold

How to Study
  Arthur W. Kornhauser

Succeeding as an International Student in the United States and Canada
  Charles Lipson

Doing Honest Work in College

. . . .

HOW TO PREPARE CITATIONS,

AVOID PLAGIARISM, AND ACHIEVE

REAL ACADEMIC SUCCESS

Second Edition

Charles Lipson

The University of Chicago Press CHICAGO AND LONDON

Charles Lipson

is professor and

director of

undergraduate

studies in political

science at the

University of

Chicago.

The University of Chicago Press, Chicago 60637
The University of Chicago Press, Ltd., London
© 2004, 2008 by Charles Lipson
All rights reserved. Published 2008
Printed in the United States of America

17 16 15 14 13 12 11 10 09 08   2 3 4 5

ISBN-13: 978-0-226-48476-1 (cloth)
ISBN-13: 978-0-226-48477-8 (paper)
ISBN-10: 0-226-48476-9 (cloth)
ISBN-10: 0-226-48477-7 (paper)

Library of Congress Cataloging-in-Publication Data
Lipson, Charles.
    Doing honest work in college: how to prepare
citations, avoid plagiarism, and achieve real
academic success / Charles Lipson. — 2nd ed.
        p.   cm. — (Chicago guides to academic life)
    Includes bibliographical references and index.
    ISBN-13: 978-0-226-48476-1 (cloth: alk. paper)
    ISBN-13: 978-0-226-48477-8 (pbk.: alk. paper)
    ISBN-10: 0-226-48476-9 (cloth: alk. paper)
    ISBN-10: 0-226-48477-7 (pbk.: alk. paper)
    1. Bibliographical citations. 2. Plagiarism. I. Title.
PN171.F56L56   2008
808'.027—dc22

                                    2007033551

♾ The paper used in this publication meets the
minimum requirements of the American National
Standard for Information Sciences—Permanence
of Paper for Printed Library Materials, ANSI
Z39.48-1992.

To the memory of

Dorothy Kohn Lipson

and Harry M. Lipson Jr.

Models of integrity

SIGNS OF THE TIMES:

Number of Wisconsin accounting students
given take-home tests to accommodate an Enron
whistle-blower's April speech: 78
Number later found to have cheated: 40
—"Harper's Index," *Harper's Magazine,* July 2003

Google search: "ethics paper"
Top two results: ready-to-use term papers on the topic
—Search on July 6, 2007

CONTENTS

. . . .

Academic Honesty

THE THREE PRINCIPLES
OF ACADEMIC HONESTY

• • • • • • • • • • • • • •

Academic honesty boils down to three simple but powerful principles:

- When you say you did the work yourself, you actually did it.
- When you rely on someone else's work, you cite it. When you use their words, you quote them openly and accurately, and you cite them, too.
- When you present research materials, you present them fairly and truthfully. That's true whether the research involves data, documents, or the writings of other scholars.

These are bedrock principles, easy to remember and follow. They apply to all your classes, labs, papers, and exams. They cover everything from English papers to chemistry experiments, from computer codes to architectural drawings. They apply to everyone in the university, from freshmen to professors. They're not just principles for students. They're principles for academic honesty across the entire university.

Of course, each university has its own code of conduct, and each class its own rules for specific assignments. In the next chapter, I'll discuss these detailed rules and explain how to follow them in papers, labs, study groups, and exams.

I'll also discuss how to use the Internet properly for assignments and show you how to cite Web pages, online articles, and blogs, as well as books, articles, poems, and films. With this brief book, you can avoid plagiarism and handle nearly every citation you'll ever do, from anthropology to astrophysics.

Speaking of sciences, what about honesty in study groups and labs? That can be confusing because you sometimes work with fellow students and sometimes by yourself. What exactly are you supposed to do on your own, without any help? I'll pass along useful advice from lab supervisors, who explain how to use study groups more effectively and how to avoid any problems.

On all these issues, I'll report on conversations with deans of students. They deal with academic honesty every day and know the issues well. Believe me, it's a lot better to read their advice here than to have them explain it to you privately! That is a meeting you do *not* want to have.

The most important advice is to *listen* to your professors' rules for each assignment, *ask* for clarification if you're unsure, and then *follow the three basic principles:* If you say you did this work, then you really did it. If you quoted others or used their research, you acknowledge it openly. If you say the data or lab experiment came out a particular way, then it really did. Never make up data, hide bad results, or steal others' work. Don't misrepresent your findings or anyone else's. Don't misrepresent their ideas, either.

If you follow this straightforward advice, you'll stay on the right side of your university's rules and meet the highest standards of academic integrity. Your grades will be honestly earned.

Now, let's get down to nuts and bolts.

2

ACADEMIC HONESTY
FROM YOUR FIRST CLASS
TO YOUR FINAL EXAM

· · · · · · · · · · · · · ·

What does it mean to do honest work in college? This chapter explores everyday issues and offers practical solutions, beginning with reading assignments and exams. From the first day of classes, you'll be required to read books, articles, and electronic documents, so it's important to know what's expected. It's also important to know what's expected in seminars and discussion sections, as well as specialized classes such as foreign languages. I'll cover all of those and offer concrete advice.

Within a few weeks, you'll be taking midterm exams. Whether they are in-class or take-home, all exams share one basic rule: You have to do your own work, without "borrowing" from others. But beyond that, the rules vary. I'll discuss these different rules and explain what to do if you're unsure about them.

Next, I'll turn to one of the most important tasks in college, writing papers. Research for these papers requires you to draw on others' work and combine it with your own ideas. That means taking clear notes and using quotes and citations properly. I'll explain that in this chapter and the next, showing how to take notes that clearly separate your words and ideas from another author's. I'll explain how to quote and paraphrase in your papers and how to cite the works you rely on, whether they're in print or on the Web.

Readings, exams, and papers are all individual assignments. Other assignments, however, require you to work closely with fellow students. In chemistry and biology, for example, you'll work alongside a lab partner. In math and statistics, you may join a study group. What are you supposed to do together? And what are you supposed to do separately? I'll explain.

I'll also explain what to do about a low grade. One thing you can always do is get advice about how to do better next time. Teachers *want* to help students, especially those who want to improve and are willing to work at it. You can also appeal if you think your paper was graded too harshly. To do that, though, you need to follow some basic guidelines. You can't change anything on the paper or exam, and you should offer a clear, sensible reason for the appeal. I'll explain that later in the chapter.

Finally, I'll discuss honor codes, which some colleges use to encourage honest work and personal responsibility.

The aim of this chapter, then, is to give you an overview of what it means to do honest work in college and take you step-by-step through the issues you'll confront. I'll discuss reading assignments, exams, papers, study groups, and labs, and I'll offer some suggestions about problems that occasionally crop up. I'll also pass along some tips about studying more effectively. All these ideas point toward a single goal: honest learning.

READING ASSIGNMENTS

From the first day of class, you'll get reading assignments. It's a mistake to skip the reading—but it's not cheating. Some students read summaries (such as CliffsNotes) to supplement their readings or even to substitute for them. As a supplement they're fine, if you think they help. As a substitute, they shortchange your education. But you aren't violating any academic rules.

> *Tip on reading more efficiently:* Don't sit down, open an article or nonfiction book to the first page, and try to read it straight through. It helps to get an overview first. Look at the introduction, conclusion, and table of contents. If it's an article, read the abstract and section headings. Then read the introduction and conclusion. You don't have to keep the ending secret. It's not a mystery novel. After this overview, you'll have a good sense of the overall work and can begin more detailed reading.

EXAMS

Exams come in two delicious flavors: in-class and take-home. Because the formats are different, so are the rules governing them. Let's consider each briefly.

In-Class Exams

Most in-class exams are "closed book." They don't allow you to consult any materials, including handwritten notes or data stored on your computer or PDA. You might be asked to bring your own blue books to an exam—blank ones, of course. Those are the default rules for in-class exams, and they are rarely changed. Stick to them unless you are explicitly told otherwise. If you are unsure about a particular exam, simply ask your professor.

Along the same lines, you should not have access to an exam before it is given. You may be able to guess what's on the exam, and it's fine to look at last year's or last semester's. But current exams are off-limits until you take them. It's cheating to pass the questions from this morning's exam to a friend who takes it this afternoon.

Occasionally, teachers give open-book exams in class. Students can use their notes, thumb through their books, and type answers on their computers during the test (though not prior to it). That certainly cuts down on dull work and rote memorization, but it doesn't make the tests any easier. Students still need to know the material well so they can write compelling answers and, if necessary, find essential information quickly.

In one legendary test, a teacher explained that his next exam would be open book and students could use "anything they can carry into class." One carried in a graduate student. I highly recommend this approach. It cuts down on needless studying.

Actually, you have to write your exams without any help. That's true whether they are open or closed book. No glances at other students' papers. No downloading precooked answers from the Internet or from your own hard drive. No text messages. No using others' words and ideas without proper quotes and citations. And, unfortunately, no carrying in graduate students, even very light ones.

> *Tip on in-class exams:* You can't use notes, books, articles, or electronic data when you write in-class exams, unless you are specifically told otherwise.

It's fine to study together before exams. Practicing answers is a great way to study—or, rather, it's great if you participate actively in the group. It doesn't help much if you just sit and listen. (That's one reason why small study groups are better than large ones.) Once you are inside the exam room, however, you are on your own. That's a central pillar of academic honesty.

Learn from Woody Allen's experience: "I was thrown out of NYU my freshman year for cheating on the metaphysics final. . . . I looked within the soul of the boy sitting next to me."[1]

Take-Home Exams

Take-home exams are usually open book. You are permitted to use books, articles, notes, and the Web. That's the standard policy, although it pays to check the rules for each exam.

Even if you are allowed to use published works and your own notes, you cannot ask others for help. That's cheating, just as it would be in class.

Similarly, if you incorporate ideas from books, articles, or the Web, you need to indicate that they are others' ideas. Even though it's an exam rather than a research paper, play it safe and cite any work you rely on. (Later, I'll show you exactly how to do that.) If it's a direct quote, enclose it in quotation marks and include a specific citation. If you've paraphrased something, use your own words, not a close imitation of the author's. And, of course, you still need to cite the original source.

Even with proper citations and quotes, the work has to be your own. You can't copy chunks of text off the Internet, drop them into your exam or research paper, pop in a citation or two, and call it your own. It's not. Cutting and pasting doesn't make it truly *your* exam or *your* paper. It's simply a patchwork quilt of others' work.

Actually, the rules are even more strict, for both exams and papers. You cannot copy as much as a single sentence—from the Web, a book, or anything else—*unless* you clearly mark it as a quote and cite it properly. Remember the basic principle: When you rely on someone else's work, you cite it; when you use their words, you quote them openly and accurately.

> *Tip on take-home exams:* You are usually permitted to use books, articles, notes, and the Web for take-home exams, although it always pays to check. What you can *never* do is copy answers or ask anyone for help. The exam is still yours alone to complete. Whatever sources you use, phrase the answers in your own words and cite the source. If you copy anything directly from these sources, place it in quotation marks and cite it.

---

1. The quote is from *Annie Hall*, DVD, directed by Woody Allen, written by Woody Allen and Marshall Brickman, MGM/UA Studios (1977; Santa Monica: MGM Home Video, 2003).

PAPERS

Paper assignments are almost always meant to be done individually. (Later, I'll discuss group assignments. For now, let's concentrate on individual work.) You need to do the reading, research, and writing by yourself and take responsibility for the results. It's great to talk about the project, and it's fine to consult teachers, writing tutors, and friends. Feel free to show them a draft version and get their feedback. But you need to do your own research, organize the paper, and write it yourself.

You will almost always utilize the work of others. That's essential to good research. You should read the best works and draw on them with a critical eye—sometimes agreeing, sometimes disagreeing. Learning to do that well is a major goal of higher education. It's one way you'll become a more thoughtful and informed person.

This is not the place to discuss how to write papers. My goal here is more limited. I simply want to say what it means to write papers honestly. That's really very simple. First, whenever you rely on the work of anyone else, cite it so your readers know. That's true whether you agree or disagree with the cited works. If you use anyone else's ideas, include a citation. If you use their exact words, use quotation marks *and* a citation.

Second, whenever you quote someone directly, use quotation marks. Longer quotes, running more than a few sentences, are indented rather than enclosed with quotation marks, but the principle is the same. Readers will understand this block indent is a quotation:

> Fourscore and seven years ago our fathers brought forth on this continent, a new nation, conceived in Liberty, and dedicated to the proposition that all men are created equal.
>
> Now we are engaged in a great civil war, testing whether that nation, or any nation so conceived and so dedicated, can long endure.[2]

No one will ever think you meant to plagiarize the Gettysburg Address. Still, you need to cite it. Citations are especially important when your sources are obscure or controversial. You must show readers exactly which sources you used, whether they're for data, analysis, or direct quotes.

---

2. Abraham Lincoln, Gettysburg Address, November 19, 1863, reprinted in Gary Wills, *Lincoln at Gettysburg: The Words That Remade America* (New York: Simon and Schuster, 1992), app. I, pp. 202–3 and app. III D 2, p. 263.

To put it a little differently, your references (or their absence) shouldn't mislead readers. Use them to strengthen your analysis and amplify your ideas, never as a substitute for doing your own work.

One more important point about papers: you cannot hand in the same paper to more than one class. That's also true for homework assignments. If you write a paper on the Great Depression for an economics class, you can't turn it in to an American history class, too. You have to write another paper. You're not allowed to plagiarize your own work. You are still welcome to write about the Great Depression and even to rely on some of the same books and articles, but the paper itself should be substantially different. (If you *really* want to expand on an earlier paper, explain that to your current teacher and get approval. If you want to turn in the same paper to two current classes, talk to both teachers and get their approval.)

Tips on writing honest papers:

- Cite others' work whenever you rely on it.
- When you use someone's words, quote them accurately, mark them as a quotation, and include a citation.
- When you paraphrase, use your own distinctive voice, not a facsimile of the author's. Be sure to include a citation.
- Never represent anyone else's work as your own.
- Never hand in the same paper to two classes unless you have permission from both instructors.
- Never buy, sell, or "borrow" papers. Do your own work.

In the next chapter, I'll expand on how to write papers honestly. But these are the key ideas: do the work yourself, quote accurately, cite the work you use and the ideas you draw upon, and present all materials fairly.

Buying Papers on the Internet
Don't.

It's dishonest to buy (or sell!) papers. For that matter, it's dishonest to turn in papers you have lifted from friends, downloaded from the Internet, or cut-and-pasted from two or three sources. It doesn't matter whether your friends gave you permission or whether the information is freely available on the Web. It is dishonest to represent anyone else's work as your own. It's just as dishonest to provide your work to others.

This kind of cheating is often caught. Professors have seen lots of papers, and they have developed good antennae to pick up dishonest ones. There are usually telltale signs. Some papers just don't sound like a particular student. Others don't quite address the assignment. Occasionally, the introduction doesn't sound like the conclusion. For example, a paper might begin: "It's for sure America will sign to this international treaty." Then it might conclude, without quotation marks: "Having ratified this pact with such lofty ideals and soaring hopes, America will soon confront its harsh realities." The writer who fumbled through the first sentence could not have written the last one. Someone else did, and the student copied it. Still other papers include obvious signs of cheating such as antiquated citations or out-of-date references. "President Lincoln will probably defeat the Confederacy and win reelection." I'm betting he will. I just hope he doesn't go to the theater.

Faculty have also become more sophisticated about detecting fraud via the Internet. Although it's easy to cheat using the Web, it's easy to catch cheating the same way. Faculty simply select some text from a questionable student paper and do a Google search for it. They can also use computer services that now work with universities to detect plagiarism and cheating. These services compare newly submitted student papers to everything in their databases, which include thousands of previously submitted student papers, all publicly available Web sites, and nearly all published articles. They automatically flag sentences in new papers matching those in the database. Then each newly submitted paper, honest or not, becomes part of this ever-expanding database.

This may sound like a cat-and-mouse game, but it's not. It's about honest work, personal integrity, and real learning. Buying papers is cheating. Universities take it seriously with good reason. It's a direct assault on honest learning. Equally important, it's a self-inflicted wound on your own education.

USING THE INTERNET FOR RESEARCH

The Web has become integral to academic work. It's the fastest way to scan lots of sources, compare authors, gain access to specialized materials, and much more. It's a great research tool and an easy way to grab some quick facts. When did women get the vote in America? Does India have more people than China? How many miles, roughly, is the Indianapolis 500?

When you use the Internet, just remember a few basic points. One is that the quality of information varies widely. Anybody with a Web site or blog can say whatever they want. There's no quality control. If the *Encyclopaedia Britannica* Web site says D-day was June 6, 1944, you can count on it. If the *Encyclopedia Brittany* says it was April 1, 1984, check somewhere else. You need to use solid sources, and, even then, you may want to cross-check them. If you're unsure which sources to use, ask your professor or a reference librarian for guidance. They know the literature and can help.

Second, Web research allows you to zero in on a topic, but it sometimes strips away the context. The context may be essential, however, for you to understand the topic and explore its significance. If you search for "Iraq War + 2008," for instance, you'll get thousands of hits on the war itself, but you may not learn much about its setting in American politics or its implications throughout the Middle East. If that's important to you, you'll need to refocus your online search.

Third, it's soooo easy to drag-and-drop information from the Web into your computer. That's great for taking notes, but it can easily become great trouble. Since you already know the value of Internet research, let me mention a couple of potential problems so you can avoid them. One is that it's often easier to copy information than to read or understand it. (That's true of photocopying, too.) Another is that it invites cheating. Just drop a paragraph or two from someone's article into your paper. Unless you quote and cite it, however, you're plagiarizing. Finally, even if you are not trying to cheat, it's easy to lose track of what you copied and what you actually wrote yourself.

How should you handle these problems? First, you need to screen your sources of information. Some, like electronic journals, publish only high-quality articles, evaluated by professionals in their field. They reject papers that fall short of their standards. At the other extreme are Web sites run by the same people who write e-mails explaining that their father was a corrupt Nigerian millionaire and that they will generously share his fortune with you, if you would please send them your bank account and credit card numbers.

There are no gatekeepers online, no global editors to guarantee the quality of information. You have to judge it yourself. You have to determine which Web sites are reliable and which ones aren't.

Second, you need to decide if the wider context is important for understanding your topic. If it is, then you'll need to expand the scope of your research. On the Web, you'll probably want to search for additional text strings (for example, "Iraq war + polling" or "Iraq war + Saudi") and follow hyperlinks to background readings. To provide the political, social, and historical setting, you'll want to read significant articles and books. That's not always necessary, but for some issues it's crucial. To hit the bull's-eye, it helps to see the surrounding circles.

Third, don't drag-and-drop too much from the Web into your notes. It's hard to keep straight just who wrote what, and it invites trouble. When you do drag-and-drop some material, it's important to have a consistent system to mark someone else's words and ideas and where they came from. You need to identify the source page, first in your notes and later in your papers. Also, once you begin writing and drawing on your notes, you need a way to keep your words separate from those you've copied. In the next chapter, I'll describe a simple method for doing that—a way that works with quotations from books, articles, and electronic sources. Just put the letter Q at the beginning and end of any quoted materials. It works well because it's simple and stands out clearly in your notes. It's equally effective in your handwritten notes.

When you copy something from a Web site, be sure to copy the URL so you can cite it later. It's a good idea to write down the date you accessed it, too. Some citation styles require it, mainly because Internet content changes so often. If you use professional databases like Medline or Math-SciNet, jot down the document ID number (DOI) so you can add it to citations or return easily for more research.

Tips on Web research:

- Screen the quality of information you get off the Internet.
- Move beyond your targeted search and look for background materials to provide essential context. That means reading books and articles as well as Web content.
- Don't drag-and-drop too much into your notes. Summarize the information in your own words.
- Have a clear system, such as Q-quotes, to mark any material you drag-and-drop.
- Be sure to write down the URL of Web pages you use and the date you accessed them so you can cite them later. It's also a time-saver if you need to go back to the site. That's true for database identification numbers, too. Be sure to write them down.

LANGUAGE CLASSES

Learning a foreign language is one of the most common college experiences. Fortunately, it presents very few difficulties for doing honest work. The rules are straightforward and familiar. You can't copy homework or exams from anyone—from classmates, answer books, or published translations. You can't use computer-assisted translations, either. You know the basic principle: When you say you did the work yourself, you actually did it. That's as true for classes in Mandarin as it is for classes in Chinese art or history.

What about using a Chinese-English dictionary? Rules vary from teacher to teacher, and sometimes from assignment to assignment. You can generally use dictionaries for take-home work. They may help you learn new words and remind you of old ones. On the other hand, some teachers don't permit them for in-class quizzes and translations since they want you to master the vocabulary. One student passed along an important practical point, based on her classes in Arabic. Although she was allowed to use dictionaries for all her assignments, the translations in class "were generally timed, so thumbing through dictionaries was a disadvantage."[3] If you use dictionaries, then use them mainly as aids to learning vocabulary. You'll eventually need to know that anyway.

Beyond these basic issues, it's important to know how honest work actually helps you learn a foreign language.

"My goal," said one Italian professor, "is to help students become good listeners, good readers, and spontaneous speakers and writers." For classical languages, the goal is to read easily and translate accurately. Whatever the language, you'll master it only with practice. That means repeating oral exercises, listening to conversations, working on grammar and vocabulary, and writing translations. Homework exercises are designed to guide you along this path by immersing you in the language and gradually building on what you've already covered. Besides giving you practice, the exercises allow you to learn from your mistakes. "Mistakes are actually quite important," one professor told me. "Correcting them is how you learn the language."

---

3. Some students need more time for other important reasons. Some have learning disabilities, and others are still mastering English. If you need more time for an exam or an assignment, speak with your teacher *in advance* and explain your situation. You may be asked to provide a letter documenting your needs.

That's why it undercuts learning simply to copy the answers instead of working on the assignments. (It's obvious to teachers, too, according to everyone I spoke with.) To learn, you need to practice. It will give you an easy familiarity with what you already know and a chance to identify and correct mistakes. Remember that the goal is not simply to translate a few paragraphs correctly. The goal is to understand the language, to grasp the general rules of Spanish, Russian, or Japanese, and to learn how they apply to specific words and sentences.

Can you ever use published translations or answer keys? Yes, occasionally, if your teacher doesn't mind. But use them *only* to double-check your work or solve a sticky problem. "Don't use them until you've already wrestled with the problem yourself," one Latin professor explained. "Then, you can turn to a published translation to check your work or get past a rough spot." In other words, use prepared translations for self-guided teaching, not as substitutes for doing your own work.

Faculty in physics, chemistry, math, and economics told me exactly the same thing about answer books in their fields. As a way to check your work, they can serve as silent teachers. As a way to avoid work, they are dishonest and self-defeating.

> *Tip for all classes:* Don't use answer keys, published translations, or work by others as substitutes for doing your own work. You can use them occasionally, if your teacher approves, as guides to help you learn—to check your work, for example, or to overcome specific obstacles.

GROUP ASSIGNMENTS

While most class assignments are meant to be done individually, some are designed for small groups. Your professor may assemble these groups, or you may form your own. "I tell my students that this is an extremely efficient way to study," one scientist explained to me. "By looking for questions that will show up on the exam, students end up looking at the material differently. Three or four folks working together will put slightly different emphases on the information, and [they] may even have taken different notes."

When you work in small groups, it's important to know the professor's rules. They vary across classes and assignments, and that variation matters for doing honest work. Sometimes you are asked to study together but then to produce your own individual written work. Sometimes you are asked to produce a joint paper or group presentation. Sometimes you are simply encouraged to study together with no written assignment. It's important to know which one applies to your group and to your assignment. When in doubt, ask.

> *Tips on group assignments:* Know what the professor expects. What is to be done by the group, and what is to be done individually? If you are unsure, ask before doing the work. If one member of the group doesn't do his share, speak privately with the student first and then with the professor.

If the assignment is to study as a group and then turn in individual papers, it violates the rules to incorporate other students' work directly into yours. Talk with them, learn from them, but don't share their writing and don't copy their ideas word-for-word. "Shared writing like this will be obvious," one professor told me.

On the other hand, you may be asked to prepare a true group assignment, such as a class presentation. Encourage everyone in the group to pitch in and work honestly. When the group presents its work, give everyone credit. Working well in groups like this is rewarding in its own right. "It's good practice for the rest of [students'] lives," one scientist pointed out, "since so much of what we do is in collaboration with others." The downside is that you may also get some practice dealing with someone who doesn't pull a fair share of the load. If someone doesn't participate, or might be cheating, first speak privately with that student and then, if necessary, with the professor.

All this advice applies to group assignments. Of course, if the assignment is given to you individually, rather than as part of a group, you have to do it individually. That's true even if you study with a group. You can discuss the assignment with group members or other friends—in person, by e-mail, or in Internet chat rooms. It's fine to toss around ideas, but it's cheating to swap actual answers and submit them as your own. You have to write the assignment . . . by yourself, in your own words.

What counts as "too much cooperation" for assignments given to you individually? That differs from subject to subject and sometimes from professor to professor. Nearly all professors encourage general discussion. What they prohibit is more detailed help, unless it's a group assignment.

Take an individual assignment to write a computer program. You need to write, edit, and debug the software yourself. You need to warrant how well it works and what the problems are. That's the heart of the assignment, and it needs to be done alone, without help. There may be some gray areas about giving or receiving minor assistance, such as checking the program's syntax. Some professors encourage it; some don't allow it. All you need to do is ask. In fact, that's the best advice I can give, whether you're taking a class in computer programming, macroeconomics, or cell biology. Ask your professor what work you can do jointly and what you must do alone.

Problem Sets as Group Activities

The most common group task is to work together on problem sets. Teachers in math, economics, statistics, and the sciences encourage it, and for good reason. It's a great way to learn.

To avoid any suspicion of cheating, however, it's important to know your professor's rules about doing problem sets. What's perfectly fine for one teacher or one assignment may not be fine for another. You may be encouraged to write answers together, as a group. Or you may be explicitly told not to. There's nothing right or wrong about these varied assignments. They're just different, the same way open- and closed-book exams are different. Listen carefully to the rules governing each problem set, ask for clarification if you are unsure, and then respect the rules you are given.

There are really two issues here. One is avoiding dishonesty. If your name stands alone on a paper, it means you solved the problems yourself. You can consult others in the group—that's why it was formed—but you must do all the written work yourself. On the other hand, if you are listed as coauthor of a group paper, then you participated in the joint work.

Tip on authorship: If your name is alone on a paper, it means you did the work entirely yourself. If you are listed as a coauthor, you contributed to the group's work.

The other issue is how best to learn from group activity. This is not usually a question of cheating (although the lines are sometimes fuzzy), but it is important to your education. If there are four students in the group and four problem sets to do, the temptation is to divide the assignment. Even if your teacher permits the group to parcel out work this way, it still may not be the best way to learn. After all, you can't take exams that way, by passing the hard questions over to friends in the study group. That's why you need to learn how to think about the questions and solve the problems—all of them, not just 25 percent.

It's not enough just to "get the answers." That's why simply copying them cheats your own education. The goal of learning is not only finding answers but finding the best *paths* to answers. It's about the journey, as well as the destination. Problem sets are tools for finding these paths, or finding out if you've lost your way. It's a lot better to discover that on practice problems than on high-stakes exams.

That's why it's usually best if each group member does *all* the problem sets individually. Then you can go over some or all of them with the group, check each other's work, suggest corrections, and learn together. You'll know the material much better when it comes time to write papers and exams.

> *Tip on problem sets as group activities:* When you do problem sets as a joint activity, each person should do the entire assignment individually and then go over it with the group. That's not a rule about honesty; it's a tip about how to learn.

What if you don't understand how some problems are solved? What if you're unsure about the right methods to use? Then it's fine to ask others to explain them, whether they're in your group or not. Before you ask for help, though, try to work out the solutions yourself. If you are still puzzled, go over the questions as often as you wish with friends, roommates, professors, tutors, TAs, and members of your study group. Focus on *how to solve problems,* rather than on the solutions themselves. Try to diagnose exactly where you are having difficulty. When you understand the right methods, you'll be able to solve the problems yourself. You'll be able to explain *why* you chose one technique or solution rather than another. In fact, that's a good test of whether you really understand the solution.

This advice applies to foreign languages as well as math, science, and economics. "Based on my own experience teaching introductory Latin," one professor explained, "it can sometimes be useful for students to consult each other on a particularly tough assignment or tough patch." But don't consult others, he said, "until you've already tackled the problem

Tips on how to set up an effective study group of your own: You can learn a lot if you study with the right people in the right setting. With the wrong people in a noisy place, though, you'll simply waste time. Here are some tips, based on conversations with experienced undergraduates:

- Study with one to three other students. Larger groups spend too much time chatting. That's fun, but it's not studying.
- Work together in a quiet place, where you can talk without bothering others. The library may have some rooms for study groups. Or there may be a coffee shop near campus that's not too crowded. Do not study together in a dorm room; there are too many distractions. (Speaking of distractions, shut off your cell phone.)
- Set a specific time to begin and end the session. Make sure everybody knows you will begin on time. Most sessions last about sixty to ninety minutes, perhaps a little longer when you are studying for finals. Setting a time to end the session will push you to work efficiently.
- Pick specific topics in advance to discuss and make sure everybody studies the same thing beforehand. Do not parcel out the work you'll discuss, with some people studying one thing and some another. Hypothetically, that seems efficient. In practice, it doesn't work. If there is a study guide, decide in advance which part you'll discuss. If there are ten assigned problems and you only want to discuss half, make sure everybody does the same odd (or even) ones.
- Select people you'll enjoy working with.
  - They should be at about your academic level, so you can keep up with them, and they can keep up with you. That way, you can teach each other, and it won't be a one-way street.
  - Choose people who want to work and will contribute to the group. Avoid those who don't study for class and just want a free ride. Again, you want a two-way street for mutual teaching and learning.

How do you select the right study partners? One student told me his approach. "I try to pick other students who always come to class and show up on time instead of fifteen minutes late. I like those who say something valuable in class instead of just trying to impress the teacher. They'll have something to say in the study group, too." Excellent advice.

yourself." If the help you receive is extensive or crucial, he suggested acknowledging it in the written assignment. That's not required, but it's a good idea for a couple of reasons. It eliminates any confusion about who did what work and, just as important, it lets your teacher know exactly which issues are troublesome and need more instruction. If they are hard for you, they are probably hard for your classmates, too.

As you learn together, don't cross the line and copy down answers directly from someone else and hand them in as your own work (unless you are specifically allowed to coauthor assignments and include others' names on the paper). The same standards apply to copying from answer books or old problem sets. If your name stands alone on the paper, then you must write all the answers yourself, in your own words. Discuss. Contribute. Learn from friends or your study group. Feel free to ask for help again and again. Then do your own work. That's the best way to learn.

At the Blackboard with Your Study Group

The most inviting time to copy answers is when everyone works together at the blackboard. After one student solves a physics or engineering problem, it's easy for everyone else to scribble down the answer. "Most teachers consider this cheating," the head of one math program told me, "and we can easily spot identical work like this."

There's a better approach and a more honest one, she explained. Work through the problems—individually and collectively—and make sure everyone understands them. Then *erase the solutions on the blackboard* and let everyone do the work individually. Reworking the solutions for yourself is not useless "make work." It's useful practice and genuine learning.

That's true even if the person writing answers on the blackboard is the teaching assistant for your section. It's not cheating to copy the TA's answers. After all, they are written out for the whole class. But you won't learn much by rote copying. The goal is to understand the process and master the technique, not repeat the answers mechanically. If the TA skips over these key elements or if you still don't understand, be sure to ask.

Final Thoughts on Group Learning

One scientist summarized his advice on group work like this, "I generally want the students to figure out *how* to solve the problem together. The actual solution should be done individually. The point [of solving problems individually] is to give each student practice with skills that can only be acquired by doing them." To see if you've actually acquired these skills, try to defend your answer to the group or even to yourself. *Why* is this answer the right one? *How* exactly did you reach it? Be sure you can answer these questions.

Time and again, teachers mentioned the importance of participating actively in group sessions. "You can't really learn in groups if you're passive," one physicist told me. "After all, it's not about getting the answers to specific questions. It's really about understanding the process, learning how to answer hard questions." You can learn that in groups, but only if you join in. First, work together to master the process; then solve the problems yourself. If you're still stumped, ask for help. Then try again— on your own.

That's probably the best approach even if your teacher permits joint written work. Students who simply copy the answers might not understand them. *Their learning gaps will show up later on exams, papers, and more advanced work.*

Tips on how to use study groups:

- Be active, not passive, in study groups.
- Learn how to answer questions and how to think about problems, rather than what the specific answers are. Once you truly understand the process, you'll be able to answer the questions yourself—on homework, papers, and exams—and you'll be able to defend the answers you've got.

That's also why published answer manuals can impede learning. They're easy to buy and provide ready solutions to problem sets in major textbooks. Some teachers think it's okay to use them; others don't. In any case, it's not a good idea to lean too heavily on them. As a quick way to check your answers, they can be a useful source of feedback. As a substitute for doing the work, they short-circuit your education. Just remember how we all learned to ride bicycles. Eventually, the training wheels had to come off.

These manuals also raise the crucial issue of honest work. If you copy the answers from a book, you're cheating. It's the same as copying answers from another student or downloading them from the Web. It's simply not your own work.

Tips on honesty in group assignments: In some classes, you work with study groups but are expected to complete assignments individually (rather than hand in joint projects). It's vital to know what you can and cannot do together. A few pointers:

- Know your professor's expectations for group work *before you hand in your work.* What should the group do together and what should be done individually?
- It's fine for the group to discuss problem sets, class topics, and so forth. It's fine to ask others to explain methods and solutions you don't understand. Together, you can go over the problems several times until you understand.
- But it's cheating for others to provide answers to you—on paper, on the blackboard, or in a printed answer manual—and for you to copy them and turn them in as your own individual work. It's also a terrible way to learn and will come back to bite you on exams and in more advanced work.

Once you understand the material, you should write your own answers, in your own words.

LABS

The most common group assignments, aside from problem sets, are science labs. Together with your lab partner, you calibrate instruments, perform experiments, collect data, clean up explosions, and call the fire department. Better yet, you can follow safety procedures. After doing all this activity together, however, you should write your lab reports separately and reach your own conclusions.

The rules here are straightforward. Do the lab experiments jointly (if that's the assignment), but keep your own personal lab notes and write your own reports. *Never* borrow data or written work without your professor's explicit permission.

Accurate Lab Notes

Whenever you do lab work, keep accurate records of both your procedures and results. Different laboratories do this in different ways. Some use traditional lab notebooks; others use computers; and still others use

Tip on working with lab partners: It's fine to do lab work together with your partners, but you should keep your own lab notes and write up the results individually.

questionnaires designed for specific experiments. Whichever method you use, write down the results as soon as possible. Don't trust your memory. Don't fudge the results. And don't use anyone else's data without your teacher's permission.

Teachers *do* sometimes give permission to use others' data. If an experiment misfires, for example, your instructor may give you other results to evaluate. Or she may provide some data to the entire class. The reason is simple: labs are designed to teach you how to analyze data as well as how to conduct experiments. But unless your instructor allows you to use other data, stick with your own.

Traditionally, scientists record their results in special notebooks—bound volumes with numbered pages—which are tailor-made for the purpose. It's hard to cover up mistakes using lab books like this. That's the point. "Never use Wite-Out or rip pages from a lab notebook," one chemistry professor told me. "That's one reason the notebooks have numbered pages. If you make an error, cross it out neatly and continue documenting your observations and results."

Tips on lab records:

- Check with your instructor (or head of your lab) about record keeping. You may be asked to use lab notebooks, computers, or packets designed for specific experiments.
- Enter data as soon as possible after an experiment. Don't rely on your memory.
- Record even your experimental mistakes. Later, after performing the experiment correctly, neatly cross out the errors in your lab notebook. Don't rip out pages or use correction fluid. The original data should still be readable. If you record data on computers instead of notebooks, label the old data "incorrect" (or use a strike-through font) but don't wipe it out. With some help from your instructors, you may be able to learn from these mistakes.

Why should you save your mistakes? "Because your observations and procedures are just as important as your results," one scientist emphasized to me. "If you record your procedures and results accurately, your teachers can help you figure out the problems, if there are any." That's exactly what math and physics professors say about showing your work. It shows them how you think about a problem. If any difficulties crop up, it helps you pin them down.

Today, most labs have replaced notebooks with computers, equipped with software for data analysis. The technologies may change, but the rules for entering data remain the same.

- Do it as soon as possible after the experiment.
- Record your results accurately, even if the experiment failed.
- When you repeat an experiment, don't erase the old data. Label it as "incorrect," but keep it so you can check what went wrong, or perhaps discover it was okay after all.
- Use only your own data, unless you are explicitly told otherwise.

Then write up the conclusions on your own.

Honest Data

The crux of honest lab work is the truthful presentation of experimental data. Your lab notebook and computer records should be honest, complete, and reliable, showing exactly how you did experiments and what results you obtained, even if they weren't up to expectations.

Never make up lab results, borrow them from others, or bend the results to fit your needs. Don't modify the results arbitrarily. Don't draw perfect graphs and fill in the observations later.

The National Science Foundation calls such violations "scientific misconduct." Misconduct, it says, means "fabrication, falsification, plagiarism, or other serious deviations from accepted practices in preparing, carrying out, or reporting results" from scientific activities.[4] You may not be working on an NSF grant, but the same sensible rules apply: don't cheat on your data.

There are temptations, of course. Sometimes, you are running late and could finish quickly if you invented some numbers or "borrowed" them from a friend. Sometimes, your experimental results don't match

---

4. *Federal Register* 56 (May 14, 1991): 22286–90.

the expected numbers. Again, it's tempting to insert the "right" numbers rather than figure out exactly what went wrong. Were the measurements off? Was the equipment calibrated incorrectly? Did you make a simple mistake in the experiment? Everybody makes mistakes. One way to learn how science is practiced is to review the proper procedures and compare them with what you actually did.

The most common lab mistakes, one biologist told me, come *before* the experiments begin. Students sometimes fail to read the instructions carefully or forget to line up all the equipment and materials. If you're missing a chemical or beaker in the midst of an experiment, it may be too late to recover. You'll learn much more by using orderly procedures, and you'll generate much better data to work with.

Tip: Before beginning any experiment, read the instructions carefully and assemble all the equipment and materials you need. Also, be prepared to record your data.

When you're finished, your instructor or lab supervisor might ask to see your records. That's perfectly appropriate. In introductory courses, it's to teach you the best methods. In more advanced work, it's to evaluate your research progress, improve collaboration, and ensure integrity throughout the lab.

Honest data is the foundation of lab integrity, and it is expected from everyone, from undergraduates to professors. Violations are treated seriously at all levels. A physicist at Bell Labs, one of the world's leading research facilities, was recently fired for fabricating results in nanoelectronics and superconductivity. Another physicist was dismissed from Berkeley's Lawrence Livermore National Laboratory when his celebrated discovery of elements 116 and 118 proved fraudulent.[5] The investigations began when other scientists could not repeat his experimental results.

It's not just scientists who must present honest, complete data. Everyone should, just as they should present reliable quotes and citations. A prize-winning book on early American gun ownership raised questions when no one else could locate many key documents on which it was alleg-

5. Robert L. Park, "The Lost Innocence of Physics," *Times Education Supplement* (London), July 24, 2002.

edly based.[6] Outside experts investigated and sustained the most serious charges of misconduct. The professor was dismissed.

Not only must you present honest data; you must present it fairly. You can't leave out the bad news. Let's say you are testing a hypothesis and some of your experimental results don't support it. It's perfectly fine to double-check the experiment, see if you made a mistake, and try again. All that should be recorded faithfully in your lab notes. But once you have completed the reevaluation and fixed any problems, you should present the results fully and candidly, whether they agree with your hypothesis or not.

Tips on honest lab work:

- Lab partners may work together on experiments and discuss their work, but they are always required to keep their own notebooks and write up the results individually, without assistance.
- Never copy or make up data on experiments.
- Don't omit or hide unfavorable results. Record them in your lab notes.
- Present your experimental results honestly, even if you know they are "wrong" and even if they contradict your hypothesis.

The same is true in history, sociology, political science, economics . . . in every field. One of the most damning findings about the book on gun ownership was its "egregious misrepresentation" of historical data. Outside experts found the author simply excluded some findings that disagreed with his.[7]

Whatever your subject, it violates basic research ethics to leave out unfavorable results. It's tempting to omit them from your papers or presentations, but you shouldn't. Remember, this is not a court case or debating

---

6. Michael A. Bellesiles, *Arming America: The Origins of a National Gun Culture* (New York: Knopf, 2000). Bellesiles was both professor of history and director of Emory University's Center for the Study of Violence.

7. When Bellesiles's critics could not find some crucial documents he had cited, they cried foul. Emory appointed an outside committee of eminent historians to investigate. They reached a number of damning conclusions and used the term "egregious misrepresentation," quoted above. "No one," they said, "has been able to replicate Professor Bellesiles' results [of low percentage of guns] for the places or dates he lists." They also found he had excluded data that contradicted his findings, notably

contest where you present only selected facts, chosen to help your side. Your aim should be to present the results honestly and completely, warts and all. That's how good scholarship moves forward. Using this data, you may come up with a better hypothesis or more powerful interpretation. Or maybe someone else will. In any case, you should present your results fully and accurately.

CLASS PARTICIPATION

In many classes, especially seminars, part of your grade depends on class participation. Teachers *love* active, engaged discussions, where students raise useful questions, listen carefully to each other, and make thoughtful points, based on the readings. There's no more rewarding way to teach . . . or learn.

Honesty is not an issue in class discussions, but students do have legitimate questions about what counts as "participation" and what grade they should receive for it. Some questions are inevitable since judgments about participation are subjective. Others arise because teachers rarely specify what counts as participation.

There is no way to avoid subjective judgments, but it's easy to say what counts as effective participation. Most teachers agree on three main elements:

- Do you attend class regularly?
- Have you done the assigned work so your comments and questions are solidly based?
- Do your contributions advance the class discussion?

You can contribute in lots of ways—by raising questions, offering answers, or playing off other student comments. To do that effectively, though, you need to keep pace with the assignments and listen respectfully to your classmates as well as your teacher. That way, you can respond to each other and to the material, a fruitful give-and-take from which everyone can learn.

Alice Hanson Jones's higher figures on gun ownership. They concluded that Bellesiles's "scholarly integrity is seriously in question." The report, made on July 10, 2002, is available at http://www.emory.edu/central/NEWS/Releases/Final_Report.pdf. Bellesiles's response is at http://www.emory.edu/central/NEWS/Releases/B_statement.pdf.

Keep in mind that a seminar is *not* a lecture, where you sit quietly, take notes, and perhaps ask a question or two. A seminar (or weekly discussion section for a lecture course) is a guided dialogue, based on assigned work. You won't get the most out of it if you sit mute, talk over others, or arrive without preparing. "Passive learning is not the way we do things," one seminar leader told me. "It is expected that a student plays an active part in learning."

To play that active part, you need to do the readings beforehand. Your goal should be to engage the material fully—to grapple with it—first when you read it and later when you discuss it in class.

Don't worry about "showing the teacher what you know." Papers and exams give you plenty of opportunity to do that. Don't worry about agreeing with everyone else. It's perfectly fine to take a different perspective, as long as you keep an open mind, respect others' opinions, and offer reasons for your views. As one professor put it, "Dialogue and debate are fundamental norms of our system of higher education."

It's also fine to try out new ideas, new angles on the subject, even if you're not completely sure what you think about them. Consider it a "test drive" for your ideas. You have my permission (and your teachers'!) to probe your own thinking in these group discussions. Just make sure you have done the readings and homework first.

The focus should be on joining the conversation, exploring the material, and discussing it openly with your classmates. That fosters a more lively seminar and a richer learning experience. In the process, it reveals how you approach the subject and what you think about it.

> *Tips on how to participate profitably in class discussions:*
>
> - Attend regularly and arrive on time.
> - Keep up with the assigned work.
> - Listen to your fellow students as well as your teacher.
> - Advance the discussion with your own questions, answers, and responses to others' comments.

One final point: try to say something during the first or second class session, even if it's just a small comment. Make an effort to break the ice early. Don't wait silently, hoping you'll find the perfect moment to say the perfect thing. Class discussions don't work that way. They are not about making perfect comments. They're about learning through give-and-take, through questions and answers, including mistakes and missteps. Believe me, we all make them. If you don't speak during the first few sessions, you can easily slip into the routine of never participating. There's a simple solution: pitch in early, even if it's just a small comment or question. Once you've joined the conversation, you'll feel more comfortable participating again.

Your teacher wants exactly the same thing: to get the discussion rolling, with lots of students contributing. One experienced professor told me he "might begin by calling on students and asking them to share their thoughts on a reading or on another student's previous comment. Students should not feel as though they are being picked on. [My goal] is not to 'test' or 'intimidate' students," but to foster discussion and encourage students to "feel confident sharing their ideas with their classmates and teacher."

If you are shy or simply uncomfortable about speaking in class, you may need to push yourself a little. If you're nervous about speaking off the cuff, jot down an idea or two from the readings and use them to ask a question or make a comment in class. If you are uncomfortable speaking in groups, drop by the professor's office hours and begin a conversation there. After a one-on-one discussion, you may feel better about participating in class. You can also get some help from your college learning skills center. It deals with these issues all the time and will have lots of useful suggestions.

> *Tip on class participation:* Try to say something during the first session or two, even if it's only a small comment. It will open the door to more participation later.
>
> *Another tip:* Sit at the table in seminars and discussion sections. Slouching in the back row, behind everyone else, invites passive listening instead of active participation.

APPEALING A LOW GRADE

Sometimes, when your professor hands back lab reports, papers, or exams, you think your grade is too low. As you hear the answers explained, you realize yours was correct and you weren't given full credit. My advice: give yourself some time to calm down, mull it over, and review your answer. Maybe, on second look, it's not quite the Nobel Prize winner you remembered.

If you still think you deserve additional credit, it's perfectly fine to discuss it with your professor and appeal the grade. But don't do that until you have reread the exam and settled on specific reasons for your appeal. "I really need a better grade" is *not* a reason.

A little courtesy helps, too. Keep the discussion positive and concrete. Snarling about incompetent grading will only make your teacher grumpy. Generally speaking, you should avoid all phrases that include the word "moron." Instead, you might say, "I think my answer is very close to what you mentioned in your last lecture, and I'd really appreciate your taking another look." Or, "You said the answer should cover three main points, and I think mine did." And it's always fine to ask, "How could I do better?"

Your professor undoubtedly has some standard procedures for regrading, and you should ask about them. Your grade might be raised. Even if it isn't, you might learn what you did wrong so you can do better next time. That's valuable, too, because there will be many "next times," in many other classes.

One common problem, especially in math, statistics, and some sciences, is failing to show all your work. It's not enough simply to write down the answer, even if it's correct. You won't get full credit if you don't show full work. That's partly to prevent cheating, but there are other reasons, too. It also allows the professor to give you partial credit for what you got right. If you got the answer wrong, it allows the professor to identify the problem and show you how to correct it.

By showing your work, you're showing how you think through a problem. That's exactly what teachers want to know. "Just writing down an answer merits no (or almost no) credit at all," one physicist told me. "We're trying to teach students how to approach problems: how to set them up, how to carry through the calculations, and how to interpret the final results. In other words, how to think physically. . . . *If a student does not show his work, he is leaving out the very thing I'm trying to assess.*"

So, follow the advice you've heard from every math teacher since third grade: show your work.

Finally, if you appeal your grades, you must follow one hard-and-fast rule. You cannot modify your work in any way before regrading. That's cheating.

Tips on appealing low grades:

- Reread your answer before deciding whether to appeal.
- Courteously explain the specific reasons for your appeal.
- Never change anything on the exam before regrading.

HONOR CODES

Some schools use honor codes to ensure academic integrity. Students typically sign a pledge to do honest work, monitor each other, and report violations. They are not only responsible for doing honest work themselves; they must report cheating by others. They also promise to behave responsibly outside class and play a major role in judging infractions.

Problems are usually dealt with by honors councils, rather than college deans. Some councils are run entirely by students; others include faculty and administrators. In either case, students play a critical role in making honor codes work, mostly by taking responsibility for academic honesty and by emphasizing its central place in education.

The actual content of honest work and responsible behavior is no different from that of other schools. Students pledge to do their own work; not to plagiarize, cheat, or purchase papers; and to follow their professors' rules for papers, lab reports, and exams. Outside class, they pledge not to harass, intimidate, or threaten others—the same rules that apply in most universities, whether or not they use honor codes.

What is different is the responsibility students take upon themselves, individually and collectively, for maintaining and promoting these high ethical standards. "Students should constantly evaluate their own actions, inside or outside of the classroom," one student told me. "This covers everything from day-to-day interactions between students to academic honesty to the manner in which the [university] Senate allocates student body funds."

Professors rely on students living up to these standards, and students count on each other. Faculty don't monitor in-class exams, for instance, and often allow students to take closed-book exams in the library or their dorm rooms. They are confident students will adhere to the rules. Everyone knows that widespread violations would sabotage the whole system.

The purpose of honor codes goes well beyond catching dishonesty or even discouraging it by monitoring and punishment. As one student put it, "The feeling of being watched runs completely counter to the point of the [honor code], as it leaves people feeling infantilized and mistrusted. The benefit of the [honor code] is that students can feel secure in making their own ethical choices because they know that they will be treated like adults, that is, rationally, with compassion and understanding."

I heard that again and again from students. *The most profound goal of the honor system, they said, was a positive one: to create an ethos of honesty and responsibility in academic and social life.*

These codes are more common in teaching colleges than in large universities. That's no surprise. They work best where students know each other well and have a strong sense of community. Indeed, the codes usually become central pillars of that community, vital elements in the school's self-definition. They encourage a student culture of fairness and integrity, promote individual and collective responsibility, and foster strong bonds of trust between students and faculty.

These are goals well worth aspiring to, whether or not your school uses an honor code.

3

TAKING GOOD NOTES
. . . .

Good notes can help you learn more from readings, seminars, and lectures. Whether you are preparing for a final exam or writing a research paper, you'll need notes that highlight the main ideas, organize the materials, and remind you what you have read and heard. In this chapter, I'll show you how to take effective notes and avoid problems.

The most important advice I can give you is actually the simplest: listen carefully in class and take notes on all your lectures and readings. "The simple act of writing notes in class really helps," a biologist told me. "It forces students to pay attention, write down what they think is important, and look for whatever is coming next." That advice applies with equal force to books and articles. Taking notes will help you organize the materials and understand them. It helps a second time when you review the notes.

> *Tip:* Take notes on all your readings and lectures and be sure to review them. The top line should say what they cover, such as "Coleridge and English Romantic Poetry." If it's a lecture, include the course, topic, and date. If it's a book or article, include all the bibliographic information.

WHAT *ARE* GOOD NOTES?

As long as you are taking notes, you might as well take good ones. But what exactly *are* good notes? They are notes and reminders you actually find useful when you write papers, study for exams, or prepare for the next class session. To do that, your notes need to

- Highlight the key points and conclusions in the readings or lectures;

- Say how these points fit together; and
- Remind you what evidence and reasoning were used.

You should include *all* definitions, plus the most important equations, formulas, and algorithms. In English class, you can skip the equations.

Of course, it's fine to include some helpful details: a few choice quotes, key dates, or other data you might need for papers and exams. Add them when you think they are important in their own right or illustrate some larger point. But don't let the details swamp your notes. The goal is to understand the important issues: the argument, the supporting logic and evidence, and the connective tissue that ties it all together. That's what you should focus on. You are not a dictation machine, trying to capture every word.

> *Tip:* The goal of notes is not to include everything, but to highlight and organize the most important material.

Clear, simple notes like this are an effective way to review what you have covered. But that's only half the story. To understand the material, you need to do more than repeat it. You need to think about it, grapple with it, figure out what it means. Good notes will help you do that.

LECTURE NOTES AND BOOK NOTES

Notes on lectures and articles differ in a few obvious ways, and a few less obvious ones. With books and articles, you can read and take notes at your own pace. With lectures, you have to dash along with the professor. That means your lecture notes are probably incomplete, so you'll need to fill them in after class. It's smart to do that the same day, while you still remember the lecture. Again, concentrate on major points and helpful examples, not minor details. Figuring out what really matters is a critical part of your education. Your notes should reflect that judgment.

Most of the time, it's easier to organize your notes on books and articles than on lectures and seminars. That's because written work comes with its own built-in structure. The text is divided into major sections, usually with titles. You should use these sections and titles to organize your notes. Take Robert Lieber's book, *The American Era: Power and Strategy for the*

21st Century.[1] His chapter on U.S. policy toward Europe has sections entitled "Sources of Conflict," "Sources of Solidarity," and "Radical Change?" Each one should translate into a heading in your notes.

Lectures have a structure, too, but it's not always so clear. That's why you should pay special attention to the introduction and conclusion, where the professor emphasizes these central elements. Listen for phrases that indicate what's coming, such as "the three main theories are" or "turning to a slightly different topic." When you hear phrases like this, you'll want to list the three theories or signal a new topic with a section heading.

> *Tip:* Your notes should be organized into sections, reflecting the structure of the reading or lecture.

Third, while notes on lectures are often skimpy and hurried, notes on books and articles are often too detailed. That's because you can copy materials so easily from online texts into your notes. That's fine, up to a point. But remember, you still need to read the material—copying is *not* reading—and you still need to select what to copy. In fact, you need to select it carefully. It's enticing to copy paragraph after paragraph instead of choosing what's important. But you cannot produce sharp, useful notes unless you pare down what you include. Remember, too, that you still need to organize it into meaningful sections and highlight what's vital.

> *Tip:* Good notes highlight what's really important. If you are typing, you can do that with boldface. If you are scribbling, you can do it with arrows or underlining. When you don't understand something, signal it to yourself with three question marks (???). Later, you can look it up or ask your professor, teaching assistant, or classmate.

As you accumulate these notes, be sure to differentiate anything you copy from anything you write yourself. Otherwise, when you use the notes to write a paper, you might inadvertently treat words you copied as if you wrote them yourself. Big mistake. Even if it's an accident, it's no fun trying to prove that to a skeptical professor or dean.

---

1. Robert Lieber, *The American Era: Power and Strategy for the 21st Century* (Cambridge: Cambridge University Press, 2005).

Fortunately, it's a mistake that's easy to avoid. In a section below, I'll show you a few simple techniques, beginning with Q-quotes, to keep your notes straight. By using them, you can tell exactly what you wrote and what someone else did. Problem solved.

> *Tip:* When taking notes on books, clearly mark any direct quotations and note the page they are on. Doing that will prevent inadvertent plagiarism if you use the quote later. Put the letter "Q" before and after each quote so it stands out in your notes.

These differences between notes on articles and lectures are significant, but so are the similarities. All your notes should help you recall the central points, organize them into coherent sections, and integrate them into a meaningful whole. That's why, whether they are notes on an article or a lecture, they should emphasize the introduction and conclusion. The introduction lays out the main topics to be covered. The conclusion recaps these topics, draws them together, and offers some insights into what they mean. That's exactly what you want to grasp.

> *Tip:* Before reading an article closely, read the introduction and conclusion and glance at the section headings. That will give you a quick overview, let you to focus on the main issues as you read, and help you take better notes.

REVIEWING AND IMPROVING YOUR NOTES

The main reason you are taking these notes is so you can review them and think about them. To file them away and forget them is to lose most of your effort—and most of the benefits. My suggestion is to review your notes a few hours after you draft them.

This initial review has two goals. One is to recall the material. The other is to annotate and expand your notes, especially those on lectures and seminars. Sometimes you'll discover that they're too brief, too cryptic, especially if you are jotting them down rapidly. It helps to expand them now, while your memories are fresh.

As you review your notes, you can improve them. You can add that example the professor mentioned. You can clarify your writing if it's hard to decipher. You can insert your own conclusions or observations. (I do that in brackets to keep my comments separate.) Finally, you can organize your notes by inserting a few major headings along the way. If you are reviewing lecture notes on the French Revolution, for instance, you might label one section "The Fall of the Bastille" and the next one "Deposing the King." Adding headers like this clarifies the basic structure of the lecture. Later, it will help you prepare for exams.

> *Tip:* Your notes are *not* complete when you have finished reading the article or listening to the lecture. You've still got two brief but vital jobs to do. The first is to review your notes. The second is to clarify and expand them.

None of this takes very long—a few minutes at most—and it has some obvious benefits. It will imprint the material more deeply. It will give you a better overview of the course. Most important of all, it will turn you from a passive recipient into an active learner.

Each time you review your notes, ask yourself: What's the overall point here? What are the three or four most important subsidiary points? How does the author or teacher develop them? What's the evidence? What's the logic? What are the best examples? You should be able to reconstruct these central elements of a lecture or article *by yourself, in your own words.* If you cannot explain them to yourself, in plain, sensible language, then you don't really understand the material. That's important to know, right now, while you still have time to go over the material or ask the professor.

TAKING NOTES WITH Q-QUOTES

Some honest writers find themselves in hot water, accused of plagiarism, because their notes are so bad they cannot tell what they copied and what they wrote themselves. You can avoid that by clearly distinguishing your words from others'.

All you need is a simple way to identify quotes and keep them separate from your own words and ideas.

The common solution—using ordinary quotation marks in your notes—doesn't actually work so well in practice. For one thing, quotation marks are small, so it's easy to overlook them later when you return to your notes to write a paper. Second, they don't tell you which page the quote comes from, something you need to know for proper citations. Third, if there's a quote within a quote, it's hard to keep your markings straight.

There's a better way. To avoid all this confusion, simply use the letter Q and the page number to begin all quotations in your notes. To end the quote, write Q again. It's painless, and it's easy to spot the Q's when you read your notes and write your papers.

Begin your notes for each new item by writing down the author, title, and other essential data. (The exact information you need is described in part 2, in the citation chapters.) You'll need this information for each book, article, and Web site you use. With this publication data plus Q-quotes, you'll be able to cite effectively from your own notes, without having to return to the original publication.

> *Tip on using Q-quotes to identify exact words:*
> Q157 Churchill's eloquence rallied the nation during the worst days of the war.Q

This system is simple, clear, and effective. It works equally well for typed and handwritten notes. It easily handles quotes within quotes. Looking at your notes, you'll know exactly which words are the author's, and which page they are on. You'll know if he is quoting anyone else. And you'll know that anything *outside* the Q-quotes is your own paraphrase.

> *Tip on paraphrasing:* Make sure your paraphrase does not closely resemble the author's words. When in doubt, double-check your wording against the original.

Because quotes can be complicated, let's see how these Q-quotes work in more detail. First, some quotes begin on one page and end on another. To show where the page break falls, insert a double slash (//) inside the quote. (A double slash stands out, just as Q does.) That way, if you use only part of the quote, you can cite the correct page without having to chase down the original again. To illustrate:

> Q324–25 Mark Twain's most important works deal with his boyhood on the river. He remembered // that distant time with great affection. He returned to it again and again for inspiration.Q

The first sentence is on page 324; the next one is on both pages; the third is only on page 325. Using Q-quotes with a double slash gives you all this information quickly and easily.

Quotes can be complicated in other ways, too. You may wish to cut out some needless words or add a few to make the quote understandable. Fortunately, there are straightforward rules to handle both changes.

SHORTENING QUOTATIONS WITH ELLIPSES . . .

Although quotes need to be exact, you are allowed to shorten them if you follow two rules. First, your cuts cannot change the quote's meaning. Second, you must show the reader exactly where you omitted any words. That's done with an ellipsis, which is simply three dots . . . with spaces before and after each one.

If the omitted words come in the middle of a sentence, an ellipsis is all you need.

Original	I walked downtown, which took at least thirty minutes, and saw her.
Shortened	I walked downtown . . . and saw her.

If the two parts of your quote come from two separate sentences, use an ellipsis plus a period (that is, three dots plus a period) to separate the two parts.

Original	I walked downtown. After walking more than thirty minutes, I rounded the corner and saw her.
Shortened 1	I walked downtown. . . . and saw her.
Shortened 2	I walked . . . . more than thirty minutes.
Explanation	Both shortened sentences use three ellipses plus a period. In the first, the period comes immediately after the word "downtown," because that's where the period falls in the original sentence. In the second, there is a space before the period because the original sentence continues.

Because ellipses are sometimes confusing, it may help to go over them again. Remember that they have a simple purpose: to signal deliberate omissions from any text you quote. These omissions can come in three places, and each is handled slightly differently.

	LOCATION OF OMISSION	HOW YOU SIGNAL THE OMISSION
A	In the middle of a single sentence	Simple ellipsis
B	Immediately after the end of a sentence	Period in its normal place, followed by an ellipsis
C	Starting in the middle of a sentence, ending at the conclusion of that sentence or later	Ellipsis, followed by a period

Now let me illustrate A, B, and C, using a simple example.

Example   Granted, this example is easy and simple. Perhaps it is silly. But I hope it is clear and useful.

LOCATION OF OMISSION	ILLUSTRATION
A In the middle of a single sentence	Granted, this example is . . . simple.
B Immediately after the end of a sentence	Granted, this example is easy and simple. . . . But I hope it is clear and useful.
C Starting in the middle of a sentence, ending at the conclusion of that sentence or later.	Granted, this example is easy . . . . But I hope it is clear and useful.

Omissions like these are perfectly acceptable as long as you signal them (with ellipses) and you don't change the quoted author's meaning.

ADDING WORDS [IN BRACKETS] TO CLARIFY A QUOTE

Occasionally, you need to add a word or two to clarify a quote. Perhaps the original sentence uses a pronoun instead of a person's name. For clarity, you might wish to include the name. Again, you cannot change the quote's meaning, and you need to signal the reader that you are modifying it slightly. You do that by using [brackets] to show exactly what you have inserted. Consider this original text:

Original text   "Condoleezza Rice, President Bush's closest advisor, was speaking in New York that day. The President called and asked her to return to Washington immediately."

Now, let's say you want to quote only the second sentence. An exact quote wouldn't make much sense since the reader won't know whom the president was summoning. To correct that, you need to add a few words and bracket them to make it clear that you've added them to the original:

Your quote with brackets
"The President called and asked [his National Security Advisor, Condoleezza Rice] to return to Washington immediately."

That's an accurate quote even though you added several bracketed words. If you added the same words without brackets, however, it would be a misquotation.

One important rule: These additions [with brackets] and omissions (with ellipses . . .) should not change the quote's meaning in any way. The statement belongs to another writer, not to you. You're welcome to praise it or to damn it, but not to twist it.

QUOTES WITHIN QUOTES

The phrase you are quoting may itself contain a quotation. One advantage of using Q-quotes for your notes is that you can simply put quotation marks wherever they appear in the text. For example: Q47 He yelled, "Come here, quick," and I ran over.Q Since you are using Q's to mark off the entire quote, there will be no confusion later when you write a paper with these notes.

USING Q-QUOTES TO HANDLE COMPLICATED QUOTATIONS

Now that we've covered the basics of Q-quotes plus ellipses, brackets, and quotes within quotes, you are equipped to handle even the most complex quotes, first in your notes and then in your papers. To illustrate that, let's combine all these elements in one example:

> Q157–58 Some of Churchill's most famous speeches // were actually recorded by professional actors imitating his distinctive voice and cadence. . . . The recordings were so good that [one friend] said, "I knew Winston well and still can't tell who is speaking."Q

This notation makes it clear that

- the first few words appear on page 157 and the rest are on page 158;
- some words from the original are omitted after the word "cadence";
- there is a period after "cadence" and then three dots, indicating that the first sentence ended at the word "cadence" and that the omission came after that;
- the bracketed words "one friend" are not in the original text; and
- the final words are actually a quotation from someone else. They are included as a quote by the author you are citing.

With clear notation like this, you will be able to cite portions of this complicated quote later, without returning to the original article and with no chance of accidental plagiarism. It's not difficult. Actually, it takes more time to explain it than to use it!

PLAGIARISM AND
ACADEMIC HONESTY

. . . .

The last chapter included some basic ideas about taking notes to write honest, effective papers. In this chapter, I'll expand on them and show you how to avoid problems.

The biggest problem is misrepresenting someone else's work as your own. That's plagiarism, and it's a serious breach of academic rules, whether it's borrowed words, proofs, data, drawings, computer code, or ideas. When it's caught—and it often is—it leads to severe consequences, anything from failing a paper to failing a course. In extreme cases, it leads to suspension or expulsion. It's not a parking ticket. It's a highway crash. If it looks deliberate, it's a highway crash without seat belts.

Plagiarism is rare, but it does happen occasionally. The reason is sometimes a simple, innocent mistake. If book notes are garbled, a student may be unable to separate another author's words from his own. Later, when those notes are used for writing a paper, he might inadvertently treat the other author's words as his own original language. Even if it's an accident, it's no fun trying to prove that to a skeptical professor or dean.

Fortunately, this problem is easily prevented. I'll show you a few simple techniques, beginning with Q-quotes, to keep your notes straight. Using them, you can tell exactly what you wrote and what someone else did. Problem solved.

Of course, bad notes are not the only reason for plagiarism. Students rushing to finish a paper may forget to include the necessary citations. Some students are just sloppy, and others don't understand the citation rules. Sadly, a few cheat deliberately.[1]

---

1. It is always wrong to use others' work without proper attribution. The most troubling cases involve intentional use of another author's work without full attribu-

Whatever the cause, plagiarism is a serious violation of academic rules—for undergraduates, graduate students, and faculty. Misrepresenting someone else's words or ideas as your own constitutes fraud. Remember the basic principles of academic integrity: When you say you did the work yourself, you actually did it. When you rely on someone else's work, you cite it. When you use someone else's words, you quote them openly and accurately. When you present research materials, you present them fairly and truthfully. Quotations, data, lab experiments, and the ideas of others should never be falsified or distorted. They should never be fabricated.

CITE OTHERS' WORK TO AVOID PLAGIARISM

Citation rules follow from these basic principles of openness and honesty. If the words are someone else's, they must be clearly marked as quotations, either by quotation marks or block indentation, followed by a citation. It's not enough merely to mention an author's name. If it's a direct quote, use quotation marks and a full citation. If it's a paraphrase of someone else's words, use your own language, not a close imitation of the work being cited, and include a proper reference.

The same rules apply to visual images, architectural drawings, databases, graphs, statistical tables, computer algorithms, spoken words, and information taken from the Internet. If you use someone else's work, cite it. Cite it even if you think the work is wrong and you intend to criticize it. Cite it even if the work is freely available in the public domain. Cite it even if the author gave you permission to use the work. All these rules follow from the same idea: acknowledge what you take from others. The only exception is when you rely on commonly known information. (What counts as "commonly known" depends on your audience.) When you discuss gravity, you don't need to footnote Isaac Newton.

The penalties for violating these rules are serious. For students, they can lead to failed courses and even expulsion. For faculty, they can lead

---

tion. That is the classic definition of plagiarism. Some use a wider definition, which includes *unintentional* copying and borrowing. I call that "accidental plagiarism." Even if it's accidental borrowing—the spoiled fruits of sloppy notes rather than deliberate theft—it is still a serious problem. Whether or not you call it plagiarism, it's a major breach of academic rules.

to demotion or even loss of tenure. The penalties are severe because academic honesty is central to the university.

Tips on avoiding plagiarism: When in doubt, give credit by citing the original source.

- If you use an author's exact words, enclose them in quotation marks and include a citation.
- If you paraphrase another author, use your own language. Don't imitate the original. Be sure to include a citation.
- If you rely on or report someone else's ideas, credit their source, whether you agree with them or not.

USING THE INTERNET WITHOUT PLAGIARIZING

You need to be especially alert to these citation issues when you use the Web. Internet research is very efficient, especially when you don't need to read long stretches of text. You can do extensive targeted searches, quickly check out multiple sources, access sophisticated databases, click on article summaries or key sentences, and then drag-and-drop material into your notes. That's all perfectly fine. In fact, it's often the best way to conduct research. But it's also crucial to be a good bookkeeper. You need to use a simple, consistent method to keep straight what some author said and what you paraphrased.

The easiest way is to stick with the method for printed books and articles, described in chapter 3: *put Q-quotes around everything you drag-and-drop from electronic sources.* You can supplement that, if you wish, by coloring the author's text red or blue, or by using a different font. Just be consistent. That way you won't be confused in three or four weeks, when you are reviewing your notes and writing your paper.

One more thing: be sure to write down the Web site's address so you can cite it or return to it for more research. Just copy the URL into your notes. It's probably a good idea to include the date you accessed it, too. Some citation styles ask for it. If the item appears in a database and has a document identification number, copy that, too.

QUOTING AND PARAPHRASING WITHOUT
PLAGIARIZING: A TABLE OF EXAMPLES

A simple example can illustrate how to quote and paraphrase properly, and how to avoid some common mistakes. The following table shows the main rules for citation and academic honesty, using a sentence written by "Jay Scrivener" about Joe Blow. I'll use footnote 99 to show when that sentence is cited.

QUOTING WITHOUT PLAGIARIZING	
Joe Blow was a happy man, who often walked down the road whistling and singing.	**Sentence in the book *Joe Blow: His Life and Times,* by Jay Scrivener**

WHAT'S RIGHT	
"Joe Blow was a happy man, who often walked down the road whistling and singing."[99]	**Correct:** Full quote is inside quotation marks, followed by citation to *Joe Blow: His Life and Times.*
According to Scrivener, Blow "often walked down the road whistling and singing."[99]	**Correct:** The partial quote is inside quote marks, followed by a citation. The partial quote is not misleading.
"Joe Blow was a happy man," writes Scrivener.[99]	**Correct:** The partial quote is inside quote marks, followed by a citation.
According to Scrivener, Blow was "a happy man," who often showed it by singing tunes to himself.[99]	**Correct:** Partial quote is inside quotation marks; nonquoted materials are outside. The paraphrase (about singing tunes to himself) accurately conveys the original author's meaning without mimicking his actual words. Citation properly follows the sentence.
Joe Blow seemed like "a happy man," the kind who enjoyed "whistling and singing."[99]	**Correct:** Two partial quotes are each inside quotation marks; nonquoted materials are outside. Citation properly follows sentence.
Joe appeared happy and enjoyed whistling and singing to himself.[99]	**Correct:** This paraphrase is fine. It's not too close to Scrivener's original wording. The citation acknowledges the source.

WHAT'S WRONG

Joe Blow was a happy man, who often walked down the road whistling and singing. (no citation)

Wrong: It is plagiarism to quote an author's exact words or to paraphrase them closely without *both* quotation marks and proper citation. Acknowledge your sources!

Joe Blow was a happy man, who often walked down the road whistling and singing.[99]

Wrong: These are actually Scrivener's exact words. It is plagiarism to use them without indicating explicitly that it is a quote. It is essential to use quotation marks (or block indentation for longer quotes), *even if* you give accurate citation to the author. So, this example is wrong because it doesn't use quotation marks, even though it cites the source.

Joe Blow was a happy man and often walked down the road singing and whistling. (no citation)

Wrong: Although the words are not exactly the author's, they are *very similar.* (The words "singing" and "whistling" are simply reversed.) Either use an exact quote or paraphrase in ways that are clearly different from the author's wording.

Joe Blow was a happy man. (no citation)

Wrong: There are two problems here. First, it's an exact quote so it should be quoted *and* cited. Second, even if the quote were modified slightly, Scrivener should still be cited because it is *his personal judgment* (and not a simple fact) that Joe Blow is happy.

Joe Blow often walked down the road whistling and singing. (no citation)

Wrong: Same two problems as the previous example: (1) exact words should be both quoted and cited; and (2) Scrivener's personal judgment needs to be credited to him.

Joe Blow appeared to be "a happy man" and often walked down the road whistling and singing.[99]

Wrong: Despite the citation, some of Scrivener's exact words are outside the quotation marks. That creates the misleading impression that the words are original, rather than Scrivener's. This is a small violation, like going a few miles over the speed limit. But if such miscitations occur often or include significant portions of text, then they can become serious cases of plagiarism.

"Joe Blow was an anxious man, who often ran down the road."[99]	**Wrong:** The quote is not accurate. According to Scrivener, Joe Blow was not anxious; he was "happy." And he didn't run, he "walked." Although this misquotation is not plagiarism, it is an error. You should quote properly, and your work should be reliable. If such mistakes are repeated, if they are seriously misleading, or, worst of all, if they appear to be intentional, they may be considered academic fraud. (Plagiarism is fraud, too, but a different kind.)
Joe Blow "walked down the road" quietly.[99]	**Wrong:** The words inside the partial quotation are accurate, but the word following it distorts Scrivener's plain meaning. Again, this is not plagiarism, but it does violate the basic principle of presenting materials fairly and accurately. If such mistakes are repeated or if they show consistent bias (for example, to prove Joe Blow is a quiet person or hates music), they may be considered a type of academic fraud. At the very least, they are misleading.

The table refers to single sentences, but some citation issues involve paragraphs or whole sections of your paper. Let's say you are writing about urban poverty and that William Julius Wilson's analysis of the subject is central to one section. Whether or not you quote Wilson directly, you should include several citations of his work in that section, reflecting its importance for your paper. You could accomplish the same thing by including an explanatory citation early in the section. The footnote might say, "My analysis in this section draws heavily on William Julius Wilson's work, particularly *The Truly Disadvantaged: The Inner City, the Under-class, and Public Policy* (Chicago: University of Chicago Press, 1987), 87–122." Or you could include a similar comment in the text itself. Of course, you still need to include citations for any direct quotes.

PARAPHRASING

When you paraphrase an author's sentence, don't veer too close to her words. That's plagiarism, *even if it's unintentional and even if you cite the author.*

So, what's the best technique for rephrasing a quote? Set aside the other author's text and think about the point *you* want to get across. Write it down in your own words (with a citation) and then compare your sentence to the author's original. If they contain several identical words or merely substitute a couple of synonyms, rewrite yours. Try to put aside the other author's distinctive language and rhythm as you write. That's sometimes hard because the original sticks in your mind or seems just right. Still, you have to try. Your sentences and paragraphs should look and sound different from anyone you cite.

If you have trouble rephrasing an idea in your own words, jot down a brief note to yourself stating the point you want to make. Then back away, wait a little while, and try again. When you begin rewriting, look at your brief note but *don't look at the author's original sentence.* Once you have finished, check your new sentence against the author's original. You may have to try several times to get it right. Don't keep using the same words again and again. Approach the sentence from a fresh angle. If you still can't solve the problem, give up and use a direct quote (perhaps a whole sentence, perhaps only a few key words). It should either be a direct quote or your distinctive rephrasing. It cannot be lip-synching.

Why not use direct quotes in the first place? Sometimes that's the best solution—when the author's language is compelling, or when it says something important about the writer. When Franklin Roosevelt spoke about the attack on Pearl Harbor, he told America: "Yesterday, December 7, 1941—a date which will live in infamy—the United States was suddenly and deliberately attacked . . . ."[2] No one would want to paraphrase that. It's perfect as it is, and it's historically significant. When you analyze novels and poems, you'll want to quote extensively to reveal the author's creative expression. Other phrases speak volumes about the people who utter them. That's why you might quote Islamic fundamentalists calling the United States "the Great Satan" or George W. Bush responding that they are "evil." These quotes convey the flavor of the conflict.

Because there are so many times when direct quotations are essential, you should avoid them where they're not. Overuse cheapens their value. Don't trot them out to express ordinary thoughts in ordinary words. Paraphrase. Just remember the basic rules: Cite the source and don't mimic the original language.

These rules apply to the whole academic community, from freshmen to faculty. A senior professor at the U.S. Naval Academy was recently stripped of tenure for violating them. Although Brian VanDeMark had written several well-regarded books, his *Pandora's Keepers: Nine Men and the Atomic Bomb* (2003) contains numerous passages that closely resemble other books.[3] Most were footnoted, but, as you now know, that doesn't eliminate the problem.[4]

Here are a few of the questionable passages, compiled by Robert Norris. (Norris compiled an even longer list of similarities between VanDeMark's work and his own 2002 book *Racing for the Bomb*.)[5]

***

2. President Franklin D. Roosevelt, Joint Address to Congress Leading to a Declaration of War against Japan, December 8, 1941, http://www.fdrlibrary.marist.edu/oddec7.html (accessed June 1, 2004).

3. Brian VanDeMark, *Pandora's Keepers: Nine Men and the Atomic Bomb* (Boston: Little, Brown, 2003).

4. Jacques Steinberg, "U.S. Naval Academy Demotes Professor over Copied Work," *New York Times* (national ed.), October 29, 2003, A23.

5. Robert Norris, *Racing for the Bomb: General Leslie R. Groves, the Manhattan Project's Indispensable Man* (South Royalton, VT: Steerforth Press, 2002); Robert Norris, "Parallels with Richard Rhodes's Books [referring to Brian VanDeMark's *Pandora's Keepers*]," History News Network Web site, http://hnn.us/articles/1485.html (accessed June 22, 2004). For convenience, I have rearranged the last two rows in the table, without changing the words.

BRIAN VANDEMARK, PANDORA'S KEEPERS (2003)	RICHARD RHODES, THE MAKING OF THE ATOMIC BOMB (1986) AND DARK SUN (1995)
". . . Vannevar Bush. A fit man of fifty-two who looked uncannily like a beardless Uncle Sam, Bush was a shrewd Yankee . . ." (60)	"Vannevar Bush made a similar choice that spring. The sharp-eyed Yankee engineer, who looked like a beardless Uncle Sam, had left his MIT vice presidency . . ." (*Making of the Atomic Bomb,* 336)
"Oppenheimer wondered aloud if the dead at Hiroshima and Nagasaki were not luckier than the survivors, whose exposure to radiation would have painful and lasting effects." (194–195)	"Lawrence found Oppenheimer weary, guilty and depressed, wondering if the dead at Hiroshima and Nagasaki were not luckier than the survivors, whose exposure to the bombs would have lifetime effects." (*Dark Sun,* 203)
"To toughen him up and round him out, Oppenheimer's parents had one of his teachers, Herbert Smith, take him out West during the summer before he entered Harvard College." (82)	"To round off Robert's convalescence and toughen him up, his father arranged for a favorite English teacher at Ethical Culture, a warm, supportive Harvard graduate named Herbert Smith, to take him out West for the summer." (*The Making of the Atomic Bomb,* 120–121)
"For the next three months, both sides marshaled their forces. At Strauss's request, the FBI tapping of Oppenheimer's home and office phones continued. The FBI also followed the physicist whenever he left Princeton." (259)	"For the next three months, both sides marshaled their forces. The FBI tapped Oppenheimer's home and office phones at Strauss's specific request and followed the physicist whenever he left Princeton." (*Dark Sun,* 539)

Source: Robert Norris, "Parallels with Richard Rhodes's Books [referring to Brian VaDe-Mark's *Pandora's Keepers*], History News Network Web site, http://hnn.us/articles/1485 .html (accessed June 22, 2004). For convenience, I have rearranged the last two rows in the table, without changing the words.

Unfortunately, VanDeMark does not cite Rhodes or quote him directly in any of these passages. Some, like the last one, are virtual quotations and would raise red flags even if they occurred only once. A few others are a little too close for comfort, but raise problems mostly because there are so many of them in VanDeMark's book.[6] This is only one of several tables, covering VanDeMark's poor paraphrasing or unquoted sources. Each was prepared by a different author who felt violated. According to the Naval Academy's academic dean, "The whole approach to documenting the sources of the book was flawed."[7] The dean and VanDeMark himself attributed the problem to sloppiness rather than purposeful theft (which is why VanDeMark was demoted rather than fired outright). Still, the punishment was severe and shows how seriously plagiarism is taken at every level of the university.

PLAGIARIZING IDEAS

Plagiarizing doesn't just mean borrowing someone else's words. It also means borrowing someone else's ideas. Let's say you are impressed by an article comparing *Catcher in the Rye* and *Hamlet*.[8] The article concludes that these works are variations on a single theme: a young man's profound anguish and mental instability, as shown through his troubled internal monologues. If your paper incorporates this striking idea, credit the author who proposed it, *even if every word you say about it is your own.*

---

6. Besides copying words and phrases from Richard Rhodes and Robert Norris, VanDeMark took passages from Greg Herken, William Lanouette, and Mary Palevsky without proper quotations or full attribution. Some passages are *not* obvious cases of plagiarism—deliberate or accidental—but some are nearly identical to other works and still others are too close for comfort. The overall pattern is troubling.

These parallels between VanDeMark's work and other books are documented online with similar tables. See History News Network, "Brian VanDeMark: Accused of Plagiarism," May 31, 2003, http://hnn.us/articles/1477.html (accessed February 26, 2004). That page links to several tables comparing VanDeMark's wording to various authors'.

7. Nelson Hernández, "Scholar's Tenure Pulled for Plagiarism: Acts Not Deliberate, Naval Academy Says," *Washington Post,* October 29, 2003, B06, http://www.washingtonpost.com/wp-dyn/articles/A32551-2003Oct28.html (accessed March 5, 2004).

8. Although I thought of this comparison between Hamlet and Holden Caulfield myself, I suspected others had, too. Just to be on the safe side, I decided to do a Google search. The top item offered to sell me a term paper on the subject! After this depressing discovery, I decided to search for "Catcher in the Rye + phony." I was deluged with offers. What a delicious irony: to buy a term paper on Holden Caulfield's hatred of all things phony.

Otherwise, your paper will wrongly imply you came up with the idea yourself. Holden Caulfield would call you a phony. The moral of the tale: It's perfectly fine to draw on others' ideas, as long as you give them credit. The only exception is when the ideas are commonplace.

DISTORTING IDEAS

A recurrent theme of this chapter is that you should acknowledge others' words and ideas and represent them faithfully, without distortion. When you paraphrase them, you should keep the author's meaning, even if you disagree with it. When you shorten a quote, you should indicate that you've shortened it and keep the essential idea.

There are really two goals here. The first is to maintain honesty in your own work. The second is to engage others' ideas fully, on a level playing field. That's the best way to confront diverse ideas, whether you agree with them or not. That's fair play, of course, but it's more than that. It's how you make your own work better. You are proving the mettle of your approach by passing a tough, fair test—one that compares your ideas to others without stacking the deck in your favor.

The danger to avoid is setting up flimsy straw men so you can knock them down without much effort. That's not only dishonest; it's intellectually lazy. Believe me, your own position will be much stronger and more effective if you confront the best opposing arguments, presented fairly, and show why yours is better.

CONCLUSION: THE RIGHT WAY TO PARAPHRASE AND CITE

The rules for paraphrasing and citation are based on a few core ideas:

- You are responsible for your written work, including the ideas, facts, and interpretations you include.
- Unless you say otherwise, every word you write is assumed to be your own.
- When you rely on others' work or ideas, acknowledge it openly.
  - When you use their ideas or data, give them credit.
  - When you use their exact words, use quotation marks plus a citation.

- ○ When you paraphrase, use your own distinctive voice and cite the original source. Make sure your language doesn't mimic the original. If it still does after rewriting, then use direct quotes.
- When you draw on others' work, present it fairly. No distortions. No straw men.
- When you present empirical material, show where you acquired it so others can check the data for themselves. (The exception is commonly known material, which does not need to be cited.)

These principles of fairness and disclosure are more than simple rules for citation. They are more than just "good housekeeping" in your paper. They are fundamental rules for academic integrity. They promote real learning. They apply to teachers and students alike and encourage free, fair, and open discussion of ideas—the heart and soul of a university.

Citations
A Quick Guide

• • • • • • • • • • • •

In the chapters to come, I'll cover citation styles in nearly every field. If the world were simple, they'd all be the same. In fact, each one has its little idiosyncrasies, its own twists and turns. Fortunately, none of them is complicated.

Chapter 5 covers the basics of citation for all fields. It deals with issues that crop up no matter which style you use.

After that, I'll describe each style in its own chapter. Each chapter shows you exactly how to cite the works you'll use, whether it's a journal article, the second volume of a three-volume work, an online newspaper, or a Web site. Because each style (or each format—they mean the same thing) is presented separately, you only need to turn to one chapter when you write a paper.

Which style should you use? That depends on which field your paper is in, what your professor suggests, and which one you prefer. If your paper is in the humanities, you'll use either Chicago or MLA citations. If it's in the social sciences, engineering, education, or business, you'll use either Chicago or APA. Anthropology, the biological sciences, chemistry, computer sciences, mathematics, and physics all have their own individual styles and sometimes more than one per field. I'll cover each one and include plenty of examples.

In the final chapter, I'll answer some frequently asked questions dealing with all types of citations, in all styles. For example, should you cite your background readings? How many sources should your paper have? Can you include analysis in your footnotes?

Now, on to the basics of citation and, after that, the specifics of each style.

THE BASICS OF CITATION

5

. . . .

Acknowledging your sources is crucial to doing honest academic work. That means citing them properly, using one of several styles. The one you choose depends on your field, your professor's advice if you are a student, and your own preferences.

There are three major citation styles:

- Chicago (or Turabian), used in many fields
- MLA, used in the humanities
- APA, used in social sciences, education, engineering, and business

Anthropology has its own citation style, which is different from any of these. Several sciences have also developed their own distinctive styles:

- CSE for the biological sciences
- AMA for the biomedical sciences, medicine, nursing, and dentistry
- ACS for chemistry
- AIP for physics, plus other styles for astrophysics and astronomy
- AMS for mathematics and computer sciences

I will cover each one, providing clear directions and plenty of examples so you won't have any trouble writing correct citations. That way, you can concentrate on your paper, not on the type of citation you're using. I'll cover each style separately so you can turn directly to the one you need. Using this information, you'll be able to cite books, articles, Web sites, films, musical performances, government documents—whatever you use in your papers.

Why would you ever want to use different citation styles? Why can't you just pick one and stick with it? Because different fields won't let you. They have designed citation styles to meet their special needs, whether it's genetics or German, and you'll just have to use them. In some sciences, for instance, proper citations list only the author, journal, and pages. They omit the article's title. If you did that in the humanities or social sciences, you'd be incorrect because proper citations for those fields *require* the title. Go figure.

Compare these bibliographic citations for an article of mine:

Chicago	Lipson, Charles. "Why Are Some International Agreements Informal?" *International Organization* 45 (Autumn 1991): 495–538.
APA	Lipson, C. (1991). Why are some international agreements informal? *International Organization, 45,* 495–538.
ACS	Lipson, C. *Int. Org.* **1991,** *45,* 495–501.

None of these is complicated, but they *are* different. When you leave the chemistry lab to take a course on Shakespeare, you'll leave behind your citation style as well as your beakers. Not to worry. For chemistry papers, just turn to chapter 12. For Shakespeare, turn to chapter 7, which covers MLA citations for the humanities. Both chapters include lots of examples, presented in simple tables, so it won't be "double, double toil and trouble."

Despite their differences, *all these citation styles have the same basic goals:*

- to identify and credit the sources you use; and
- to give readers specific information so they can go to these sources themselves, if they wish.

Fortunately, the different styles include a lot of the same information. That means you can write down the same things as you take notes, without worrying about what kind of citations you will ultimately use. You should write down that information as soon as you start taking notes on a new book or article. If you photocopy an article, write all the reference information on the first page. If you do it first, you won't forget. You'll need it later for citations.

How these citations will ultimately look depends on which style you use. Chicago notes are either complete citations or shortened versions plus a complete description in the bibliography or in a previous note. Their name comes from their original source, *The Chicago Manual of Style,* published by the University of Chicago Press. This format is sometimes called "Turabian" after a popular book based on that style, Kate Turabian's *A Manual for Writers of Research Papers, Theses, and Dissertations.*[1]

If you use complete-citation notes, you might not need a bibliography at all since the first note for each item includes all the necessary data. If you use the shortened form, though, you definitely need a bibliography since the notes skip vital information.

Whether you use complete-citation notes or the shortened version, you can place them either at the bottom of each page or at the end of the document. Footnotes and endnotes are identical, except for their placement. Footnotes appear on the same page as the citation in the text. Endnotes are bunched together at the end of the paper, article, chapter, or book. Word processors give you an easy choice between the two.

MLA, APA, and the science citation styles were developed to provide alternative ways of referencing materials. They use in-text citations such as (Stewart 154) or (Stewart, 2004) with full information provided only in a reference list at the end.[2] Because these in-text citations are brief, they require a full bibliography. I'll describe each style in detail and provide lots of examples, just as I will for Chicago citations.

In case you are wondering about the initials: APA stands for the American Psychological Association, which uses this style in its professional journals. MLA stands for the Modern Language Association. Both styles have been adopted well beyond their original fields. APA is widely used in the social sciences, MLA in the humanities. Chicago citations are widely used in both. I will discuss the science styles (and what their initials mean) a little later.

Your department, school, or publisher may prefer one style or even require it, or they might leave it up to you. Check on that as soon as you begin handing in papers with citations. Why not do it consistently from the beginning?

---

1. Kate L. Turabian, *A Manual for Writers of Research Papers, Theses, and Dissertations,* 7th ed., revised by Wayne C. Booth, Gregory C. Colomb, Joseph M. Williams, and the University of Chicago Press Editorial Staff (Chicago: University of Chicago Press, 2007); *The Chicago Manual of Style,* 15th ed. (Chicago: University of Chicago Press, 2003).

2. Reference lists are similar to bibliographies, but there are some technical differences. In later chapters, I'll explain the details (and nomenclature) for each style. To avoid a needless proliferation of citation styles, I include only the most common ones in each academic field.

> *Tip on selecting a citation style:* Check with your teachers in each class to find out what style citations they prefer. Then use that style consistently.

Speaking of consistency . . . it's an important aspect of footnoting. Stick with the same abbreviations, capitalizations, and don't mix styles within a paper. It's easy to write "Volume" in one footnote, "Vol." in another, and "vol." in a third. We all do it, and then we have to correct it. We all abbreviate "chapter" as both "chap." and "ch." Just try your best the first time around and then go back and fix the mistakes when you revise. That's why they invented the search-and-replace function.

My goal here is to provide a one-stop reference so that you can handle nearly all citation issues you'll face, regardless of which style you use and what kinds of items you cite. For each style, I'll show you how to cite books, articles, unpublished papers, Web sites, and lots more. For specialized documents, such as musical scores or scientific preprints, I show citations only in the fields that actually use them. Physicists often cite preprints, but they don't cite Beethoven. The physics chapter reflects those needs. Students in the humanities not only cite Beethoven; they cite dance performances, plays, and poems. I have included MLA citations for all of them. In case you need to cite something well off the beaten path, I'll explain where to find additional information for each style.

HANGING INDENTS

One final point about shared bibliographic style. Most bibliographies—Chicago, MLA, APA, and some of the sciences—use a special style known as "hanging indents." This applies only to the bibliography and not to footnotes or endnotes. It is the opposite of regular paragraph indention, where the first line is indented and the rest are regular length. In a hanging indent, the first line of each citation is regular length and the rest are indented. For example:

Rothenberg, Gunther E. "Maurice of Nassau, Gustavus Adolphus, Raimondo Montecuccoli, and the 'Military Revolution' of the Seventeenth Century." In *Makers of Modern Strategy from Machiavelli to the Nuclear Age,* edited by Peter Paret, 32–63. Princeton, NJ: Princeton University Press, 1986.

Spooner, Frank C. *Risks at Sea: Amsterdam Insurance and Maritime Europe, 1766–1780.* Cambridge: Cambridge University Press, 1983.

There's a good reason for this unusual format. Hanging indents are designed to make it easy to skim down the list of references and see the authors' names. To remind you to use this format, I'll use it myself when I illustrate references in the citation styles that use it. (The only ones that don't use hanging indents are science styles with numbered citations. It's actually not complicated, and I'll explain it later.)

To make the authors' names stand out further, most bibliographies list their last names first. If an author's name is repeated, however, the styles differ. APA repeats the full name for each citation. MLA uses three hyphens, followed by a period. Chicago uses three em dashes (that is, long dashes), followed by a period.[3]

Lipson, Charles. *Barbecue, Cole Slaw, and Extra Hot Sauce.* Midnight, MS: Hushpuppy, 2006.
———. *More Gumbo, Please.* Thibodeaux, LA: Andouille Press, 2005.

You can arrange hanging indents easily on your word processor. Go to the format feature and, within it, the section on paragraphs. Choose hanging indentation instead of regular or none.

WHERE TO FIND MORE

So far, we have covered some basic issues that apply to most citation styles. There are, of course, lots more questions, some that apply to all styles and some that apply only to one or two. Rather than cover these questions now, I'll handle them in the chapters on individual citation styles and in a final chapter on frequently asked questions (FAQs).

If you have questions that aren't covered in the chapter on your citation style, be sure to check the FAQ chapter. If you still have questions, you can always go to the reference books for each style. Most styles have them (but not all). I'll list them in the chapters for individual styles.

---

3. Because em dashes are longer than hyphens, they show up differently on-screen and in print. The em dashes show up as a solid line, the hyphens as separate dashes. Three em dashes: ———. Three hyphens: ---. Frankly, you don't need to worry about this for your papers. Use the preferred one if you can, but either is fine.

ON TO THE NUTS AND BOLTS

I have organized the references so they are most convenient for you, putting all the documentation for each style in its own chapter.

Chapter 6: Chicago (or Turabian) citations
Chapter 7: MLA citations for the humanities
Chapter 8: APA citations for the social sciences, education, engineering, and business
Chapter 9: AAA citations for anthropology and ethnography
Chapter 10: CSE citations for the biological sciences
Chapter 11: AMA citations for the biomedical sciences, medicine, nursing, and dentistry
Chapter 12: ACS citations for chemistry
Chapter 13: Physics, astrophysics, and astronomy citations
Chapter 14: Mathematics and computer science citations

Fortunately, they're very straightforward. They're mostly examples, showing you how to cite specific kinds of sources, such as the third edition of a popular book or a chapter in an edited volume. I've included lots of examples of electronic documents, too, from Weblogs and databases to electronic versions of print documents.

Some of the official style guides do not yet cover the latest forms of electronic communications, such as video blogs. The problem is that you might wish to cite such blogs—or perhaps music videos, podcasts, or debates among bloggers—in a paper using one of these styles. My response is to include these newer electronic communications and to base the citations on each style's general rules and citations for similar items. I hope these "unofficial" citations will prove useful.

Don't bother trying to memorize any of these styles. There are simply too many minor details. Just follow the tables, and you'll be able to handle different sources—from journal articles to Web pages—in whichever style you need to use. Later, as you write more papers, you'll become familiar with the style you use most.

After explaining each style, I'll answer some common questions that apply to all of them. That's in chapter 15. Now, let's see how to do citations and bibliographies in the specific style you want to use.

6

CHICAGO (OR TURABIAN) CITATIONS

. . . .

Chicago citations are based on the authoritative *Chicago Manual of Style.* The manual, now in its fifteenth edition, is the bible for references and academic style. A briefer version, covering most aspects of student papers, is Kate Turabian's *A Manual for Writers of Research Papers, Theses, and Dissertations.* This section, however, should cover all you need to document your sources, even if they're unusual.

FULL NOTES, SHORT NOTES, AND BIBLIOGRAPHY

Chicago-style notes come in two flavors, and I include both in this section.[1]

1. A complete first note + short follow-up notes.
   The first note for any item is a full one, giving complete information about the book, article, or other document. Subsequent entries for that item are brief. There is no need for a bibliography since all the information is covered in the first note.
2. Short notes only + bibliography.
   All notes are brief. Full information about the sources appears only in the bibliography.

This means there are three ways to cite individual items. All of them are illustrated in this chapter.

---

1. *The Chicago Manual of Style* and Turabian also describe another style, the author-date system. These citations appear in parentheses in the text, listing the author and the date of publication. For example: (Larmore 2006). Full citations appear in a reference list at the end. For simplicity, I have omitted this style since it is similar to APA, discussed in chapter 8.

A. Full first notes
B. Short notes
C. Bibliographic entries

The first flavor combines A + B, the second combines B + C.

This chapter covers everything from edited books to reference works, from sheet music to online databases, and lots of things in between. To make it easy to find what you need, I've listed them here alphabetically, together with the pages they are on. At the end of this chapter, I answer some questions about using this style.

INDEX OF CHICAGO CITATIONS IN THIS CHAPTER

CHICAGO MANUAL OF STYLE: NOTES AND BIBLIOGRAPHY

Book, one author	Full first note	[99] Charles Lipson, *Reliable Partners: How Democracies Have Made a Separate Peace* (Princeton, NJ: Princeton University Press, 2003), 22–23.

▸ This is note number 99 and refers to pages 22–23.

▸ Footnotes and endnotes do not have hanging indents. Only the bibliography does.

[99] Pauline W. Chen, *Final Exam: A Surgeon's Reflections on Mortality* (New York: Random House, 2007), 203–6.

Short note

[99] Lipson, *Reliable Partners,* 22–23.

[99] Chen, *Final Exam,* 203–6.

▸ Shorten titles to four words or fewer, if possible.

Bibliography

Lipson, Charles. *Reliable Partners: How Democracies Have Made a Separate Peace.* Princeton, NJ: Princeton University Press, 2003.

Chen, Pauline W. *Final Exam: A Surgeon's Reflections on Mortality.* New York: Random House, 2007.

Books, several by same author

First note

[99] William R. Easterly, *The White Man's Burden: Why the West's Efforts to Aid the Rest Have Done So Much Ill and So Little Good* (New York: Penguin, 2006).

[100] William R. Easterly, *The Elusive Quest for Growth: Economists' Adventures and Misadventures in the Tropics* (Cambridge, MA: MIT Press, 2001).

Short note

[99] Easterly, *White Man's Burden.*

[100] Easterly, *Elusive Quest for Growth.*

Bibliography

Easterly, William R. *The Elusive Quest for Growth: Economists' Adventures and Misadventures in the Tropics.* Cambridge, MA: MIT Press, 2001.

———. *The White Man's Burden: Why the West's Efforts to Aid the Rest Have Done*

Books, several by same author (*continued*)		*So Much Ill and So Little Good.* New York: Penguin, 2006.

- The repetition of the author's name uses three em dashes (which are simply long dashes), followed by a period. You can find em dashes by digging around in Microsoft Word. Go to "Insert," then "Symbols," then "Special Characters." After you do it once, you can simply copy and paste it. If, for some reason, you can't find the em dash, just use three hyphens.
- List works for each author alphabetically, by title. In alphabetizing, skip any initial article: *a, an, the.*

Book, multiple authors	First note	[99] Edward D. Mansfield and Jack Snyder, *Electing to Fight: Why Emerging Democracies Go to War* (Cambridge, MA: MIT Press, 2005), 15–26.

- For four or more authors, only use the first author's name plus "and others" or "et al." For example, Edward D. Mansfield and others, *Electing* . . .

	Short note	[99] Mansfield and Snyder, *Electing to Fight,* 15–26.

- Titles with four words or fewer are not shortened.

	Bibliography	Mansfield, Edward D., and Jack Snyder. *Electing to Fight: Why Emerging Democracies Go to War.* Cambridge, MA: MIT Press, 2005.

- Only the first author's name is inverted.
- List up to ten coauthors in the bibliography. If there are more, list the first seven, followed by "and others" or "et al."

Book, multiple editions	First note	[99] Stuart O. Schweitzer, *Pharmaceutical Economics and Policy,* 2nd ed. (New York: Oxford University Press, 2007). [99] William Strunk Jr. and E. B. White, *The Elements of Style,* 4th ed. (New York: Longman, 2000), 12.

	Short note	[99] Schweitzer, *Pharmaceutical Economics.* [99] Strunk and White, *Elements of Style,* 12. ▸ To keep the note short, the title doesn't include the initial article (~~The~~ *Elements of Style*) or the edition number.
	Bibliography	Schweitzer, Stuart O. *Pharmaceutical Economics and Policy.* 2nd ed. New York: Oxford University Press, 2007. Strunk, William, Jr., and E. B. White. *The Elements of Style.* 4th ed. New York: Longman, 2000.

Book, edited	First note	[99] Karen Bakker, ed., *Eau Canada: The Future of Canada's Water* (Vancouver, BC: University of British Columbia Press, 2007). [99] John Bowker, ed., *Cambridge Illustrated History of Religions* (Cambridge: Cambridge University Press, 2002). [99] David Taras, Frits Pannekoek, and Maria Bakardjieva, eds., *How Canadians Communicate II* (Calgary, AB: University of Calgary Press, 2007). ▸ Use standard two-letter abbreviations for Canadian provinces.
	Short note	[99] Bakker, *Eau Canada.* ▸ Do not include the abbreviation for editor in short notes. [99] Bowker, *History of Religions.* ▸ Choose the most relevant words when shortening the title. [99] Taras, Pannekoek, and Bakardjieva, *How Canadians Communicate II.*
	Bibliography	Bakker, Karen, ed. *Eau Canada: The Future of Canada's Water.* Vancouver, BC: University of British Columbia Press, 2007. Bowker, John, ed. *Cambridge Illustrated History of Religions.* Cambridge: Cambridge University Press, 2002.

Book, edited (*continued*)		Taras, David, Frits Pannekoek, and Maria Bakardjieva, eds. *How Canadians Communicate II*. Calgary, AB: University of Calgary Press, 2007.
Book, anonymous or no author	First note	[99] Anonymous, *Through Our Enemies' Eyes: Osama Bin Laden, Radical Islam, and the Future of America* (Washington, DC: Brassey's, 2003). [99] *Golden Verses of the Pythagoreans* (Whitefish, MT: Kessinger, 2003).
	Short note	[99] Anonymous, *Through Our Enemies' Eyes*. [99] *Golden Verses of Pythagoreans*.
	Bibliography	Anonymous, *Through Our Enemies' Eyes: Osama Bin Laden, Radical Islam, and the Future of America*. Washington, DC: Brassey's, 2003. *Golden Verses of the Pythagoreans*. Whitefish, MT: Kessinger, 2003. ▸ If a book lists "anonymous" as the author, then that word should be included. If no author is listed, then you may list "anonymous" or simply begin with the title.
Book, online and e-books	First note	[99] Charles Dickens, *Great Expectations* (1860–61; Project Gutenberg, 1998), etext 1400, http://www.gutenberg.net/etext98/grexp10.txt. ▸ The etext number is helpful but not essential. [99] John Willinksy, *Empire of Words: The Reign of the OED* (Princeton, NJ: Princeton University Press, 2001), Microsoft Reader e-book. ▸ For e-books, include the specific type, such as "Microsoft Reader e-book."
	Short note	[99] Dickens, *Great Expectations*. [99] Willinksy, *Empire of Words*.
	Bibliography	Dickens, Charles. *Great Expectations*. 1860–61. Project Gutenberg, 1998. Etext 1400. http://www.gutenberg.net/etext98/grexp10.txt.

Willinksy, John. *Empire of Words: The Reign of the OED*. Princeton, NJ: Princeton University Press, 2001. Microsoft Reader e-book.

Multivolume work	First note	[99] Otto Pflanze, *Bismarck and the Development of Germany,* 3 vols. (Princeton, NJ: Princeton University Press, 1963–90), 1:153. [99] Bruce E. Johansen, *Global Warming in the 21st Century,* 3 vols. (Westport, CT: Praeger, 2006), 2:75.
	Short note	[99] Pflanze, *Bismarck,* 1:153. [99] Johansen, *Global Warming,* 2:75.
	Bibliography	Pflanze, Otto. *Bismarck and the Development of Germany.* 3 vols. Princeton, NJ: Princeton University Press, 1963–90. Johansen, Bruce E. *Global Warming in the 21st Century.* 3 vols. Westport, CT: Praeger, 2006.
Single volume in a multivolume work	First note	[99] Robert A. Caro, *The Years of Lyndon Johnson,* vol. 3, *Master of the Senate* (New York: Knopf, 2002), 237. [99] Bruce E. Johansen, *Global Warming in the 21st Century,* vol. 2, *Melting Ice and Warming Seas* (Westport, CT: Praeger, 2006), 71. [99] Akira Iriye, *The Globalizing of America,* Cambridge History of American Foreign Relations, edited by Warren I. Cohen, vol. 3 (Cambridge: Cambridge University Press, 1993), 124. ▸ Caro wrote all three volumes. Iriye wrote only the third volume in a series edited by Cohen.
	Short note	[99] Caro, *Years of Lyndon Johnson,* 3:237. ▸ Or [99] Caro, *Master of the Senate,* 237. [99] Johansen, *Global Warming,* 2:71. ▸ Or [99] Johansen, *Melting Ice and Warming Seas,* 71. [99] Iriye, *Globalizing of America,* 124.

Single volume in a multivolume work (*continued*)	Bibliography	Caro, Robert A. *The Years of Lyndon Johnson.* Vol. 3, *Master of the Senate.* New York: Knopf, 2002. Johansen, Bruce E. *Global Warming in the 21st Century.* Vol. 2, *Melting Ice and Warming Seas.* Westport, CT: Praeger, 2006. Iriye, Akira. *The Globalizing of America.* Cambridge History of American Foreign Relations, edited by Warren I. Cohen, vol. 3. Cambridge: Cambridge University Press, 1993.

Reprint of earlier edition	First note	[99] Jacques Barzun, *Simple and Direct: A Rhetoric for Writers,* rev. ed. (1985; repr., Chicago: University of Chicago Press, 1994), 27. [99] Adam Smith, *An Inquiry into the Nature and Causes of the Wealth of Nations* (1776), ed. Edwin Cannan (Chicago: University of Chicago Press, 1976). ▸ The year 1776 appears immediately after the title because that's when Smith's original work appeared. The editor, Edwin Cannan, worked only on its modern publication. The Barzun volume, by contrast, is simply a reprint so the original year appears as part of the publication information.
	Short note	[99] Barzun, *Simple and Direct,* 27. [99] Smith, *Wealth of Nations,* vol. I, bk. IV, chap. II: 477. ▸ This modern edition of Smith is actually a single volume, but it retains the volume numbering of the 1776 original. You could simply cite the page number, but the full citation helps readers with other editions.
	Bibliography	Barzun, Jacques. *Simple and Direct: A Rhetoric for Writers.* 1985. Reprint, Chicago: University of Chicago Press, 1994. Smith, Adam. *An Inquiry into the Nature and Causes of the Wealth of Nations.* 1776. Edited by Edwin Cannan. Chicago: University of Chicago Press, 1976.

Translated volume	First note	[99] Max Weber, *The Protestant Ethic and the Spirit of Capitalism* (1904–5), trans. Talcott Parsons (New York: Charles Scribner's Sons, 1958), 176–77. [99] Alexis de Tocqueville, *Democracy in America* (1835), ed. J. P. Mayer, trans. George Lawrence (New York: HarperCollins, 2000). ▸ Translator and editor are listed in the order they appear on the book's title page. [99] Seamus Heaney, trans., *Beowulf: A New Verse Translation* (New York: Farrar, Straus and Giroux, 2000). ▸ For *Beowulf,* the translator's name appears before the book title because Heaney's is the only name on the title page. (The poem is anonymous.) The same treatment would be given to an editor or compiler whose name appeared alone on the title page.
	Short note	[99] Weber, *Protestant Ethic,* 176–77. [99] Tocqueville, *Democracy in America.* [99] *Beowulf.* ▸ Or [99] Heaney, *Beowulf.*
	Bibliography	Weber, Max. *The Protestant Ethic and the Spirit of Capitalism.* 1904–5. Translated by Talcott Parsons. New York: Charles Scribner's Sons, 1958. Tocqueville, Alexis de. *Democracy in America.* 1835. Edited by J. P. Mayer. Translated by George Lawrence. New York: HarperCollins, 2000. Heaney, Seamus, trans. *Beowulf: A New Verse Translation.* New York: Farrar, Straus and Giroux, 2000.
Chapter in edited book	First note	[99] Benjamin J. Cohen, "The Macrofoundations of Monetary Power," in *International Monetary Power,* ed. David M. Andrews (Ithaca, NY: Cornell University Press, 2006), 31–50.

Chapter in edited book (*continued*)	Short note	[99] Cohen, "The Macrofoundations of Monetary Power," 31–50.
	Bibliography	Cohen, Benjamin J. "The Macrofoundations of Monetary Power." In *International Monetary Power,* edited by David M. Andrews, 31–50. Ithaca, NY: Cornell University Press, 2006.
Journal article, one author	First note	[99] Adam Meirowitz, "Communication and Bargaining in the Spatial Model," *International Journal of Game Theory* 35 (January 2007): 251–66.
	Short note	[99] Meirowitz, "Communication and Bargaining," 251–66.
	Bibliography	Meirowitz, Adam. "Communication and Bargaining in the Spatial Model." *International Journal of Game Theory* 35 (January 2007): 251–66.
Journal article, multiple authors	First note	[99] William G. Thomas III and Edward L. Ayers, "An Overview: The Differences Slavery Made; a Close Analysis of Two American Communities," *American Historical Review* 108 (December 2003): 1299–307. [99] Jeffery J. Mondak and others, "Does Familiarity Breed Contempt? The Impact of Information on Mass Attitudes toward Congress," *American Journal of Political Science* 51 (January 2007): 34–48. ▸ For four or more authors, only use the first author's name plus "and others" or "et al." [99] Michael Tomz, Judith Goldstein, and Doug Rivers, "Membership Has Its Privileges: Understanding the Effects of the GATT and the WTO on World Trade," *American Economic Review* (forthcoming). ▸ Or [99] Michael Tomz, Judith Goldstein, and Doug Rivers, "Membership Has Its Privileges: Understanding the Effects of the GATT and the WTO on World Trade," *American Economic*

		Review (forthcoming), http://www.stanford .edu/~tomz/working/intlagmts.pdf (accessed February 16, 2007).
	Short note	[99] Thomas and Ayers, "Differences Slavery Made," 1299–307. [99] Mondak and others, "Does Familiarity Breed Contempt?" 34–48. [99] Tomz, Goldstein, and Rivers, "Membership Has Its Privileges."
	Bibliography	Thomas, William G., III, and Edward L. Ayers. "An Overview: The Differences Slavery Made; a Close Analysis of Two American Communities." *American Historical Review* 108 (December 2003): 1299–307. Mondak, Jeffery J., Edward G. Carmines, Robert Huckfeldt, Dona-Gene Mitchell, and Scot Schraufnagel. "Does Familiarity Breed Contempt? The Impact of Information on Mass Attitudes toward Congress." *American Journal of Political Science* 51 (January 2007): 34–48. ▸ Only the first author's name is inverted. ▸ List up to ten coauthors in the bibliography. If there are more, list the first seven, followed by "et al."
Journal article, online	First note	[99] Janice B. Stockigt and Michael Talbot, "Two More New Vivaldi Finds in Dresden," *Eighteenth-Century Music* 3, no. 1 (Spring 2006): 35–61, http://journals.cambridge .org.proxy.uchicago.edu/download. php?file=%2FECM%2FECM3_01 %2FS1478570606000480a.pdf&code =60f4acfcf2410f745695a37a3d8fa71f (accessed February 11, 2007).
	Short note	[99] Stockigt and Talbot, "Two More New Vivaldi Finds," 35–61.
	Bibliography	Stockigt, Janice B., and Michael Talbot. "Two More New Vivaldi Finds in Dresden." *Eighteenth-Century Music* 3, no. 1

Journal article, online (*continued*)		(Spring 2006): 35–61. http://journals. cambridge.org.proxy.uchicago.edu/ download.php?file=%2FECM%2FECM3_ 01%2FS1478570606000480a.pdf&code=60 f4acfcf2410f745695a37a3d8fa71f (accessed February 11, 2007).
Journal article, foreign language	First note	99 Zvi Uri Ma'oz, "Y a-t-il des juifs sans synagogue?" *Revue des Études Juives* 163 (juillet–décembre 2004): 483–93. ▸ Or 99 Zvi Uri Ma'oz, "Y a-t-il des juifs sans synagogue?" [Are there Jews without a synagogue?] *Revue des Études Juives* 163 (juillet–décembre 2004): 483–93.
	Short note	99 Ma'oz, "Y a-t-il des juifs sans synagogue?" 483–93.
	Bibliography	Ma'oz, Zvi Uri. "Y a-t-il des juifs sans synagogue?" *Revue des Études Juives* 163 (juillet–décembre 2004): 483–93. ▸ Or Ma'oz, Zvi Uri. "Y a-t-il des juifs sans synagogue?" [Are there Jews without a synagogue?] *Revue des Études Juives* 163 (juillet–décembre 2004): 483–93.
Newspaper or magazine article, no author	First note	99 "State Senator's Indictment Details Demands on Staff," *New York Times,* February 11, 2007, national edition, 23. ▸ This refers to page 23. You may omit page numbers, if you wish, since many newspapers have different editions with different pagination. ▸ If the article has a byline and you wish to include the reporter's name, you certainly can: Jeff Zeleny, "State Senator's Staff . . ." ▸ Short articles in newsweeklies like *Time* are treated the same as newspaper articles. Longer articles with bylines are treated like journal articles.

	Short note	⁹⁹ "State Senator's Indictment," *New York Times*, 23.
		▸ Since newspapers are usually omitted from the bibliography, use a full citation for the first reference. You may omit pagination if you wish.
	Bibliography	▸ Newspapers articles are left out of bibliographies, but you can include an especially important article:
		"State Senator's Indictment Details Demands on Staff." *New York Times*, February 11, 2007, national edition, 23.

Newspaper or magazine article, with author	First note	⁹⁹ David M. Halbfinger, "Politicians Are Doing Hollywood Star Turns," *New York Times*, February 6, 2007, national edition, B1, B7.
		▸ You may omit pagination from newspapers, if you wish, since these vary from edition to edition.
	Short note	⁹⁹ Halbfinger, "Politicians Are Doing Hollywood," B1, B7.
	Bibliography	▸ Newspaper and magazine articles are rarely included in bibliographies, but you can include an especially important article:
		Halbfinger, David M. "Politicians Are Doing Hollywood Star Turns." *New York Times*, February 6, 2007, national edition, B1, B7.

Newspaper or magazine article, online	First note	⁹⁹ Charles Babington, "Democrats Urge Tighter FCC Rules," *Washington Post*, February 5, 2007, http://www.washingtonpost.com/wp-dyn/content/article/2007/02/01/AR2007020101997.html (accessed February 7, 2007).
	Short note	⁹⁹ Babington, "Democrats Urge Tighter FCC Rules."
	Bibliography	▸ Rarely included, but you may include an especially important article:
		Babington, Charles. "Democrats Urge Tighter

Newspaper or magazine article, online (*continued*)		FCC Rules." *Washington Post,* February 5, 2007, national edition. http://www .washingtonpost.com/wp-dyn/content/ article/2007/02/01/AR2007020101997.html (accessed February 7, 2007).
Review	First note	[99] Joseph H. Lane, review of *A Kinder, Gentler America: Melancholia and the Mythical 1950s,* by Mary Caputi, *Perspectives on Politics* 4 (December 2006): 749–50. [99] Niall Ferguson, "Ameliorate, Contain, Coerce, Destroy," review of *The Utility of Force: The Art of War in the Modern World,* by Rupert Smith, *New York Times Book Review,* February 4, 2007, 14–15.
	Short note	[99] Lane, review of *Kinder, Gentler America.* [99] Ferguson, "Ameliorate, Contain, Coerce, Destroy." ▸ Or [99] Ferguson, review of *The Utility of Force.*
	Bibliography	Ferguson, Niall. "Ameliorate, Contain, Coerce, Destroy." Review of *The Utility of Force: The Art of War in the Modern World,* by Rupert Smith. *New York Times Book Review,* February 4, 2007, 14–15. Lane, Joseph H. Review of *A Kinder, Gentler America: Melancholia and the Mythical 1950s,* by Mary Caputi. *Perspectives on Politics* 4 (December 2006): 749–50.
Unpublished paper, thesis, or dissertation	First note	[99] Ashley Leeds, "Interests, Institutions, and Foreign Policy Consistency" (paper presented at the Program on International Politics, Economics, and Security, University of Chicago, February 15, 2007), 1–25. [99] Lance Noble, "One Goal, Multiple Strategies: Engagement in Sino-American WTO Accession Negotiations" (master's thesis, University of British Columbia, 2006), 15. [99] Deborah Talmi, "The Role of Attention

and Organization in Emotional Memory
Enhancement" (PhD diss., University of
Toronto, 2006).

Short note
[99] Leeds, "Interests, Institutions, and Foreign
Policy."
[99] Noble, "One Goal, Multiple Strategies."
[99] Talmi, "Attention and Organization."

Bibliography
Leeds, Ashley. "Interests, Institutions,
and Foreign Policy Consistency." Paper
presented at the Program on International
Politics, Economics, and Security, University
of Chicago, February 15, 2007.
Noble, Lance. "One Goal, Multiple Strategies:
Engagement in Sino-American WTO
Accession Negotiations." Master's thesis,
University of British Columbia, 2006.
Talmi, Deborah. "The Role of Attention
and Organization in Emotional Memory
Enhancement." PhD diss., University of
Toronto, 2006.

Preprint
First note
[99] Mary Eschelbach Hansen and Daniel Pollack,
"Transracial Adoption of Black Children: An
Economic Analysis," preprint, January 17, 2007,
http://law.bepress.com/expresso/eps/1942
(accessed February 6, 2007).
[99] Francis Heylighen, "Five Questions on
Complexity," preprint, February 2007, arXiv:
nlin.AO/0702016, http://arxiv.org/ftp/nlin/
papers/0702/0702016.pdf (accessed February
12, 2007).

Short note
[99] Hansen and Pollack, "Transracial Adoption."
[99] Heylighen, "Five Questions on Complexity."

Bibliography
Hansen, Mary Eschelbach, and Daniel Pollack.
"Transracial Adoption of Black Children: An
Economic Analysis," preprint, January 17,
2007. http://law.bepress.com/expresso/
eps/1942 (accessed February 6, 2007).
Heylighen, Francis. "Five Questions on
Complexity," preprint, February 2007, arXiv:

Preprint (*continued*)		nlin.AO/0702016. http://arxiv.org/ftp/ nlin/papers/0702/0702016.pdf (accessed February 12, 2007).

Abstract	First note	[99] Carlos Barahona and Sarah Levy, "The Best of Both Worlds: Producing National Statistics Using Participatory Methods," abstract, *World Development* 35 (February 2007): 326–41. [99] John Hatchard, "Combating Transnational Crime in Africa: Problems and Perspectives," *Journal of African Law* 50 (October 2006): 145–60, abstract in *African Studies Abstracts Online* 17, abstract no. 21 (2007): 28.
	Short note	[99] Barahona and Levy, "Best of Both Worlds," 326–41. [99] Hatchard, "Combating Transnational Crime in Africa,"28.
	Bibliography	Barahona, Carlos, and Sarah Levy. "The Best of Both Worlds: Producing National Statistics Using Participatory Methods." Abstract. *World Development* 35 (February 2007): 326–41. Hatchard, John. "Combating Transnational Crime in Africa: Problems and Perspectives." *Journal of African Law* 50 (October 2006): 145–60. Abstract in *African Studies Abstracts Online* 17, Abstract No. 21 (2007): 28.

Microfilm, microfiche	First note	[99] Martin Luther King Jr., *FBI File,* ed. David J. Garrow (Frederick, MD: University Publications of America, 1984), microform. [99] Alice Irving Abbott, *Circumstantial Evidence* (New York: W. B. Smith, 1882), in *American Fiction, 1774–1910* (Woodbridge, CT: Gale/ Primary Source Microfilm, 1998), microfilm, reel A-1.
	Short note	[99] King, *FBI File,* 11:23–24. [99] Abbott, *Circumstantial Evidence,* 73.

Bibliography

King, Martin Luther, Jr., *FBI File*. Edited by David J. Garrow. Frederick, MD: University Publications of America, 1984. Microform.

Abbott, Alice Irving. *Circumstantial Evidence.* New York: W. B. Smith, 1882. In *American Fiction, 1774–1910*. Reel A-1. Woodbridge, CT: Gale/Primary Source Microfilm, 1998.

▸ You can omit any mention of microfilm or microfiche if it simply preserves a source in its original form. Just cite the work as if it were the published version. So, to cite the Abbott book:

Abbott, Alice Irving. *Circumstantial Evidence.* New York: W. B. Smith, 1882.

Archival materials and manuscript collections, hard copies and online

First note

[99] Isaac Franklin to R. C. Ballard, February 28, 1831, series 1.1, folder 1, Rice Ballard Papers, Southern Historical Collection, Wilson Library, University of North Carolina, Chapel Hill.

▸ Here is the order of items within the citation:

1. Author and brief description of the item
2. Date, if possible
3. Identification number for item or manuscript
4. Title of the series or collection
5. Library (or depository) and its location; for well-known libraries and archives, the location may be omitted.

[99] Mary Swift Lamson, "An Account of the Beginning of the B.Y.W.C.A.," MS, [n.d.], and accompanying letter, 1891, series I, I-A-2, Boston YWCA Papers, Schlesinger Library, Radcliffe Institute for Advanced Study, Harvard University.

▸ "MS" = manuscript = papers (plural: "MSS")

[99] Sigismundo Taraval, Journal recounting Indian uprisings in Baja California [handwritten ms.], 1734–1737, ¶ 23, Edward E. Ayer Manuscript Collection No. 1240, Newberry Library, Chicago, IL.

▸ This journal has numbered paragraphs. Page numbers, paragraphs, or other identifiers aid readers.

Archival
materials and
manuscript
collections,
hard copies
and online
(*continued*)

[99] Horatio Nelson Taft, Diary, February 20, 1862, p. 149 (vol. 1, January 1, 1861–April 11, 1862), Manuscript Division, Library of Congress, http://memory.loc.gov/ammem/tafthtml/tafthome.html (accessed July 9, 2007).

[99] Henrietta Szold to Rose Jacobs, February 3, 1932, reel 1, book 1, Rose Jacobs–Alice L. Seligsberg Collection, Judaica Microforms, Brandeis Library, Waltham, MA.

▸ Abbreviations: When a collection's name and location are often repeated, they may be abbreviated after the first use:

[99] Henrietta Szold to Rose Jacobs, March 9, 1936, A/125/112, Central Zionist Archives, Jerusalem (hereafter cited as CZA).

[100] Szold to Eva Stern, July 27, 1936, A/125/912, CZA.

Short note

[99] Isaac Franklin to R. C. Ballard, February 28, 1831, series 1.1, folder 1, Rice Ballard Papers.

▸ Short-form citation varies for archival items. The main concerns are readers' convenience and the proximity of full information in nearby notes.

[99] Mary Swift Lamson, "Beginning of the B.Y.W.C.A.," MS, [1891], Boston YWCA Papers, Schlesinger Library.

[99] Sigismundo Taraval, Journal recounting Indian uprisings in Baja California, Edward E. Ayer Manuscript Collection, Newberry Library.

▸ Or

[99] Taraval, Journal, Ayer MS Collection, Newberry Library.

[99] Horatio Nelson Taft, Diary, February 20, 1862, 149.

[99] Henrietta Szold to Rose Jacobs, February 3, 1932, reel 1, book 1, Rose Jacobs–Alice L. Seligsberg Collection.

[100] Szold to Jacobs, March 9, 1936, A/125/112, CZA.

[101] Szold to Eva Stern, July 27, 1936, A/125/912, CZA.

Bibliography Rice Ballard Papers. Southern Historical
Collection. Wilson Library. University of
North Carolina, Chapel Hill.

▸ In footnotes and endnotes, the specific
archival item is usually listed first because
it is the most important element in the
note. For example: Isaac Franklin to R. C.
Ballard, February 28, 1831. In bibliographies,
however, the collection itself is usually listed
first because it is more important. Individual
items are not mentioned in the bibliography
unless only one item is cited from a particular
collection.

Boston YWCA Papers. Schlesinger Library.
Radcliffe Institute for Advanced Study,
Harvard University.

▸ Or

Lamson, Mary Swift. "An Account of the
Beginning of the B.Y.W.C.A." MS, [n.d.],
and accompanying letter. 1891. Boston
YWCA Papers. Schlesinger Library. Radcliffe
Institute for Advanced Study, Harvard
University.

▸ If Lamson's account is the only item cited from
these papers, then it would be listed in the
bibliography.

Ayer, Edward E. Manuscript Collection.
Newberry Library, Chicago, IL.

Taft, Horatio Nelson. Diary. Vol. 1, January 1,
1861–April 11, 1862. Manuscript Division,
Library of Congress. http://memory.loc
.gov/ammem/tafthtml/tafthome.html
(accessed May 30, 2004).

Rose Jacobs–Alice L. Seligsberg Collection.
Judaica Microforms. Brandeis Library,
Waltham, MA.

Central Zionist Archives, Jerusalem.

Encyclopedia, First note [99] *Encyclopaedia Britannica,* 15th ed., s.vv.
hard copy "Balkans: History," "World War I."
and online
▸ s.v. (*sub verbo*) means "under the word."
Plural: s.vv.

Encyclopedia,
hard copy and
online
(*continued*)

▸ You must include the edition but, according
to the *Chicago Manual of Style,* you can omit
the publisher, location, and page numbers for
well-known references like the *Encyclopaedia
Britannica.*

⁹⁹ *Encyclopaedia Britannica Online,* s.v.
"Balkans," http://search.eb.com.proxy
.uchicago.edu/eb/article-9110555 (accessed
February 6, 2007).

⁹⁹ George Graham, "Behaviorism," in *Stanford
Encyclopedia of Philosophy,* http://plato
.stanford.edu/entries/behaviorism/ (accessed
February 10, 2007).

▸ Or

⁹⁹ *Stanford Encyclopedia of Philosophy,*
"Behaviorism" (by George Graham), http://
plato.stanford.edu/entries/behaviorism/
(accessed February 10, 2007).

⁹⁹ *Wikipedia,* "Stamford Raffles," http://
en.wikipedia.org/wiki/Stamford_Raffles
(accessed February 14, 2007).

Short note

⁹⁹ *Encyclopaedia Britannica,* s.v. "World
War I."

⁹⁹ *Encyclopaedia Britannica Online,* s.v.
"Balkans."

⁹⁹ Graham, "Behaviorism."

▸ Or

⁹⁹ *Stanford Encyclopedia,* "Behaviorism."

⁹⁹ *Wikipedia,* "Stamford Raffles."

Bibliography

Encyclopaedia Britannica. 15th ed. s.vv.
"Balkans: History." "World War I."

Encyclopaedia Britannica Online. s.v.
"Balkans." http://search.eb.com.proxy
.uchicago.edu/eb/article-9110555 (accessed
February 6, 2007).

Graham, George. "Behaviorism." In *Stanford
Encyclopedia of Philosophy.* http://plato
.stanford.edu/entries/behaviorism/
(accessed February 10, 2007).

▸ Or

Stanford Encyclopedia of Philosophy.
    "Behaviorism" (by George Graham). http://
    plato.stanford.edu/entries/behaviorism/
    (accessed February 10, 2007).
Wikipedia. "Stamford Raffles." http://
    en.wikipedia.org/wiki/Stamford_Raffles
    (accessed February 14, 2007).

Reference book, hard copy and online	First note	[99] *Reference Guide to World Literature,* 3rd ed., 2 vols., ed. Sara Pendergast and Tom Pendergast (Detroit: St. James Press/ Thomson-Gale, 2003).
		[99] *Reference Guide to World Literature,* 3rd ed., ed. Sara Pendergast and Tom Pendergast (Detroit: St. James Press, 2003), e-book.
		[99] Edmund Cusick, "The Snow Queen, story by Hans Christian Andersen," in *Reference Guide to World Literature,* 3rd ed., 2 vols., ed. Sara Pendergast and Tom Pendergast (Detroit: St. James Press/Thomson-Gale, 2003), 2:1511–12.
		[99] "Great Britain: Queen's Speech Opens Parliament," November 26, 2003, *FirstSearch,* Facts On File database, accession no. 2003302680.
	Short note	[99] *Reference Guide to World Literature.*
		[99] Cusick, "Snow Queen," 2:1511–12.
		[99] "Great Britain: Queen's Speech."
	Bibliography	*Reference Guide to World Literature.* 3rd ed. 2 vols., edited by Sara Pendergast and Tom Pendergast. Detroit: St. James Press/ Thomson-Gale, 2003.
		Reference Guide to World Literature. 3rd ed., edited by Sara Pendergast and Tom Pendergast. Detroit: St. James Press, 2003. E-book.
		Cusick, Edmund. "The Snow Queen, story by Hans Christian Andersen." In *Reference Guide to World Literature.* 3rd ed. 2 vols., edited by Sara Pendergast and Tom

Reference book, hard copy and online (*continued*)		Pendergast, 2:1511–12. Detroit: St. James Press/Thomson-Gale, 2003. "Great Britain: Queen's Speech Opens Parliament." November 26, 2003. *FirstSearch.* Facts On File database. Accession no. 2003302680.
Dictionary, hard copy, online, and CD-ROM	First note	[99] *Merriam-Webster's Collegiate Dictionary,* 11th ed., s.v. "chronology."
		▸ You must include the edition but can omit the publisher, location, and page numbers for well-known references like *Merriam-Webster's.*
		[99] *Compact Edition of the Oxford English Dictionary,* s.vv. "class, *n.,*" "state, *n.*"
		▸ The words "class" and "state" can be either nouns or verbs, and this reference is to the nouns.
		[99] Dictionary.com, s.v. "status," http://dictionary.reference.com/search?q=status (accessed February 2, 2004).
		[99] *American Heritage Dictionary of the English Language,* 4th ed., CD-ROM.
	Short note	[99] *Merriam-Webster's,* s.v. "chronology." [99] *Compact O.E.D.,* s.vv. "class, *n.,*" "state, *n.*" [99] Dictionary.com, s.v. "status." [99] *American Heritage Dictionary of the English Language* on CD-ROM.
	Bibliography	▸ Standard dictionaries are not normally listed in bibliographies, but you may wish to include more specialized reference works:
		Middle English Dictionary, W.2, edited by Robert E. Lewis. Ann Arbor: University of Michigan Press, 1999.
		Middle English Dictionary. http://ets.umdl .umich.edu/cgi/m/mec/med-idx?type=id &id=MED5390 (accessed February 14, 2007).
Bible, Qur'an (Koran)	First note	[99] Genesis 1:1, 1:3–5, 2:4. [99] Genesis 1:1, 1:3–5, 2:4 (New Revised Standard Version).

- Books of the Bible can be abbreviated: Gen. 1:1.
- Abbreviations for the next four books are Exod., Lev., Num., and Deut. Abbreviations for other books are easily found with a Web search for "abbreviations + Bible."

⁹⁹ Qur'an 18:65–82.

Short note   ⁹⁹ Genesis 1:1, 1:3–5, 2:4.
⁹⁹ Qur'an 18:65–82.

Bibliography

- References to the Bible, Qur'an, and other sacred texts are not normally included in the bibliography, but you may wish to include a particular version or translation:

Tanakh: The Holy Scriptures: The New JPS Translation according to the Traditional Hebrew Text. Philadelphia: Jewish Publication Society, 1985.

- Thou shalt omit the Divine Author's name.

Classical works

First note

- Ordinarily, classical Greek and Latin works are referred to in the text itself or in notes. They are not included in the bibliography except to reference the specific translation or commentary by a modern author. Here is an in-text reference:

  In Pericles' Funeral Oration (2.34–46), Thucydides gives us one of history's most moving speeches.
- If you do need to include a note, here is the format:

⁹⁹ Plato, *The Republic,* trans. R. E. Allen (New Haven, CT: Yale University Press, 2006).
⁹⁹ Virgil, *The Aeneid,* introd. Bernard Knox, trans. Robert Fagles (New York: Viking, 2006).

Short note   ⁹⁹ Plato *Republic* 3.212b–414b.
⁹⁹ Virgil *Aeneid* 5.6–31.

Bibliography

- Classical Greek and Latin works are not normally included in the bibliography except to reference the specific translation or commentary by a modern author.

Classical works (*continued*)		Plato. *The Republic.* Translated by R. E. Allen. New Haven, CT: Yale University Press, 2006. Virgil. *The Aeneid.* Introduction by Bernard Knox. Translated by Robert Fagles. New York: Viking, 2006.
Speech, academic talk, or course lecture	First note	[99] David J. Skorton, "State of the University Speech" (Cornell University, Ithaca, NY, October 27, 2006). [99] Ira Katznelson, "At the Court of Chaos: Political Science in an Age of Perpetual Fear" (presidential address, annual meeting of the American Political Science Association, Philadelphia, PA, August 31, 2006). [99] Gary Sick, lecture on U.S. policy toward Iran (course on U.S. Foreign Policy Making in the Persian Gulf, Columbia University, New York, March 22, 2007).
		▸ The title of Professor Sick's talk is not in quotes because it is a regular course lecture and does not have a specific title. I have given a description, but you could simply call it a lecture and omit the description. For example: Gary Sick (lecture, course on U.S. Foreign . . .).
	Short note	[99] Skorton, "State of the University Speech."
		▸ Or, to differentiate it from Skorton's 2007 talk: [99] Skorton, "State of the University Speech," 2006. [99] Katznelson, "At the Court of Chaos." [99] Sick, lecture on U.S. policy toward Iran.
	Bibliography	Skorton, David J. "State of the University Speech." Cornell University, Ithaca, NY, October 27, 2006. Katznelson, Ira. "At the Court of Chaos: Political Science in an Age of Perpetual Fear." Presidential address, annual meeting of the American Political Science Association, Philadelphia, PA, August 31, 2006. Sick, Gary. Lecture on U.S. policy toward Iran. Course on U.S. Foreign Policy Making in

the Persian Gulf, Columbia University, New York, March 22, 2007.

Interview, personal, telephone, or in print	First note	[99] J. M. Coetzee, personal interview, May 14, 2007. [99] Gordon Brown, telephone interview, March 16, 2007. [99] Anonymous U.S. Marine, recently returned from Iraq, interview by author, June 4, 2007. [99] Margaret MacMillan, "On Her New Book, *Nixon in China: The Week That Changed the World*," interview by Kenneth Whyte, *Macleans,* September 27, 2006, http://www.macleans .ca/culture/books/article.jsp?content =20061002_133865_133865 (accessed February 10, 2007).
	Short note	[99] J. M. Coetzee, personal interview, May 14, 2007. [99] Gordon Brown, telephone interview, March 16, 2007. [99] Anonymous U.S. Marine, interview by author, June 4, 2007. [99] MacMillan, "On *Nixon in China*."
	Bibliography	▸ Interviews should be included in the bibliography if they are in print, online, or archived (so that they are available to other researchers). Personal interviews and communications that are not accessible to others should be described fully in the notes and omitted from the bibliography. Hence, there is a bibliographic item for Macmillan but none for Coetzee, Brown, or the anonymous U.S. Marine. MacMillan, Margaret. "On Her New Book, *Nixon in China: The Week That Changed the World*." Interview by Kenneth Whyte. *Macleans,* September 27, 2006. http:// www.macleans.ca/culture/books/article .jsp?content=20061002_133865_133865 (accessed February 10, 2007).

Personal communication	First note	[99] Ron Chernow, personal communication, May 25, 2007. [99] Dr. Adam Rowen, telephone conversation with author, May 21, 2007. [99] Professor Gayle McKeen, letter to author, July 3, 2007. [99] Discussion with senior official at Department of Homeland Security, Washington, DC, June 1, 2007.
		▸ Sometimes you may not wish to reveal the source of an interview or conversation, or you may have promised not to reveal your source. If so, then you should (a) reveal as much descriptive data as you can, such as "a police officer who works with an anti-gang unit," instead of just "a police officer" and (b) explain to readers, in some footnote, why you are omitting names, such as "Interviews with State Department officials were conducted with guarantees of anonymity."
	Short note	[99] Ron Chernow, personal communication, May 25, 2007. [99] Dr. Adam Rowen, telephone conversation with author, May 21, 2007. [99] Professor Gayle McKeen, letter to author, July 3, 2007. [99] Discussion with senior official at Department of Homeland Security, Washington, DC, June 1, 2007.
	Bibliography	▸ Personal communications are typically omitted from the bibliography, unless they are archived and available to others. For example: Kaster, Robert. Comment posted October 10, 2004. http://www.charleslipson.com/ Honesty-Reviews.htm (accessed February 15, 2007).
Poem	First note	[99] Elizabeth Bishop, "The Fish," in *The Complete Poems, 1927–1979* (New York: Noonday Press/ Farrar, Straus and Giroux, 1983), 42–44.

	Short note	[99] Bishop, "The Fish," 42–44.
	Bibliography	Bishop, Elizabeth. "The Fish." In *The Complete Poems, 1927–1979,* 42–44. New York: Noonday Press/Farrar, Straus and Giroux, 1983.

Play, text	First note	[99] Shakespeare, *Hamlet, Prince of Denmark,* 2.1.1–9.
		▸ Refers to act 2, scene 1, lines 1–9.
		▸ If you wish to cite a specific edition, then:
		[99] William Shakespeare, *Hamlet, Prince of Denmark,* ed. Constance Jordan (New York: Pearson/Longman, 2005).
		[99] William Shakespeare, *The Three-Text Hamlet: Parallel Texts of the First and Second Quartos and First Folio,* ed. Bernice W. Kliman and Paul Bertram, introd. Eric Rasmussen (New York: AMS Press, 2003).
	Short note	[99] Shakespeare, *Hamlet,* 2.1.1–9.
	Bibliography	Shakespeare, William. *William Shakespeare's Hamlet, Prince of Denmark.* Edited by Constance Jordan. New York: Pearson/Longman, 2005.
		Shakespeare, William. *The Three-Text Hamlet: Parallel Texts of the First and Second Quartos and First Folio.* Edited by Bernice W. Kliman and Paul Bertram. Introduction by Eric Rasmussen. New York: AMS Press, 2003.

Performance of play or dance	First note	[99] *Kiss,* choreography by Susan Marshall, music by Arvo Pärt, performed by Cheryl Mann, Tobin Del Cuore, Hubbard Street Dance Chicago, Chicago, March 12, 2004.
		[99] *Topdog/Underdog,* by Suzan Lori-Parks, directed by Amy Morton, performed by K. Todd Freeman, David Rainey, Steppenwolf Theater, Chicago, November 2, 2003.
		▸ If you are concentrating on one person or one position such as director, put that

Performance of play or dance (*continued*)		person's name first. For example, if you are concentrating on David Rainey's acting: ⁹⁹ David Rainey, performance, *Topdog/Underdog,* by Suzan Lori-Parks, directed by Amy Morton . . .
	Short note	⁹⁹ *Kiss.* ⁹⁹ *Topdog/Underdog.*
	Bibliography	*Kiss.* Choreography by Susan Marshall. Music by Arvo Pärt. Performed by Cheryl Mann, Tobin Del Cuore. Hubbard Street Dance Chicago, Chicago, March 12, 2004. *Topdog/Underdog.* By Suzan Lori-Parks. Directed by Amy Morton. Performed by K. Todd Freeman, David Rainey. Steppenwolf Theater, Chicago, November 2, 2003. ▸ Or, if you are concentrating on Rainey's acting: Rainey, David, performance. *Topdog/Underdog.* By Suzan Lori-Parks. Directed by Amy Morton . . .
Television program	First note	⁹⁹ *Seinfeld,* "The Soup Nazi," episode 116, November 2, 1995. ▸ Or, a fuller citation: ⁹⁹ *Seinfeld,* "The Soup Nazi," by Spike Feresten, episode 116, directed by Andy Ackerman, performed by Jerry Seinfeld, Jason Alexander, Julia Louis-Dreyfus, Michael Richards, Alexandra Wentworth, Larry Thomas, NBC, November 2, 1995.
	Short note	⁹⁹ *Seinfeld,* "Soup Nazi."
	Bibliography	*Seinfeld,* "The Soup Nazi." Episode 116. Directed by Andy Ackerman. Written by Spike Feresten. Performed by Jerry Seinfeld, Jason Alexander, Julia Louis-Dreyfus, Michael Richards, Alexandra Wentworth, Larry Thomas. NBC, November 2, 1995.
Film	First note	⁹⁹ *Godfather II,* DVD, directed by Francis Ford Coppola (1974; Los Angeles: Paramount Home Video, 2003).

▸ If you wish to cite individual scenes, which are accessible on DVDs, treat them like chapters in books. "Murder of Fredo," *Godfather II* . . .

Short note	[99] *Godfather II.*
Bibliography	*Godfather II,* DVD. Directed by Francis Ford Coppola. Performed by Al Pacino, Robert De Niro, Robert Duvall, Diane Keaton. Screenplay by Francis Ford Coppola and Mario Puzo based on novel by Mario Puzo. 1974; Paramount Home Video, 2003.

▸ Title, director, studio, and year of release are all required. So is the year the video recording was released, if that's what you are citing.

▸ Optional: the actors, producers, screenwriters, editors, cinematographers, and other information. You can include what you need for your paper, in order of their importance to your analysis. Their names appear between the title and the distributor.

Artwork, original	First note	[99] Jacopo Robusti Tintoretto, *The Birth of John the Baptist,* ca. 1550, Hermitage, St. Petersburg.

▸ If the exact date of an artwork is not available, give an approximate one. A painting from "circa 1550" would be abbreviated "ca. 1550."

Short note	[99] Tintoretto, *Birth of John the Baptist.*
Bibliography	▸ Do not include any artwork, sculptures, or photographs in the bibliography.

Artwork, reproduction	First note	[99] Jacopo Robusti Tintoretto, *The Birth of John the Baptist,* 1550s, in Tom Nichols, *Tintoretto: Tradition and Identity* (London: Reaktion Books, 1999), 47.

Short note	[99] Tintoretto, *The Birth of John the Baptist.*
Bibliography	▸ Do not include any artwork, sculptures, or photographs in the bibliography.

Artwork, online	First note	[99] Jacopo Robusti Tintoretto, *The Birth of John the Baptist,* 1550s, Hermitage, St. Petersburg, http://www.hermitage.ru/html_En/index.html (accessed February 1, 2004). [99] Jacopo Robusti Tintoretto, *The Birth of John the Baptist* (detail), 1550s, Hermitage, St. Petersburg, http://cgfa.floridaimaging.com/t/p-tintore1.htm (accessed January 6, 2004).
	Short note	[99] Tintoretto, *The Birth of John the Baptist.*
	Bibliography	▸ Do not include any artwork, sculptures, or photographs in the bibliography.
Photograph	First note	[99] Ansel Adams, *Monolith, the Face of Half Dome, Yosemite National Park,* 1927, Art Institute, Chicago.
	Short note	[99] Adams, *Monolith.*
	Bibliography	▸ Do not include any artwork, sculptures, or photographs in the bibliography.
Photograph, online	First note	[99] Ansel Adams, *Monolith, the Face of Half Dome, Yosemite National Park,* 1927, Art Institute, Chicago, http://www.hctc.commnet .edu/artmuseum/anseladams/details/pdf/monlith.pdf (accessed February 14, 2007).
	Short note	[99] Adams, *Monolith.*
	Bibliography	▸ Do not include any artwork, sculptures, or photographs in the bibliography.
Figures: map, chart, graph, or table	First citation	▸ Citation for a map, chart, graph, or table normally appears as a credit below the item rather than as a footnote or endnote. *Source:* Ken Menkhaus, "Governance without Government in Somalia: Spoilers, State Building, and the Politics of Coping," *International Security* 31 (Winter 2006/07): 79, fig. 1. *Source:* http://www-personal.umich.edu/~mejn/election/2006/ (accessed February 14, 2007).

Source: "2006 Election Results," House of
Representatives map, *Washington Post,*
n.d., http://projects.washingtonpost.com/
elections/keyraces/map/ (accessed February
10, 2007).
Source: Topographic Maps (California),
National Geographic Society, 2004, http://
mapmachine.nationalgeographic.com/
mapmachine/viewandcustomize.html?task=g
etMap&themeId=113&size=s&state=zoomBox
(accessed February 6, 2007).

Short citation   ▸ Use full citations for all figures.

Bibliography   Menkhaus, Ken. "Governance without
Government in Somalia: Spoilers, State
Building, and the Politics of Coping,"
International Security 31 (Winter 2006/07):
74–106.
"2006 Election Results." House of
Representatives map. *Washington Post,*
n.d. http://projects.washingtonpost
.com/elections/keyraces/map/ (accessed
February 10, 2007).
Topographic Maps (California). National
Geographic Society. 2004. http://
mapmachine.nationalgeographic.com/
mapmachine/viewandcustomize.html?task
=getMap&themeId=113&size=s&state=zoo
mBox (accessed February 6, 2007).

Musical   First note   ⁹⁹ Robert Johnson, "Cross Road Blues," 1937,
recording   *Robert Johnson: King of the Delta Blues
Singers,* Columbia Records 1654, 1961.
⁹⁹ Samuel Barber, "Cello Sonata, for cello and
piano, Op. 6," *Barber: Adagio for Strings,
Violin Concerto, Orchestral and Chamber
Works,* compact disc 2, St. Louis Symphony,
cond. Leonard Slatkin, Alan Stepansky (cello),
Israela Margalit (piano), EMI Classics 74287,
2001.
⁹⁹ Jimi Hendrix, "Purple Haze," 1969,
Woodstock: Three Days of Peace and Music,

Musical recording (*continued*)		compact disc 3, Atlantic/Wea, 1994, available at iTunes.
	Short note	[99] Johnson, "Cross Road Blues." [99] Barber, "Cello Sonata, Op. 6." [99] Hendrix, "Purple Haze."
	Bibliography	Johnson, Robert. "Cross Road Blues." 1937. *Robert Johnson: King of the Delta Blues Singers.* Columbia Records 1654, 1961. Barber, Samuel. "Cello Sonata, for cello and piano, Op. 6." *Barber: Adagio for Strings, Violin Concerto, Orchestral and Chamber Works.* Compact disc 2. St. Louis Symphony. Cond. Leonard Slatkin, Alan Stepansky (cello), Israela Margalit (piano). EMI Classics 74287, 2001. Hendrix, Jimi. "Purple Haze," 1969. *Woodstock: Three Days of Peace and Music.* Compact disk 3. Atlantic/Wea, 1994. Available at iTunes.
Music video, comments on music video	First note	[99] Nelly Furtado featuring Timbaland, "Promiscuous," music video, 2006, at iTunes store (accessed February 8, 2007). [99] Jay-Z, "Show Me What You Got," music video, directed by F. Gary Gray, from *Kingdom Come,* Roc-a-Fella/Def Jam, 2006, http://www.mtv.com/music/video/ (accessed February 8, 2007). [99] Delbert McClinton, "Same Kind of Crazy as Me," music video, 2007, http://www.youtube.com/watch?v=5vBEYAhXkaI (accessed February 14, 2007). [99] RobertZimmerman897, comment on music video [Bob Dylan, "Like a Rolling Stone, 1966"], February 14, 2007, http://www.youtube.com/watch?v=xOogSJGJ7Fs (accessed February 14, 2007).
	Short note	[99] Furtado, "Promiscuous." [99] Jay-Z, "Show Me What You Got." [99] McClinton, "Same Kind of Crazy as Me."

⁹⁹ RobertZimmerman897, comment on music video.

Bibliography	Furtado, Nelly, featuring Timbaland. "Promiscuous." Music video, 2006. iTunes store (accessed February 8, 2007).
	Jay-Z. "Show Me What You Got." Music video. Directed by F. Gary Gray. From *Kingdom Come*. Roc-a-Fella/Def Jam, 2006. http://www.mtv.com/music/video/ (accessed February 8, 2007).
	McClinton, Delbert. "Same Kind of Crazy as Me." Music video. 2007. http://www.youtube.com/watch?v=5vBEYAhXkaI (accessed February 14, 2007).
	RobertZimmerman897. Comment on music video [Bob Dylan, "Like a Rolling Stone, 1966"]. February 14, 2007. http://www.youtube.com/watch?v=xOogSJGJ7Fs (accessed February 14, 2007).

Sheet music	First note	⁹⁹ Johann Sebastian Bach, "Toccata and Fugue in D Minor," 1708, BWV 565, arranged by Ferruccio Benvenuto Busoni for solo piano (New York: G. Schirmer, LB1629, 1942).
	Short note	⁹⁹ Bach, "Toccata and Fugue in D Minor."
	Bibliography	Bach, Johann Sebastian. "Toccata and Fugue in D Minor." 1708. BWV 565. Arranged by Ferruccio Benvenuto Busoni for solo piano. New York: G. Schirmer LB1629, 1942.
		▸ This piece was written in 1708 and has the standard Bach classification BWV 565. This particular arrangement was published by G. Schirmer in 1942 and has their catalog number LB1629.

Liner notes	First note	⁹⁹ Steven Reich, liner notes for *Different Trains*, Elektra/Nonesuch 9 79176-2, 1988.
	Short note	⁹⁹ Reich, liner notes.
		▸ Or

Liner notes (*continued*)		[99] Reich, liner notes, *Different Trains.*
	Bibliography	Reich, Steven. Liner notes for *Different Trains.* Elektra/Nonesuch 9 79176-2, 1988.

Advertise-ment, hard copy and online	First note	[99] *Letters from Iwo Jima* advertisement, *New York Times,* February 6, 2007, B4.
		▸ You may omit pagination from newspapers, if you wish, since these vary from edition to edition.
		[99] Mercedes-Benz 2007 CL, "Pillarless" advertisement, *New Yorker,* February 12, 2007, 26.
		[99] Avis Israel Car Rentals advertisement, *Jerusalem Post,* February 7, 2007, http://www.jpost.com/, link at http://www.avis.co.il/avis/site/local/avis/english/IsraelRentals.jsp?banner=JpostHP (accessed February 7, 2007).
	Short note	[99] *Letters from Iwo Jima* advertisement.
		[99] Mercedes-Benz 2007 CL, "Pillarless" advertisement.
		[99] Avis Israel advertisement.
	Bibliography	▸ Advertisements are rarely included in bibliographies, but you may include them if they are especially important to your work.
		Letters from Iwo Jima advertisement. *New York Times,* February 6, 2007.
		Mercedes-Benz 2007 CL. "Pillarless" advertisement. *New Yorker,* February 12, 2007, 26.
		Avis Israel Car Rentals advertisement. *Jerusalem Post,* February 7, 2007. http://www.jpost.com/, link at http://www.avis.co.il/avis/site/local/avis/english/IsraelRentals.jsp?banner=JpostHP (accessed February 7, 2007).

Government document, hard copy and online	First note	[99] Senate Committee on Armed Services, *Hearings on S. 758, A Bill to Promote the National Security by Providing for a National Defense Establishment,* 80th Cong., 1st sess., 1947, S. Rep. 239, 13.

▶ "S. Rep. 239, 13" refers to report number 239, page 13.

[99] *Financial Services and General Government Appropriations Act, 2008,* HR 2829, 110th Cong., 1st sess., *Congressional Record* 153 (June 28, 2007): H7347.

[99] *Financial Services and General Government Appropriations Act, 2008,* HR 2829, 110th Cong., 1st sess., *Congressional Record* 153 (June 28, 2007): H7347, http://frwebgate .access.gpo.gov/cgi-bin/getpage.cgi?position =all&page=H7347&dbname=2007_record (accessed July 9, 2007).

[99] Environmental Protection Agency (EPA), *Final Rule, Air Pollution Control: Prevention of Significant Deterioration; Approval and Promulgation of Implementation Plans, Federal Register* 68, no. 247 (December 24, 2003): 74483–91.

[99] U.S. Department of State, Daily Press Briefing, February 12, 2007, http://www.state .gov/r/pa/prs/dpb/2007/80442.htm (accessed February 19, 2007).

Short note

[99] Senate, *Hearings on S. 758,* 13.

[99] *Financial Services and General Government Appropriations Act, 2008,* HR 2829, *Cong. Rec.,* (June 28, 2007): H7347.

[99] EPA, *Final Rule, Air Pollution Control.*

[99] U.S. State Department, Daily Press Briefing, February 12, 2007.

Bibliography

U.S. Congress. Senate. Committee on Armed Services. *Hearings on S. 758, Bill to Promote the National Security by Providing for a National Defense Establishment.* 80th Cong., 1st sess., 1947. S. Rep. 239.

U.S. Congress. House. *Congressional Record.* 110th Cong., 1st sess. June 28, 2007. Vol. 153, no. 106. H7347.

U.S. Congress. House. *Congressional Record.* 110th Cong., 1st sess. June 28, 2007. Vol. 153, no. 106. H7347. http://frwebgate .access.gpo.gov/cgi-bin/getpage.cgi

Government document, hard copy and online (*continued*)		?position=all&page=H7347&dbname =2007_record (accessed July 9, 2007). Environmental Protection Agency. *Final Rule, Air Pollution Control: Prevention of Significant Deterioration; Approval and Promulgation of Implementation Plans. Federal Register* 68, no. 247 (December 24, 2003): 74483–91. U.S. Department of State. Daily Press Briefing. February 12, 2007. http://www.state.gov/ r/pa/prs/dpb/2007/80442.htm (accessed February 19, 2007).
Software	First note	[99] *Dreamweaver 8* (San Francisco: Adobe, 2007). [99] *iTunes 7.0.2* (Cupertino, CA: Apple, 2007). [99] *Stata 9* (College Station, TX: Stata, 2007). [99] J. Scott Long and Jeremy Freese, *Regression Models for Categorical Dependent Variables Using Stata,* 2nd ed. (College Station, TX: Stata, 2006). ▸ Long and Freese's book shows how to use Stata software. It is treated like other texts.
	Short note	[99] *Dreamweaver 8.* [99] *iTunes 7.0.2.* [99] *Stata 9.* [99] Long and Freese, *Regression Models.*
	Bibliography	*Dreamweaver 8.* San Francisco: Adobe, 2007. *iTunes 7.0.2.* Cupertino, CA: Apple, 2007. *Stata 9.* College Station, TX: Stata, 2007. Long, J. Scott, and Jeremy Freese. *Regression Models for Categorical Dependent Variables Using Stata.* 2nd ed. College Station, TX: Stata, 2006.
Database	First note	[99] Corpus Scriptorum Latinorum database of Latin literature, http://www.forumromanum .org/literature/index.html (accessed July 10, 2007). ▸ For a specific item within this database: [99] Gaius Julius Caesar, *Commentarii de bello civili,* ed. A. G. Peskett (Loeb Classical Library;

London: W. Heinemann, 1914), in Corpus
Scriptorum Latinorum database of Latin
literature, http://www.thelatinlibrary.com/
caes.html (accessed July 10, 2007).

[99] Maryland Department of Assessments and
Taxation, Real Property Data Search v1.00.18,
http://sdatcert3.resiusa.org/rp_rewrite/
(accessed July 10, 2007).

[99] U.S. Copyright Office, Search Copyright
Records: Registrations and Documents,
http://www.copyright.gov/records/ (accessed
February 12, 2007).

[99] United Nations Treaty Collection, Access to
Databases, http://untreaty.un.org/English/
access.asp (accessed February 12, 2007).

▸ For a specific item within this database:

[99] "International Tropical Timber Agreement,
2006 (adopted January 27, 2006)," in United
Nations Treaty Collection, Access to Databases,
http://untreaty.un.org/English/notpubl/IV_
16_english.pdf (accessed February 12, 2007).

Short note	[99] Corpus Scriptorum Latinorum.
	[99] Maryland, Real Property Data Search.
	[99] U.S. Copyright Office, Search Copyright Records.
	[99] United Nations Treaty Collection, Access to Database.
	[99] "International Tropical Timber Agreement, 2006."
Bibliography	Corpus Scriptorum Latinorum. Database of Latin literature. http://www. forumromanum.org/literature/index.html (accessed July 10, 2007).
	Caesar, Gaius Julius. *Commentarii de bello civili*. Edited by A. G. Peskett. Loeb Classical Library. London: W. Heinemann, 1914. In Corpus Scriptorum Latinorum database of Latin literature. http://www.thelatinlibrary .com/caes.html (accessed July 10, 2007).
	Maryland Department of Assessments and Taxation. Real Property Data Search

Database (*continued*)		v1.00.18. http://sdatcert3.resiusa.org/rp_ rewrite/ (accessed July 10, 2007).
		U.S. Copyright Office. Search Copyright Records: Registrations and Documents. http://www.copyright.gov/records/ (accessed February 12, 2007).
		United Nations Treaty Collection. Access to Databases. http://untreaty.un.org/English/ access.asp (accessed February 12, 2007).
		▸ For a specific item within this database:
		"International Tropical Timber Agreement, 2006 (adopted January 27, 2006)." In United Nations Treaty Collection, Access to Databases. http://untreaty.un.org/English/ notpubl/IV_16_english.pdf (accessed February 12, 2007).
Web site, entire	First note	⁹⁹ Digital History Web site, ed. Steven Mintz, http://www.digitalhistory.uh.edu/index.cfm? (accessed February 12, 2007).
		⁹⁹ Internet Public Library (IPL), http://www.ipl .org/ (accessed February 12, 2007).
		⁹⁹ Yale University, History Department home page, http://www.yale.edu/history/ (accessed February 12, 2007).
		▸ You may omit "home page" if it is obvious.
	Short note	⁹⁹ Digital History Web site.
		⁹⁹ Internet Public Library.
		⁹⁹ Yale History Department home page.
	Bibliography	Digital History Web site. Edited by Steven Mintz. http://www.digitalhistory.uh.edu/ index.cfm? (accessed February 12, 2007).
		Internet Public Library (IPL). http://www.ipl .org/ (accessed February 12, 2007).
		Yale University. History Department home page. http://www.yale.edu/history/ (accessed February 12, 2007).
Web page, with author	First note	⁹⁹ Charles Lipson, "International News Sources," http://www.charleslipson.com/ News-links.htm (accessed February 12, 2007).

	Short note	[99] Lipson, "International News Sources."
	Bibliography	Lipson, Charles. "International News Sources." http://www.charleslipson.com/News-links .htm (accessed February 12, 2007).
		▸ Include the title or description of the Web page if available. That way, if the link changes, it may still be possible to find the page through a search.
Web page, no author	First note	[99] "*I Love Lucy:* Series Summary," *Sitcoms Online,* http://www.sitcomsonline .com/ilovelucy.html (accessed February 6, 2007).
	Short note	[99] "*I Love Lucy:* Series Summary."
	Bibliography	"*I Love Lucy:* Series Summary." *Sitcoms Online.* http://www.sitcomsonline.com/ilovelucy .html (accessed February 6, 2007).
Weblog entry or comment	First note	[99] Daniel Drezner, "Is Economic Protectionism on the Rise in China?" Daniel W. Drezner Weblog, entry posted February 2, 2007, http:// www.danieldrezner.com/archives/003136.html (accessed March 1, 2007).
		▸ If this entry had no title, it would be cited as: Daniel Drezner, untitled entry, Daniel W. Drezner Weblog . . . .
		[99] Jonathan Adler, "On *Ad Hominem* Arguments," Volokh Conspiracy Weblog, entry posted February 5, 2007, http://volokh.com/ (accessed February 7, 2007).
		[99] Nick Good, comment on "On *Ad Hominem* Arguments," Volokh Conspiracy Weblog, posted on 2:55 am February 6, 2007, http:// volokh.com/posts/1170708620.shtml#185453 (accessed February 7, 2007).
		▸ Nick Good made several comments on this entry so the time is included to specify one. There is also a specific link to this comment because this particular Weblog provides it.

Weblog entry or comment (*continued*)		[99] Peter Richards, untitled poem, Project Muse, entry posted January 24, 2007, http://www .quickmuse.com/archive/landing.php?poem=1 xM3n4DY5Ysy7x4TFKdYJ3I8BIP8eM1 (accessed February 14, 2007).
	Short note	[99] Drezner, "Economic Protectionism in China." [99] Adler, "On *Ad Hominem* Arguments." [99] Good, comment on "On *Ad Hominem* Arguments." [99] Richards, untitled poem.
	Bibliography	▸ Weblog items are not usually part of the bibliography, but you may include them if the items are important in their own right or are especially significant for your paper. Here is the format:

Drezner, Daniel. "Is Economic Protectionism on the Rise in China?" Daniel W. Drezner Weblog. Entry posted February 2, 2007. http://www.danieldrezner.com/ archives/003136.html (accessed March 1, 2007).

Adler, Jonathan. "On *Ad Hominem* Arguments." Volokh Conspiracy Weblog. Entry posted February 5, 2007. http://volokh.com/ (accessed February 7, 2007).

Good, Nick. Comment on "On *Ad Hominem* Arguments." Volokh Conspiracy Weblog. Comment posted February 6, 2007, 2:55 a.m. http://volokh.com/posts/1170708620 .shtml#185453 (accessed February 7, 2007).

Richards, Peter. Untitled poem. Project Muse. Entry posted January 24, 2007. http://www .quickmuse.com/archive/landing.php ?poem=1xM3n4DY5Ysy7x4TFKdYJ3I8BIP8eM1 (accessed February 14, 2007).

Video clip, news video	First note	[99] *Duck and Cover,* Federal Civil Defense Administration/Archer Productions, 1951, video file posted November 26, 2006, http://youtube.com/watch?v=-UVH8YRXsqo (accessed February 14, 2007).

[99] "High Speed Chase Ends in Shootout," *CNN
.com,* video news clip posted February 7, 2007,
http://dynamic.cnn.com/apps/tp/video/
us/2007/02/07/ortiz.ut.police.shootout.ktvx/
video.ws.asx?NGUserID=aa5128f-31671
-1169599598-1&adDEmas=R00%26hi
%26ameritech.net%2673%26usa%26602
%2660601%2614%2607%26U1% (accessed
February 7, 2007).

▸ When the URL is very long and the video can
be found on a searchable site, you may choose
not to include it.

Short note	[99] "High Speed Chase," *CNN.com,* February 7, 2007. [99] *Duck and Cover,* 1951.
Bibliography	"High Speed Chase Ends in Shootout." *CNN.com.* Video news clip posted February 7, 2007. http://dynamic.cnn .com/apps/tp/video/us/2007/02/07/ ortiz.ut.police.shootout.ktvx/video .ws.asx?NGUserID=aa5128f-31671 -1169599598-1&adDEmas=R00%26hi %26ameritech.net%2673%26usa%26602 %2660601%2614%2607%26U1 % (accessed February 7, 2007). ▸ When the video can be found on a searchable site and the URL is very long, you may choose not to include it. "High Speed Chase Ends in Shootout." *CNN .com.* Video news clip posted February 7, 2007.

Video blog (Vlog), video on Web site, posted comment on video	First note	[99] Steve Garfield, "Vlog Soup 23," Steve Garfield's Video Blog, video posted January 29, 2007, http://stevegarfield.blogs.com/ videoblog/2007/01/vlog_soup_23.html (accessed February 7, 2007). [99] miaarose, "Mia's First Vlog," video posted January 9, 2007, http://www.youtube.com/ watch?v=Hd3UC8kYCrk (accessed February 7, 2007).

Video blog (Vlog), video on Web site, posted comment on video (*continued*)		[99] benwsp, "Darragh's Response to Miaarose," video comment posted January 10, 2007, http://www.youtube.com/watch?v=_-SmfbUZAxo (accessed February 7, 2007). [99] lonelyinacrowd, text response to vlog, posted February 6, 2007, http://www.youtube.com/watch?v=Hd3UC8kYCrk (accessed February 7, 2007).
	Short note	[99] Garfield, "Vlog Soup 23." [99] miaarose, "Mia's First Vlog." [99] benwsp, "Darragh's Response to Miaarose." [99] lonelyinacrowd, response to vlog.
	Bibliography	Garfield, Steve. "Vlog Soup 23." Steve Garfield's Video Blog. Video posted January 29, 2007. http://stevegarfield.blogs.com/videoblog/2007/01/vlog_soup_23.html (accessed February 7, 2007). miaarose. "Mia's First Vlog." Video posted January 9, 2007. http://www.youtube.com/watch?v=Hd3UC8kYCrk (accessed February 7, 2007). benwsp. "Darragh's Response to Miaarose." Video comment posted January 10, 2007. http://www.youtube.com/watch?v=_-SmfbUZAxo (accessed February 7, 2007). lonelyinacrowd. Text response to vlog posted February 6, 2007. http://www.youtube.com/watch?v=Hd3UC8kYCrk (accessed February 7, 2007).
Podcast or video podcast (vodcast)	First note	[99] Marc Fournier, "Goals and Needs," *TVO Big Ideas Podcast,* February 3 2007, iTunes Store (accessed February 8, 2007). [99] "BBC Question Time," February 1, 2007, video podcast, http://downloads.bbc.co.uk/rmhttp/downloadtrial/bbc1/questiontime-videopodcast/questiontime-videopodcast_20070201-2200_40_pc.mp4 (accessed February 8, 2007). [99] "2057: Future of Civilization," Discovery

Channel, video podcast, n.d., iTunes Store
(accessed February 8, 2007).
▸ Or
⁹⁹ Micheo Kaku, host, "2057: Future of
Civilization," Discovery Channel, video podcast,
n.d., iTunes Store (accessed February 8, 2007).

Short note		⁹⁹ Fournier, "Goals and Needs." ⁹⁹ "BBC Question Time." ▸ Or ⁹⁹ "BBC Question Time," February 1, 2007. ⁹⁹ "2057: Future of Civilization." ▸ Or ⁹⁹ Kaku, "2057: Future of Civilization."
Bibliography		Fournier, Marc. "Goals and Needs." *TVO Big Ideas Podcast*. February 3, 2007. iTunes Store (accessed February 8, 2007). "BBC Question Time." February 1, 2007. Video podcast. http://downloads.bbc.co.uk/ rmhttp/downloadtrial/bbc1/questiontime-videopodcast/questiontime-videopodcast_20070201-2200_40_pc.mp4 (accessed February 8, 2007). "2057: Future of Civilization." Discovery Channel. Video podcast. n.d. iTunes Store (accessed February 8, 2007). ▸ Or Kaku, Micheo, host. "2057: Future of Civilization." Discovery Channel. Video podcast. n.d. iTunes Store (accessed February 8, 2007).
Personal networking site (Facebook, MySpace)	First note	⁹⁹ Barney Fife, profile at MySpace, http:// profile.myspace.com/index.cfm?fuseaction =user.viewprofile&friendid=15431304 (accessed February 8, 2007). ⁹⁹ Bobbie, comment in Barney Fife's Friends Comments, posted February 4, 2007, 10:16 a.m., at Barney Fife profile at MySpace, http:// profile.myspace.com/index.cfm?fuseaction= user.viewprofile&friendid=15431304 (accessed February 8, 2007).

Personal networking site (Facebook, MySpace) (*continued*)		[99] Aunt Bea, photograph at Barney Fife profile at MySpace, http://profile.myspace.com/index .cfm?fuseaction=user.viewprofile (accessed February 8, 2007).
	Short note	[99] Fife, profile at MySpace. [99] Bobbie, comment in Barney Fife profile at MySpace. ▸ Or [99] Bobbie, comment, February 4, 2007, in Barney Fife profile at MySpace. [99] Aunt Bea, photograph at Barney Fife profile at MySpace.
	Bibliography	Fife, Barney. Profile at MySpace. http://profile .myspace.com/index.cfm?fuseaction=user .viewprofile&friendid=15431304 (accessed February 8, 2007). Bobbie. Comment in Barney Fife's Friends Comments. Posted February 4, 2007, 10:16 a.m. Barney Fife profile at MySpace. http://profile.myspace.com/index .cfm?fuseaction=user.viewprofile&friendid =15431304 (accessed February 8, 2007). Aunt Bea. Photograph. Barney Fife profile at MySpace. http://profile.myspace.com/ index.cfm?fuseaction=user.viewprofile (accessed February 8, 2007).
E-mail, instant messages, electronic newsgroups, and listservs	First note	[99] Chicago Council on Global Affairs, "Weekly Update," *Chicago Council Calendar,* e-mail to Chicago Council on Global Affairs mailing list, February 6, 2007. [99] "Campus Events for Coming Week," University of Chicago e-mail to listserv, February 6, 2007, https://listhost.uchicago .edu/pipermail/events/2007-February/ 000228.html (accessed February 8, 2007). ▸ Include the URL if the mass e-mailing has been archived. [99] Kathy Leis, e-mail message to author, May 3, 2007.

[99] Michael Lipson, instant message to Jonathan Lipson, March 9, 2007.

> ▸ You may include the time of an electronic message if it is important or differentiates it from others. For example:

[99] Michael Lipson, instant message to Jonathan Lipson, 11:23 a.m., March 9, 2007.

Short note

[99] Chicago Council on Global Affairs, "Weekly Update," February 6, 2007.

[99] "Campus Events for the Coming Week," February 6, 2007.

[99] Kathy Leis, e-mail message to author, May 3, 2007.

> ▸ You may be able to shorten these notes. If you are citing only one person named Leis, for instance, then you can drop the first name. But if you are citing messages from Alan Leis, Kathy Leis, Elizabeth Leis, and Julia Leis, then it is much clearer to include their first names, even in short notes.

[99] Michael Lipson, instant message to Jonathan Lipson, March 9, 2007.

[99] Michael Lipson, instant message to Jonathan Lipson, 11:23 a.m., March 9, 2007.

Bibliography

> ▸ Personal e-mails, instant messages, and e-mails to listservs are not included in the bibliography unless they can be retrieved by third parties. If they are archived and can be retrieved, then include their URL.

"Campus Events for Coming Week." University of Chicago e-mail to listserv. February 6, 2007. https://listhost.uchicago.edu/pipermail/events/2007-February/000228.html (accessed February 8, 2007).

CHICAGO: CITATIONS TO TABLES AND NOTES

CITATION	REFERS TO
106	page 106
106n	only note appearing on page 106
107 n. 32	note number 32 on page 107, a page with several notes
89, table 6.2	table 6.2, which appears on page 89; similar for graphs and figures

CHICAGO: COMMON ABBREVIATIONS IN CITATIONS

and others	et al.	editor	ed.	page	p.
appendix	app.	especially	esp.	pages	pp.
book	bk.	figure	fig.	part	pt.
chapter	chap.	note	n.	pseudonym	pseud.
compare	cf.	notes	nn.	translator	trans.
document	doc.	number	no.	versus	vs.
edition	ed.	opus	op.	volume	vol.

Note: All abbreviations are lowercase, followed by a period. Most form their plurals by adding "s." The exceptions are note (n. → nn.), opus (op. → opp.), page (p. → pp.), and translator (same abbreviation).

In citing poetry, do not use abbreviations for "line" or "lines" since a lowercase "l" is easily confused with the number one.

FAQS ABOUT CHICAGO-STYLE CITATIONS

Why do you put the state after some publishers and not after others?
The Chicago Manual of Style recommends using state names for all but the largest, best-known cities. To avoid confusion, they use Cambridge, MA, for Harvard and MIT presses but just Cambridge for Cambridge University Press in the ancient English university town. Also, you can drop the state name if it is already included in the publisher's title, such as Ann Arbor: University of Michigan Press.

What if a book is forthcoming?
Use "forthcoming" just as you would use the year. Here's a bibliographic entry:

Godot, Shlomo. *Still Waiting.* London: Verso, forthcoming.

What if the date or place of publication is missing?
Same idea as "forthcoming." Where you would normally put the place or date, use "n.p." (no place) or "n.d." (no date). For example: (Montreal, QC: McGill-Queen's University Press, n.d.).

What if the author is anonymous or not listed?
Usually, you omit the anonymous author and begin with the title.

If an author is technically anonymous but is actually known, put the name in brackets, as in [Johnson, Samuel] or [Madison, James] and list it wherever the author's name falls.

One book I cite has a title that ends with a question mark. Do I still put periods or commas after it?
No.

Are notes single-spaced or double-spaced? What about the bibliography?
Space your footnotes and endnotes the same way you do your text.

As for your bibliography, I think it is easiest to read if you single space within entries and put a double space between the entries. But check what your department or publisher requires. They may require double spacing for everything.

I'm reading Mark Twain. Do I cite Twain or Samuel Clemens?
When pseudonyms are well known such as Mark Twain or Mother Teresa, you can use them alone, without explanation, if you wish.

If you want to include both the pseudonym and the given name, the rule is simple. Put the better-known name first, followed by the lesser-known one in brackets. It doesn't matter if the "real" name is the lesser-known one.

George Eliot [Mary Ann Evans]
Isak Dinesen [Karen Christence Dinesen, Baroness Blixen-Finecke]
Le Corbusier [Charles-Edouard Jeanneret]
Benjamin Disraeli [Lord Beaconsfield]
Lord Palmerston [Henry John Temple]
Krusty the Clown [Herschel S. Krustofski]

If you wish to include the pseudonym in a bibliographic entry, it reads:

Aleichem, Sholom [Solomon Rabinovitz]. *Fiddler on the Roof . . .*

Are there any differences between the rules for citations in *The Chicago Manual of Style* and those in Kate L. Turabian's *Manual for Writers of Research Papers, Theses, and Dissertations?*

Turabian's *Manual* is essentially a student version of *The Chicago Manual of Style*. In terms of citation style, the only significant difference between the two books is that Turabian requires access dates with all citations of online sources, while *The Chicago Manual of Style* considers them optional, depending on the situation. Since this book is intended for students, it follows Turabian's rule and includes access dates.

MLA CITATIONS FOR
THE HUMANITIES

. . . .

The Modern Language Association (MLA) has developed a citation style that is widely used in the humanities. Instead of footnotes or endnotes, it uses in-text citations such as (Strier 125). Full information about each item appears in the bibliography, which MLA calls "Works Cited." Like other bibliographies, it contains three essential nuggets of information about each item: the author, title, and publication data. To illustrate, let's use a book by Fouad Ajami. The full entry in the Works Cited is

> Ajami, Fouad. The Foreigner's Gift: The Americans, the Arabs, and
>   the Iraqis in Iraq. New York: Free Press, 2006.

Titles are underlined rather than italicized.

In-text citations are brief and simple. To cite the entire book, just insert (Ajami) at the end of the sentence, or (Ajami 12) to refer to page 12. If your paper happens to cite several books by Ajami, be sure your reader knows which one you are referring to. If that's not clear in the sentence, then include a very brief title: (Ajami, Gift 12).

MLA citations can be even briefer—and they should be, whenever possible. They can omit the author and the title as long as it's clear which work is being cited. For example:

> As Ajami notes, these are long-standing problems in Iraqi politics (14–33).

You can omit the in-text reference entirely if the author and title are clear and you are not citing specific pages. For instance:

> Gibbon's Decline and Fall of the Roman Empire established new standards of documentary evidence for historians.

In this case, there's nothing to put in an in-text reference that isn't already in the sentence. So, given MLA's consistent emphasis on brevity, you simply skip the reference. You still include Gibbon in your Works Cited.

Because in-text references are so brief, you can string several together in one parenthesis: (Bevington 17; Bloom 75; Vendler 51). The authors' names are separated by semicolons.

If Ajami's book were a three-volume work, then the citation to volume 3, page 17, would be (Ajami 3: 17). If you need to differentiate this work from others by the same author, then include the title: (Ajami, Gift 3: 17). If you wanted to cite the volume but not a specific page, then use (Ajami, vol. 3) or (Ajami, Gift, vol. 3). Why include "vol." here? So readers won't think you are citing page 3 of a one-volume work.

If several authors have the same last name, simply add their first initials to differentiate them: (C. Brontë, Jane Eyre), (E. Brontë, Wuthering Heights). Of course, full information about the authors and their works appears at the end, in the Works Cited.

Books like *Jane Eyre* appear in countless editions, and your readers may wish to look up passages in theirs. To make that easier, the MLA recommends that you add some information after the normal page citation. You might say, for example, that the passage appears in chapter 1. For poems, you would note the verse and lines.

Let's say that you quoted a passage from the first chapter of *Jane Eyre*, which appeared on page 7 in the edition you are using. Insert a semicolon after the page and add the chapter number, using a lowercase abbreviation for chapter: (E. Brontë, Wuthering Heights 7; ch. 1). For plays, the act, scene, and lines are separated by periods (Romeo and Juliet 1.3.12–15).

When you refer to online documents, there are often no pages to cite. As a substitute, include a section or paragraph number, if there is one. Just put a comma after the author's name, then list the section or paragraph: (Padgett, sec. 9.7) or (Snidal, pars. 12–18). If there's no numbering system, just list the author. Don't cite your printout because those pages vary from person to person, printer to printer.[1]

In-text citations normally appear at the end of sentences and are followed by the punctuation for the sentence itself. To illustrate:

---

1. These recommendations follow the MLA's own recommendation. MLA, "Frequently Asked Questions about MLA Style," http://www.mla.org/publications/style/style_faq/style_faq7.

A full discussion of these citation issues appears in the <u>MLA Handbook</u> (Gibaldi).

In this style, you can still use regular footnotes or endnotes for limited purposes. They can *only* be used for commentary, however, not for citations. If you need to cite some materials within the note itself, use in-text citations there, just as you would in the text.

For brevity—a paramount virtue of the MLA system—the names of publishers are also compressed: Princeton University Press becomes Princeton UP, the University of Chicago Press becomes U of Chicago P. For the same reason, most month names are abbreviated.

MLA throws brevity overboard, however, when referencing electronic information. If the works were originally printed, the Works Cited include all the print information, plus some extra information about the online versions, including Web sites, sponsoring organizations, access dates, and URLs. Of all citation styles, only MLA requires listing the sponsoring organization. This leads to redundancy. You are supposed to write: <u>Encyclopaedia Britannica Online</u>. 2008. Encyclopaedia Britannica . . . Or <u>CBSNews.com</u>. 5 Mar. 2008. CBS . . . The underlined titles are the works cited; the repeated name is the sponsoring organization. Actually, we'll see the name a third time in the URL, <http://www.cbs.com>. This seems like overkill to me, at least when the sponsoring organization is evident. But that's the current MLA style.

If an item is exclusively online, like a Web page or Weblog, the citation includes the author, the title of the Web page or site, the date it was created (or updated), plus information about the Web site, sponsoring organization, the date it was accessed, and the URL. It makes for a long list.

I have provided detailed information and examples in a table below. Because MLA style is often used in the humanities, where citations to plays, poems, paintings, and films are common, I include all of them. If you want still more examples or less common items, consult two useful books published by the MLA:

- Joseph Gibaldi, *MLA Style Manual and Guide to Scholarly Publishing,* 2nd ed. (New York: Modern Language Association of America, 1998), 149–254.
- Joseph Gibaldi, *MLA Handbook for Writers of Research Papers,* 6th ed. (New York: Modern Language Association of America, 2003).

They should be available in your library's reference section.

To make it easy to find the citations you need, I've listed them here al-phabetically, along with the pages where they are described. At the end of the chapter, I have listed some common MLA abbreviations.

INDEX OF MLA CITATIONS IN THIS CHAPTER

MLA: WORKS CITED AND IN-TEXT CITATIONS

Book, one author	Works Cited	Lipson, Charles. How to Write a BA Thesis: A Practical Guide from Your First Ideas to Your Finished Paper. Chicago: U Chicago P, 2005. Mavor, Carol. Reading Boyishly: Roland Barthes, J. M. Barrie, Jacques Henri Lartigue, Marcel Proust, and D. W. Winnicott. Durham: Duke UP, 2007. Robinson, Andrew M. Multiculturalism and the Foundations of Meaningful Life: Reconciling Autonomy, Identity, and Community. Vancouver: U of British Columbia P, 2007. ▸ MLA style omits the publisher's state or province.
	In-text	(Lipson 22–23) or (22–23) ▸ Refers to pages 22–23. ▸ If it is necessary to differentiate this book from others by the same author, then cite as: (Lipson, BA Thesis 22–23) (Mavor 26) or (26) (Robinson 136) or (136)
Books, several by same author	Works Cited	Easterly, William R. The Elusive Quest for Growth: Economists' Adventures and Misadventures in the Tropics. Cambridge: MIT P, 2001. ---. The White Man's Burden: Why the West's Efforts to Aid the Rest Have Done So Much Ill and So Little Good. New York: Penguin, 2006. ▸ The repetition of the author's name uses three hyphens, followed by a period.
	In-text	(Easterly, Elusive 34; Easterly, White Man's 456)
Book, multiple authors	Works Cited	Gikandi, Simon, and Evan Mwangi. The Columbia Guide to East African Literature in English since 1945. New York: Columbia UP, 2007. Heathcote, Edwin, and Laura Moffatt.

Book, multiple authors *(continued)*		Contemporary Church Architecture. Hoboken: Wiley, 2007. Nunez, Fernando, et al. Space and Place in the Mexican Landscape: The Evolution of a Colonial City. College Station: Texas A&M UP, 2007. ▸ When there are four or more authors, as there are for Space and Place, use "et al." after naming the first one.
	In-text	(Gikandi and Mwangi, Columbia Guide 15–26) or (Gikandi and Mwangi 15–26)
Book, multiple editions	Works Cited	Strunk, William, Jr., and E. B. White. The Elements of Style. 4th ed. New York: Longman, 2000. Gombrich, Richard F. Theravada Buddhism: A Social History from Ancient Benares to Modern Colombo. 2nd ed. London: Routledge, 2006. Head, Dominic, ed. The Cambridge Guide to Literature in English. 3rd ed. Cambridge: Cambridge UP, 2006. ▸ If this were a multivolume work, then the volume number would come after the edition: 3rd ed. Vol. 2.
	In-text	(Strunk and White 12) (Gombrich, 197) (Head 15)
Book, edited	Works Cited	Lutz, John Sutton, ed. Myth and Memory: Stories of Indigenous-European Contact. Vancouver: U of British Columbia P, 2007. Waugh, Patricia, ed. Literary Theory and Criticism: An Oxford Guide. New York: Oxford UP, 2006. Gilbert, Sandra, and Susan Gubar, eds. Feminist Literary Theory and Criticism: A Norton Reader. New York: Norton, 2007.

In-text		(Lutz 93) (Waugh 72) (Gilbert and Gubar 12)

Book, anonymous or no author	Works Cited	<u>Through Our Enemies' Eyes: Osama Bin Laden, Radical Islam, and the Future of America</u>. Washington: Brassey's, 2003. <u>Golden Verses of the Pythagoreans</u>. Whitefish: Kessinger, 2003. ▸ Do not use "anonymous" as the author. If the author is unknown, alphabetize by title but ignore any initial article ("a," "an," or "the"). So, <u>The Holy Koran</u> is alphabetized under "H."
	In-text	(<u>Through Our Enemies' Eyes</u>) (<u>Golden Verses</u>)

Book, online and e-books	Works Cited	Dickens, Charles. <u>Great Expectations</u>. 1860–61. <u>Project Gutenberg Archive</u>. Etext 1400. 14 July 2007 ‹http://www.gutenberg.net/ etext98/grexp10.txt›. ▸ The date when you access the online content (in this case, 14 July 2007) comes immediately before the URL. Notice that the day comes before the month; that's standard with MLA. There is no punctuation between this date and the URL.[2]
	In-text	(Dickens) ▸ Since this electronic version does not have pagination, cite the chapter numbers. (Dickens, ch. 2)

Multivolume work	Works Cited	Pflanze, Otto. <u>Bismarck and the Development of Germany</u>. 3 vols. Princeton: Princeton UP, 1963–90.
	In-text	(Pflanze) or (Pflanze 3: 21) ▸ This refers to volume 3, page 21.

---

2. This follows the MLA's most recent recommendation: http://www.mla.org/
publications/style/style_faq/style_faq4.

Multivolume work (*continued*)		(Pflanze, vol. 3) ▸ When a volume is referenced without a specific page, then use "vol." so the volume won't be confused for a page number.
Single volume in a multivolume work	Works Cited	Pflanze, Otto. The Period of Fortification, 1880–1898. Princeton: Princeton UP, 1990. Vol. 3 of Bismarck and the Development of Germany. 3 vols. 1963–90. Iriye, Akira. The Globalizing of America. Cambridge: Cambridge UP, 1993. Vol. 3 of Cambridge History of American Foreign Relations, ed. Warren I. Cohen. 4 vols. 1993.
	In-text	(Pflanze) (Iriye)
Reprint of earlier edition	Works Cited	Barzun, Jacques. Simple and Direct: A Rhetoric for Writers. 1985. Chicago: U of Chicago P, 1994. Smith, Adam. An Inquiry into the Nature and Causes of the Wealth of Nations. 1776. Ed. Edwin Cannan. Chicago: U of Chicago P, 1976.
	In-text	(Barzun, Simple) or (Barzun) (Smith, Wealth of Nations) or (Smith)
Translated volume	Works Cited	Weber, Max. The Protestant Ethic and the Spirit of Capitalism. 1904–5. Trans. Talcott Parsons. New York: Scribner's, 1958. Tocqueville, Alexis de. Democracy in America. Ed. J. P. Mayer. Trans. George Lawrence. New York: Harper, 2000. ▸ Editor and translator are listed in the order in which they appear on the book's title page. Beowulf: A New Verse Translation. Trans. Seamus Heaney. New York: Farrar, 2000. ▸ *Beowulf* is an anonymous poem. The translator's name normally comes after the title. But there is an exception. If you wish to

comment on the translator's work, then place
the translator's name first. For example:
Heaney, Seamus, trans. Beowulf: A New Verse
   Translation. New York: Farrar, 2000.
Parsons, Talcott, trans. The Protestant Ethic
   and the Spirit of Capitalism, by Max Weber.
   1904–5. New York: Scribner's, 1958.

In-text

(Weber, Protestant Ethic) or (Weber)
(Tocqueville, Democracy in America) or
(Tocqueville)
(Heaney, Beowulf) or (Beowulf)
(Parsons)

Chapter in edited book

Works Cited

Epstein, Leslie. "The Roar of the Crowd."
   Scoring from Second: Writers on Baseball.
   Ed. Philip F. Deaver. Lincoln: Bison, 2007.
   99–103.

In-text

(Epstein 99–103)

Journal article, one author

Works Cited

Egan, Shannon. " 'Yet in a Primitive Condition':
   Edward S. Curtiss's North American Indian."
   American Art 20.3 (Fall 2006): 58–83.
Leonard, Miriam. "Oedipus in the Accusative:
   Derrida and Levinas." Comparative
   Literature Studies 43.3 (2006): 224–51.
   ▸ Refers to volume 43, number 3.
   ▸ The issue number is optional if it is clear how
     to find the article (perhaps because you have
     already included the month or because the
     pages run continuously through the year). But
     if each issue begins with page 1 and you include
     only the year, then you need to add the issue
     number or month to show where the article
     appears: American Art 20.3 (2006): 58–83.

In-text

(Egan) or (Egan 64)
(Leonard) or (Leonard 226) or (Leonard,
"Oedipus" 226).
   ▸ The title may be needed to differentiate this
     article from others by the same author.

Journal article, multiple authors	Works Cited	Prendergast, Catherine, and Nancy Abelmann. "Alma Mater: College, Kinship, and the Pursuit of Diversity." Social Text 24 (Spring 2006): 37–53.
		▸ If there are four or more authors: Prendergast, Catherine, et al.
	In-text	(Prendergast and Abelmann 37–53)

Journal article, online	Works Cited	Scott, Gray. "Signifying Nothing? A Secondary Analysis of the Claremont Authorship Debates." Early Modern Literary Studies 12.2 (Sept. 2006): 6.1–50. 13 Feb. 2007 ‹http://purl.oclc.org/emls/12-2/scotsig2 .htm›.
		▸ This journal is online only, and the pagination is a little unusual (6.1–50). The citation is the same as a normal print journal. MLA recommends listing the entire URL when they are relatively brief, as this one is.
		Baggetun, Rune, and Barbara Wasson. "Self-Regulated Learning and Open Writing." European Journal of Education 41.3–4 (Sept.–Dec. 2006): 453–72. Blackwell Journals Online. 13 Feb. 2007 ‹http://www .blackwell-synergy.com.proxy.uchicago .edu/›.
		▸ This is a normal print journal, available online from multiple sources such as JSTOR, with the same pagination as the print version. Here I list it through Blackwell Journals Online. The URL is quite long, so MLA recommends listing only the search page.
		Clark, Michael, et al. "Use of Preferred Music to Reduce Emotional Distress and Symptom Activity During Radiation Therapy." Journal of Music Therapy 43.3 (Fall 2006): 247–65. 12 Feb. 2007. IIMP Full Text via ProQuest.
		▸ There are four or more authors in this case, so only the first is listed, followed by "et al."
	In-text	(Scott) or (Scott 6.1–50) or (Scott, "Signifying Nothing" 6.1–50)

(Baggetun and Wasson)
(Clark et al. 247–65)

Journal article, foreign language	Works Cited	Joosten, Jan. "Le milieu producteur du Pentateuque grec." Revue des Études Juives 165.3–4 (juillet–décembre 2006): 349–61.
	In-text	(Joosten) or (Joosten 356)

Newspaper or magazine article, no author, hard copy and online	Works Cited	"State Senator's Indictment Details Demands on Staff." New York Times 11 Feb. 2007: 23.

▸ This refers to page 23.
▸ If the article has a byline and you wish to include the reporter's name, you certainly can: Zeleny, Jeff. "State Senator's Staff . . ."
▸ Short articles in newsweeklies like *Time* or the *Economist* are treated the same as newspaper articles. Longer articles with bylines are treated like journal articles.

"Jacopo Tintoretto: A Tribute Well Earned." Economist 10–16 Feb. 2007: 90.

▸ The same article online:

"Jacopo Tintoretto: A Tribute Well Earned." Economist 10–16 Feb. 2007. 13 Feb. 2007 ‹http://www.economist.com/books/displaystory.cfm?story_id=E1_RGGPTJG›.

▸ The first date refers to the article, the second to the day it was accessed.
▸ For magazines and newspapers, there is no need to reference the sponsoring organization.

In-text

("State Senator's Indictment" 23)
("Jacopo Tintoretto" 90)
("Jacopo Tintoretto")

Newspaper or magazine article, with author, hard copy and online	Works Cited	Halbfinger, David M. "Politicians Are Doing Hollywood Star Turns." New York Times 6 Feb. 2007, national ed.: B1, B7.

▸ It's always fine to include the headline and reporter's name. The MLA says you can omit them, though, if they do not add to the point you are making in the text.

Newspaper or magazine article, with author, hard copy and online (*continued*)		Pinsky, Robert. "Poet's Choice." Washington Post 11 Feb. 2007. 13 Feb. 2007: BW12 ‹http://www.washingtonpost.com/ wp-dyn/content/article/2007/02/08/ AR2007020802552.html›.
		▸ The first date refers to the article, the second to the day it was accessed.
		▸ For magazines and newspapers, there is no need to reference the sponsoring organization.
	In-text	(Halbfinger B1, B7) or (Halbfinger, "Politicians" B1, B7) if you cite more than one article by this author.
		(Pinsky BW12)

Review, hard copy and online	Works Cited	Lane, Joseph H. Rev. of A Kinder, Gentler America: Melancholia and the Mythical 1950s, by Mary Caputi. Perspectives on Politics 4 Dec. 2006: 749–50.
		Macintyre, Ben. "Midnight's Grandchildren." Rev. of In Spite of the Gods: The Strange Rise of Modern India, by Edward Luce. New York Times Book Review 4 Feb. 2007: 16.
		▸ The same review online:
		Macintyre, Ben. "Midnight's Grandchildren." Rev. of In Spite of the Gods: The Strange Rise of Modern India, by Edward Luce. New York Times Book Review 4 Feb. 2007. 13 Feb. 2007 ‹www.nytimes.com›.
		▸ The first date refers to the article, the second to the day it was accessed.
	In-text	(Macintyre 16) or (Macintyre, "Midnight's Grandchildren" 16)
		(Lane 749) or (Lane, "Kinder, Gentler" 749)

Unpublished paper, thesis, or dissertation	Works Cited	Leeds, Ashley. "Interests, Institutions, and Foreign Policy Consistency." Paper presented at the Program on International Politics, Economy, and Security, U Chicago, 15 Feb. 2007.

Noble, Lance. "One Goal, Multiple Strategies:
Engagement in Sino-American WTO
Accession Negotiations." MA thesis. U
British Columbia, 2006.
Talmi, Deborah. "The Role of Attention
and Organization in Emotional Memory
Enhancement." Diss. U Toronto, 2006.

In-text   (Leeds)
(Noble)
(Talmi)

Abstract   Works Cited   Tyler, Tom. "Snakes, Skins and the Sphinx:
Nietzsche's Ecdysis." Journal of Visual
Culture 5.3 (2006): 365–85. Abstract.
12 Feb. 2007 ‹http://vcu.sagepub
.com.proxy.uchicago.edu/cgi/content/
abstract/5/3/365›.
Hatchard, John. "Combating Transnational
Crime in Africa: Problems and
Perspectives." Journal of African Law
50 (Oct. 2006): 145–60. African Studies
Abstracts Online 17, Abstract No. 21
(2007): 28 ‹http://www.ascleiden
.nl/Library/Abstracts/asa-online/pdf/
ASAOnline2007-17.pdf›.

In-text   (Tyler)
(Hatchard 145–60)

Microfilm,   Works Cited   Abbott, Alice Irving. Circumstantial Evidence.
microfiche   New York: W. B. Smith, 1882. American
Fiction, 1774–1910. Reel A-1. Woodbridge:
Gale/Primary Source Microfilm, 1998.
King, Martin Luther, Jr., FBI file [microform].
Ed. David J. Garrow. 16 reels. Frederick: U
Publications of Am., 1984.

In-text   (Abbott) To cite page 13 on reel A-1, use (Abbott
A-1: 13)
(King) To cite reel 2, page 12, use (King 2: 12)

Archival materials and manuscript collections, hard copy or online

Works Cited

Franklin, Isaac. Letter to R. C. Ballard. 28 Feb. 1831. Series 1.1, folder 1. Rice Ballard Papers. Southern Historical Collection. Wilson Lib. U of North Carolina, Chapel Hill.

Lamson, Mary Swift. An Account of the Beginning of the B.Y.W.C.A. Ms. Boston YWCA Papers. Schlesinger Lib. Radcliffe Institute for Advanced Study, Harvard U. Cambridge, MA. 1891.

▸ Manuscript is abbreviated "ms." Typescript is "ts." Spell out "notebook" and "unpublished essay."

Szold, Henrietta. Letter to Rose Jacobs. 3 Feb. 1932. Reel 1, book 1. Rose Jacobs–Alice L. Seligsberg Collection. Judaica Microforms. Brandeis Lib. Waltham, MA.

Szold, Henrietta. Letter to Rose Jacobs. 9 Mar. 1936. A/125/112. Central Zionist Archives, Jerusalem.

Taraval, Sigismundo. Journal Recounting Indian Uprisings in Baja California. Handwritten ms. 1734–1737. Edward E. Ayer Manuscript Collection No. 1240, Newberry Lib. Chicago, IL.

Taft, Horatio Nelson. Diary. Vol. 1, Jan. 1, 1861–Apr. 11, 1862. Manuscript Division, Lib. of Congress. 30 May 2004 ‹http://memory.loc.gov/cgi-bin/ampage?collId=mtaft&fileName=mtaft1/mtaftmtaft1.db&recNum=148›.

In-text

(Franklin) or (Franklin to Ballard) or (Franklin to Ballard, 28 Feb. 1831)

(Lamson) or (Lamson 2)

(Szold) or (Szold to Jacobs) or (Szold to Jacobs, 3 Feb. 1932)

(Szold) or (Szold to Jacobs) or (Szold to Jacobs, 9 Mar. 1936)

(Taraval) or (Taraval, par. 23)

▸ This manuscript uses paragraph numbers, not pages.

(Taft) or (Taft 149)

Encyclopedia, hard copy and online	Works Cited	"African Arts." Encyclopaedia Britannica. 15th ed. 1987. 13: 134–80.

- ▶ Alphabetize by the first significant word in title.
- ▶ Volume and page numbers are optional.
- ▶ Edition and year are required, but you can omit the city and publisher for well-known encyclopedias, dictionaries, and other references.

"Art, African." Encyclopaedia Britannica Online. 2007. Encyclopaedia Britannica. 14 Feb. 2007 ‹http://search.eb.com.proxy .uchicago.edu/eb/article-9384738›.

- ▶ Why does the name, *Encyclopaedia Britannica,* appear twice? Because it is both the publication and the "sponsoring organization," and MLA rules currently require that you list both.

Zangwill, Nick. "Aesthetic Judgment." Stanford Encyclopedia of Philosophy. 2003; rev. 2006. Metaphysics Research Lab, Stanford University. 13 Feb. 2007 ‹http://plato .stanford.edu/entries/aesthetic-judgment/›.

- ▶ This article was originally published online in 2003 and substantially revised in 2006. Both dates are included.

	In-text	("African Arts" 13: 137) ("Art, African") (Zangwill)

Reference book, hard copy and online	Works Cited	Pendergast, Sara, and Tom Pendergast, eds. Reference Guide to World Literature. 3rd ed. 2 vols. Detroit: St. James P/Thomson-Gale, 2003.

Cannon, John, ed. Oxford Companion to British History. New York: Oxford UP, 2002 ‹http:// www.oxfordreference.com/views/BOOK _SEARCH.html?book=t110&subject=s11›.

Cicioni, Mirna. "The periodic table (Il sistema periodico), prose by Primo Levi, 1975." Reference Guide to World Literature. Ed. Sara Pendergast and Tom Pendergast. 3rd

Reference book, hard copy and online (*continued*)		ed. 2 vols. Detroit: St. James P/Thomson-Gale, 2003. 2: 1447.

"Polytheism." The New Dictionary of Cultural Literacy. Ed. E. D. Hirsch Jr., Joseph F. Kett, and James Trefil. 3rd ed. Boston: Houghton, 2002. 2 Feb. 2004 ⟨http://www.bartleby.com/59/5/polytheism.html⟩.

▸ This is a hard-copy book that is also available online.

"Napoleon I." The Biographical Dictionary. 2004. S-9 Technologies. 5 Jan. 2004 ⟨http://www.s9.com/biography/search.html⟩.

In-text (Pendergast and Pendergast)
(Cannon)
(Cicioni 2: 1447)
("Polytheism")
("Napoleon I")

Dictionary, hard copy, online, and CD-ROM

Works Cited

"Historiography." Merriam-Webster's Collegiate Dictionary. 11th ed. 2003.

▸ You can omit the publisher information.

"Protest, v." Compact Edition of the Oxford English Dictionary. 1971 ed. 2: 2335.

▸ The word "protest" is both a noun and a verb, and I am citing the verb here.

"Pluck, n." Def. 1. Oxford English Dictionary. Ed. J. A. Simpson and E. S. C. Weiner. 2nd ed. Oxford: Clarendon P, 1989. Oxford UP. 5 Jan. 2004 ⟨http://dictionary.oed.com/cgi/entry/00181836⟩.

▸ There are two separate entries for the noun "pluck," and I am citing the first, hence "n. Def. 1." The second is for an obscure fish.

"Metaphor." Microsoft Encarta Online Dictionary. 2007. Microsoft. 15 Feb. 2007 ⟨http://encarta.msn.com/dictionary_/Metaphor.html⟩.

"Citation." American Heritage Dictionary of the English Language. 4th ed. CD-ROM. Boston: Houghton, 2000.

"Merci." Le Nouveau Petit Robert—Dictionnaire

de la Langue Française, 2007. Nouvelle ed. Paris: Le Robert, 2006.

	In-text	("Historiography") or (<u>Merriam-Webster's Collegiate Dict.</u>) ("Protest" 2: 2335) (<u>Compact OED</u> 2: 2335) ("Metaphor") or (<u>Microsoft Encarta Online Dict.</u>) ("Citation") or (<u>American Heritage Dict.</u>) ("Merci") or (<u>Le Nouveau Petit Robert</u>)
Bible, Qur'an (Koran)	Works Cited	<u>Tanakh: The Holy Scriptures: The New JPS Translation according to the Traditional Hebrew Text.</u> Philadelphia: Jewish Publication Society, 1985. ▸ The Bible, Qur'an, and other sacred texts do *not* usually appear in Works Cited, although you can include them if you wish to cite a particular version or translation.
	In-text	Genesis 1.1, 1.3–5, 2.4. ▸ Books may be abbreviated, such as Gen. 1.1, 1.3–5, 2.4. ▸ Abbreviations for the next four books are Ex., Lev., Num., and Deut. Abbreviations for other books are easily found with a Web search for "abbreviations + Bible." Qur'an 18.65–82.
Speech, academic talk, or course lecture	Works Cited	Herman, (Chancellor) Richard. Speech at Dr. Martin Luther King Jr. Community Celebration. U of Illinois, Urbana–Champaign. 14 Jan. 2007. MacFarlane, Seth. "Class Day Speech." Harvard, Cambridge, MA. 7 June 2006. Video [part 3 of 4]. 18 Feb. 2007 ‹http://youtube.com/watch?v=gLt73xSJlAM&mode=related&search=›. Hearn, Maxwell K. "How to Read (and Teach) Chinese Art." Speech to annual convention of the National Art Education Association. New York. 16 Mar. 2007.

Speech, academic talk, or course lecture (*continued*)		Doniger, Wendy. Course lecture. U of Chicago. 15 Mar. 2007. ▸ Or, using a more descriptive name for an untitled lecture: Doniger, Wendy. Course lecture on evil in Hindu mythology. U of Chicago. 15 Mar. 2007.
	In-text	(Herman) (MacFarlane) (Hearn) (Doniger)
Interview, personal, telephone, in print, or online	Works Cited	Coetzee, J. M. Personal interview. 14 May 2007. Brown, Gordon. Telephone interview. 16 Mar. 2007. Anonymous U.S. Marine, recently returned from Iraq. Personal interview. 4 June 2007. MacMillan, Margaret. "On Her New Book, Nixon in China: The Week That Changed the World." Interview by Kenneth Whyte, Macleans 27 Sept. 2006. 14 Feb. 2007 <http://www.macleans.ca/culture/books/article.jsp?content=20061002_133865_133865>. Rosenquist, James. "Reminiscing on the Gulf of Mexico: A Conversation with James Rosenquist." Interview by Jan van der Marck. American Art 20.3 (Fall 2006): 84–107.
	In-text	(Coetzee) (Brown) (anonymous U.S. Marine) (MacMillan) (Rosenquist 93)
Personal communication	Works Cited	Wills, Gary. Personal interview. 2 June 2007. Chandler, James. E-mail to author. 3 June 2007. ▸ Unlike some other formats, MLA includes e-mails, conversations, and other personal communications in the Works Cited, even if they are not generally available to others.

Vicinus, Martha. "Sweetland Conference; title
for talk." E-mail to author. 22 Apr. 2005.
Art Institute of Chicago. E-newsletter. Apr.
2007 [e-mail sent to members]. 14 Apr.
2007.
▸ If a personal communication is publicly
archived, add the URL at the end of the
citation.

In-text

(Wills, personal interview)
(Chandler, e-mail) or, if there are several:
(Chandler, e-mail, 3 June 2007)
(Vicinus, e-mail) or (Vicinus, "Sweetland
Conference")
(Art Institute of Chicago, E-newsletter)

Poem,
in print
or online

Works Cited

Auden, W. H. "The Shield of Achilles." <u>Collected
Poems</u>. Ed. Edward Mendelson. New York:
Random, 2007. 596–97.
Bishop, Elizabeth. "The Fish." <u>The Complete
Poems, 1927–1979</u>. New York: Noonday
P/Farrar, 1983. 42–44.
Lowell, Robert. "For the Union Dead." <u>The Top
500 Poems</u>. Ed. William Harmon. New York:
Columbia UP, 1992. 1061–63.
Yeats, W. B. "The Lake Isle of Innisfree." 1892.
<u>Poets.org</u>. n.d. Academy of American Poets.
14 Feb. 2007 ‹http://www.poets.org/
viewmedia.php/prmMID/1552›.
▸ This indicates Yeats's poem was written in 1892
and is posted at the Poets.org Web site, which
is run by the Academy of American Poets. The
site does not indicate exactly when this poem
was posted (hence "n.d."), but it was accessed
for this citation on February 14, 2007.

In-text

(596–97) or (Auden 596–97) or (Auden, "Shield
of Achilles" 596–97) or ("Shield of Achilles"
596–97)
▸ For poems such as "The Shield of Achilles,"
you can note the verse and lines separated by
periods or use (lines 10–12).

Poem, in print or online (*continued*)		(Bishop 42–44) or (Bishop, "The Fish" 42–44) or ("The Fish" 42–44) or (42–44) (Lowell 1061–63) or (Lowell, "Union Dead" 1061–63) (Yeats) or (Yeats, "The Lake Isle of Innisfree")
Play, text	Works Cited	Bunin, Keith. The Busy World Is Hushed. 2006. New York: Dramatists Play Service, 2007. ▶ The play was written in 2006, published in 2007. Shakespeare, William. Romeo and Juliet. ▶ If you wish to cite a specific edition, then: Shakespeare, William. Romeo and Juliet. Ed. Brian Gibbons. London: Methuen, 1980. ▶ For an online version: Shakespeare, William. Romeo and Juliet. Project Gutenberg. E-text 1112. 1997. 14 Feb. 2007 ‹http://www.gutenberg.org/ etext/1112›.
	In-text	(Bunin) or (Bunin, The Busy World Is Hushed) (Shakespeare, Romeo and Juliet 1.3.12–15) or (Romeo and Juliet 1.3.12–15) or (1.3.12–15) if the play's name is clear in the text. ▶ This refers to act 1, scene 3, lines 12–15 (separated by periods). ▶ If you refer repeatedly to Shakespeare's plays, you can use MLA's standard abbreviations for them, such as (Ham.) for *Hamlet.* The first time you mention a play such as *Romeo and Juliet,* you simply indicate the abbreviation (Rom.), and then use it after that for in-text citations, such as (Rom. 1.3.12–15).
Performance of play or dance	Works Cited	Kiss. Chor. Susan Marshall. Music Arvo Pärt. Perf. Cheryl Mann, Tobin Del Cuore. Hubbard Street Dance Chicago. Joan W. and Irving B. Harris Theater for Music and Dance, Chicago. 12 Mar. 2004. Topdog/Underdog. By Suzan Lori-Parks. Dir. Amy Morton. Perf. K. Todd Freeman, David

Rainey. Steppenwolf Theater, Chicago.
2 Nov. 2003.

▸ If you are concentrating on one person's
  work in theater, music, dance, or other
  collaborative arts, put that person's name first.
  For example, if you are focusing on David
  Rainey's acting:

Rainey, David, perf. Topdog/Underdog. By
Suzan Lori-Parks. Dir. Amy Morton . . .

▸ If, by contrast, you are focusing on Amy
  Morton's directing or on directing in general:

Morton, Amy, dir. Topdog/Underdog. By Suzan
Lori-Parks. Perf. David Rainey . . .

	In-text	(Kiss) (Topdog/Underdog) or (Rainey) or (Morton)
Television program	Works Cited	"Bart vs. Lisa vs. 3rd Grade." The Simpsons. Writ. T. Long. Dir. S. Moore. Fox. 17 Nov. 2002.
	In-text	("Bart vs. Lisa")
Film	Works Cited	Godfather II. Dir. Francis Ford Coppola. Perf. Al Pacino, Robert De Niro, Robert Duvall, Diane Keaton. Screenplay by Francis Ford Coppola and Mario Puzo based on the novel by Mario Puzo. Paramount Pictures, 1974. DVD. Paramount Home Video, Godfather DVD Collection, 2003.

▸ Required: title, director, studio, and year
  released. Include them, or you will sleep with
  the fishes.

▸ Optional: actors, producers, screenwriters,
  editors, cinematographers, and other
  information. Include what you need for
  analysis in your paper, in order of their
  importance to your analysis. Their names
  appear between the title and the distributor.

▸ If you are concentrating on one person's work,
  put that person's name and role (such as
  performer) first, before the title:

Film (*continued*)		Coppola, Francis Ford, dir. Godfather II. Perf. Al Pacino, Robert De Niro, Robert Duvall, Diane Keaton. Paramount Pictures, 1974. DVD. Paramount Home Video, Godfather DVD Collection, 2003.
	In-text	(Godfather II)
Artwork, original	Works Cited	Tintoretto, Jacopo Robusti. The Birth of John the Baptist. 1550s. Oil on canvas, 181 x 266 cm. Hermitage, St. Petersburg. ▸ Year, size, and artistic medium are optional.
	In-text	(Tintoretto) or (Tintoretto, Birth of John the Baptist)
Artwork, reproduction	Works Cited	Tintoretto, Jacopo Robusti. The Birth of John the Baptist. 1550s. Hermitage, St. Petersburg. In Tintoretto: Tradition and Identity. By Tom Nichols. London: Reaktion Books, 1999. 47.
	In-text	(Tintoretto) or (Tintoretto, Birth of John the Baptist)
Artwork, online	Works Cited	Tintoretto, Jacopo Robusti. The Birth of John the Baptist. 1550s. Hermitage, St. Petersburg. State Hermitage Museum. 5 Jan. 2004 ‹http://www.hermitage.ru/html_En/index.html›. Tintoretto, Jacopo Robusti. The Birth of John the Baptist (detail). 1550s. Hermitage, St. Petersburg. CGFA-Virtual Art Museum. 5 Jan. 2004 ‹http://cgfa.floridaimaging.com/t/p-tintore1.htm›. ▸ The same artwork accessed through the museum's site and another site. Note that the sponsors of the different Web sites are listed, as well as their URLs.
	In-text	(Tintoretto) or (Tintoretto, Birth of John the Baptist)

Photograph, original	Works Cited	Adams, Ansel. <u>Monolith, the Face of Half Dome, Yosemite National Park</u>. 1927. Art Institute, Chicago.
	In-text	(Adams) or (Adams, <u>Monolith</u>)
Photograph, online	Works Cited	Adams, Ansel. <u>Dunes, Oceano</u>. 1963. Ansel Adams Gallery. 2007. 14 Feb. 2007 ‹http://www.anseladams.com/index.asp?PageAction=VIEWPROD&ProdID=958›.
	In-text	(Adams) or (Adam, <u>Dunes, Oceano</u>)
Figures: map, chart, graph, or table	Works Cited	"Climate Change Vulnerability in Africa." Map. <u>UNEP/GRID-Arendal Maps and Graphics Library</u>. 2002, updated 2004, 2005. UNEP/GRID-Arendal. 14 Feb. 2007 ‹http://maps.grida.no/go/graphic/climate_change_vulnerability_in_africa›. "House of Representatives, 2006 Election Results." Map. <u>Washington Post</u>. n.d. 14 Feb. 2007 ‹http://projects.washingtonpost.com/elections/keyraces/map/›. ▸ MLA treats maps like anonymous books. "Map of Somalia, 2006." Ken Menkhaus, "Governance without Government in Somalia: Spoilers, State Building, and the Politics of Coping." <u>International Security</u> 31 (Winter 2006/07): 79. ▸ Or Menkhaus, Ken. "Governance without Government in Somalia: Spoilers, State Building, and the Politics of Coping." <u>International Security</u> 31 (Winter 2006/07): 74–106. ("Climate Change Vulnerability in Africa") ("House of Representatives, 2006" map) ("Map of Somalia, 2006") or (Menkhaus 79, map)

Musical recording	Works Cited	Johnson, Robert. "Come On in My Kitchen (Take 1)." Rec. 23 Nov. 1936. Robert Johnson: King of the Delta Blues Singers. Expanded ed. Columbia/Legacy, CK 65746, 1998.

Allman Brothers Band. "Come On in My Kitchen." By Robert Johnson. Shades of Two Worlds. Sony, 1991.

Barber, Samuel. Cello sonata, for cello and piano, op. 6. Barber: Adagio for Strings, Violin Concerto, Orchestral and Chamber Works. Disc 2. St. Louis Symphony. Cond. Leonard Slatkin. Cello, Alan Stepansky. Piano, Israela Margalit. EMI Classics 74287, 2001.

▸ The catalog numbers are optional but helpful.
▸ There is no need to say that a recording is on CD. However, if it is on cassette, LP, or some other medium, that should be listed just before the publisher. For example:

Holloway, Stanley. "Get Me to the Church on Time." My Fair Lady, Original London Cast Recording. Book and lyrics, Alan Jay Lerner. Music, Frederick Loewe. Rec. 1958. Audiocassette. Broadway/Legacy 060539, 1998.

▸ If you are concentrating on one person's work, such as the pianist, her name can come first:

Margalit, Israela, piano. Cello sonata, for cello and piano, op. 6. Barber: Adagio for Strings, Violin Concerto, Orchestral and Chamber Works. Disc 2. St. Louis Symphony. Cond. Leonard Slatkin. Cello, Alan Stepansky. EMI Classics 74287, 2001.

In-text	(Johnson) or (Johnson, "Come On in My Kitchen") (Allman Brothers) or (Allman Brothers, "Come On in My Kitchen") (Holloway) or (Holloway, "Get Me to the Church on Time") (Margalit) or (Margalit, Cello sonata)

Music video, comments on music video	Works Cited	Furtado, Nelly, featuring Timbaland. "Promiscuous." Promiscuous. Mosely Music Group/Geffen Records, 2006. Music video. Dir. Little X. 2006. 14 Feb. 2007. iTunes store.
		Jay-Z. "Show Me What You Got." Kingdom Come. Roc-a-Fella/Def Jam, 2006. Music video. Dir. F. Gary Gray. 15 Feb. 2007 <http://www.mtv.com/music/video/>.
		McClinton, Delbert. "Same Kind of Crazy as Me." Room to Breathe. New West, 2002. Music video. 15 Feb. 2007 <http://www.youtube.com/watch?v=5vBEYAhXkaI>.
		▸ This video was recorded at a live performance and posted on YouTube. No director was listed.
		RobertZimmerman897. Comment on music video [Bob Dylan, "Like a Rolling Stone, 1966"]. 14 Feb. 2007. 15 Feb. 2007 <http://www.youtube.com/watch?v=xOogSJGJ7Fs>.
	In-text	(Furtado)
		(Jay-Z)
		(McClinton)
		(RobertZimmerman897)
Sheet music	Works Cited	Bach, Johann Sebastian. Toccata and Fugue in D Minor. 1708. BWV 565. Arr. Ferruccio Benvenuto Busoni for solo piano. New York: G. Schirmer LB1629, 1942.
		▸ This piece was written in 1708 and has the standard Bach classification BWV 565. The arrangement is published by G. Schirmer, with their catalog number LB1629.
	In-text	(Toccata and Fugue in D Minor) or (Bach, Toccata and Fugue in D Minor)
Liner notes	Works Cited	Reich, Steven. Liner notes. Different Trains. Kronos Quartet. Elektra/Nonesuch 9 79176-2, 1988.
	In-text	(Reich, Different Trains)

Advertise-ment, hard copy and online	Works Cited	Letters from Iwo Jima (film). Advertisement. New York Times 6 Feb. 2007: B4. Mercedes-Benz 2007 CL-class automobiles. Advertisement. New Yorker 12 Feb. 2007: 26. Avis Israel Car Rentals. Advertisement. Jerusalem Post 7 Feb. 2007 <http://www .jpost.com/>.
	In-text	(Letters from Iwo Jima advertisement) (Mercedes-Benz advertisement) (Avis Israel advertisement)

Government document, hard copy and online	Works Cited	Cong. Rec. 12 Feb. 2007: H1425. Cong. Rec. 12 Feb. 2007: H1425. 18 Mar. 2007 <http://www.gpoaccess.gov/crecord/index .html>. United States. Cong. Senate. Committee on Armed Services. Hearings on S. 758, a Bill to Promote the National Security by Providing for a National Defense Establishment. 80th Cong., 1st sess., Washington: GPO, 1947. Freedman, Stephen. Four-Year Impacts of Ten Programs on Employment Stability and Earnings Growth. The National Evaluation of Welfare-to-Work Strategies. Washington: U.S. Department of Education. 2000. ERIC Document Reproduction Service No. ED450262. United States, Department of State. Daily Press Briefing. 12 Feb. 2007. 19 Feb. 2007 <http:// www.state.gov/r/pa/prs/dpb/2007/80442 .htm>.
	In-text	(Cong. Rec. 12 Feb. 2007: H1425) (U.S. Cong., Senate, Committee on Armed Services) ▸ If you are only referencing one item from that committee, then in-text citations don't need to include the hearing number or report. (U.S. Cong., Senate, Committee on Armed Services, Hearings on S. 758, 1947) ▸ If you refer to several items from the

committee, indicate which one you are citing. You can shorten that after the first use:
(Hearings on S. 758)
(Freedman) or (Freedman, Four-Year Impacts)
(U.S. Dept. of State) or (U.S. Dept. of State, Press Briefing, 12 Feb. 2007)

Software	Works Cited	Dreamweaver 8. San Francisco: Adobe, 2007. iTunes 7.0.2. Cupertino, CA: Apple, 2007.
	In-text	(Dreamweaver 8) (iTunes 7.0.2)
Database	Works Cited	Internet Movie Database (IMDb). 2007. Internet Movie Database. 8 Mar. 2007 ‹http://www.imdb.com/›. Corpus Scriptorum Latinorum database of Latin literature. 2003. Forum Romanum. 5 Jan. 2004 ‹http://www.forumromanum.org/literature/index.html›. ▸ For a specific item within this database: Caesar, Gaius Julius. Commentarii de bello civili. Ed. A. G. Peskett. Loeb Classical Library. London: W. Heinemann, 1914. Corpus Scriptorum Latinorum database of Latin literature. 2003. Forum Romanum. 5 Jan. 2004 ‹http://www.thelatinlibrary.com/caes.html›.
	In-text	(IMDb) (Corpus Scriptorum Latinorum) (Caesar) or (Caesar, Commentarii de bello civili)
Web site, entire	Works Cited	Digital History. Ed. Steven Mintz. 2007. U of Houston et al. 14 Feb. 2007 ‹http://www.digitalhistory.uh.edu/index.cfm?›. Internet Public Library (IPL). 2007. School of Information, U of Michigan. 14 Feb. 2007 ‹http://www.ipl.org/›.
	In-text	(Internet Public Library) or (IPL)

| Web page, with author | Works Cited | Lipson, Charles. "Advice on Getting a Great Recommendation." 2007. 14 Feb. 2007 ‹http://www.charleslipson.com/courses/ Getting-a-good-recommendation.htm›. |

- If the URL takes up more than one line, break *after* a single or double slash and *before* a period, a comma, a hyphen, an underline, or a number sign.
- MLA currently suggests listing the date when you accessed a particular Web file. *The Chicago Manual of Style* now recommends against it, unless there is a reason.

| | In-text | (Lipson) or (Lipson, "Advice") |

- Web pages and other online documents may not have pages. You may, however, be able to cite to a specific section (Lipson, sec. 7) or paragraph (Lipson, pars. 3–5).

| Web page, no author | Works Cited | "I Love Lucy: Series Summary." Sitcoms Online. 2007. 28 Apr. 2007 ‹http://www .sitcomsonline.com/ilovelucy.html›. |
| | In-text | ("I Love Lucy") or ("I Love Lucy: Series Summary") |

| Weblog, entry or comment | Works Cited | Drezner, Daniel. "Is Economic Protectionism on the Rise in China?" Online posting. 2 Feb. 2007. Daniel W. Drezner. 18 Feb. 2007 ‹http://www.danieldrezner.com/ archives/003136.html›. |

- The MLA does not cover these types of citations in its *Handbook for Writers of Research Papers,* 6th edition, or its online FAQs. The format shown here is similar to MLA's citation for "Posting to a Discussion List," http://www.mla.org/style_faq4, accessed on July 10, 2007.

Adler, Jonathan. "On *Ad Hominem* Arguments." Online posting. 5 Feb. 2007. Volokh Conspiracy. 18 Feb. 2007. ‹http://volokh .com/›.

▶ The Weblog entry was made on 5 Feb. 2007. It
was accessed on 18 Feb. 2007.

Good, Nick. Comment on "On *Ad Hominem*
Arguments." Online posting. 6 Feb. 2007.
2:55 a.m. Volokh Conspiracy. 18 Feb. 2007
‹http://volokh.com/posts/1170708620
.shtml#185453›.

▶ Good's comment had no title and is one of
several he posted to this group blog on the
same day. Listing the time identifies it.

Richards, Peter. Untitled poem. 24 Jan. 2007.
Project Muse. Weblog. 14 Feb. 2007 ‹http://
www.quickmuse.com/archive/landing.php
?poem=1xM3n4DY5Ysy7x4TFKdYJ3I8BIP8eM1›.

In-text   (Drezner) or (Drezner, "Economic
Protectionism")
(Adler) or (Adler, "On *Ad Hominem*
Arguments")
(Good) or (Good, untitled comment) or (Good,
untitled comment, 6 Feb. 2007 2:55 a.m.)

Video clip,   Works Cited   Duck and Cover. Archer Productions/Federal
news video   Civil Defense Administration. 1951. Video
posted 26 Nov. 2006. 14 Feb. 2007 ‹http://
youtube.com/watch?v=-UVH8YRXsqo›.

▶ This 1951 film was posted online in 2006 and
accessed on February 14, 2007.

"High Speed Chase Ends in Shootout." CNN
.com. Video posted 7 Feb. 2007. 14 Feb.
2007 ‹www.cnn.com›.

▶ When the URL is very long, as this one is, and
the video can be found on a searchable site,
you may simply list the site.

▶ Why is Duck and Cover underlined, but
"High Speed Chase" placed in quotation
marks? Because MLA underlines films and
TV series, but "quotes" individual episodes.
The emergence of new media blurs this once-
bright line. In this case, Duck and Cover
is underlined because it was produced as a
stand-alone film, albeit a brief one. The "high

Video clip, news video (*continued*)		speed chase," on the other hand, is a segment from one day's newscast.
	In-text	(Duck and Cover) ("High Speed Chase")
Video blog (vlog), video on Web site, posted comment on video	Works Cited	Garfield, Steve. "Vlog Soup 23." Steve Garfield's Video Blog. Video posted 29 Jan. 2007. 14 Feb. 2007 ‹http://stevegarfield .blogs.com/videoblog/2007/01/vlog_soup _23.html›.
		Miaarose. "Mia's First Vlog." Video posted 9 Jan. 2007. 7 Feb. 2007 ‹http://www .youtube.com/watch?v=Hd3UC8kYCrk›.
		Benwsp. "Darragh's Response to Miaarose." Video comment Posted 10 Jan. 2007. 7 Feb. 2007 ‹http://www.youtube.com/watch?v= _-SmfbUZAxo›.
		Lonelyinacrowd. Text response to vlog [re: "Mia's First Vlog"]. 6 Feb. 2007. 7 Feb. 2007. ‹http://www.youtube.com/ watch?v=Hd3UC8kYCrk›.
	In-text	(Garfield) (Miaarose) (Benwsp) (Lonelyinacrowd)
Podcast or video podcast (vodcast)	Works Cited	TVO Big Ideas Podcast. 2007. 18 Feb. 2007. iTunes Store.
		Fournier, Marc. "Goals and Needs." TVO Big Ideas Podcast. 3 Feb. 2007. 18 Feb. 2007. iTunes Store.
		▸ The Fournier episode was posted on February 3, 2007, and accessed on February 18, 2007.
		"BBC Question Time." Video podcast. 1 Feb. 2007. 18 Feb. 2007 ‹http://downloads .bbc.co.uk/rmhttp/downloadtrial/bbc1/ questiontime-videopodcast/questiontime -videopodcast_20070201-2200_40_pc .mp4›.

"2057: Future of Civilization." <u>Discovery Channel</u>. Video podcast. n.d. 18 Feb. 2007. iTunes Store.

▸ Or

"2057: Future of Civilization." Host Micheo Kaku. <u>Discovery Channel</u>. Video podcast. n.d. 18 Feb. 2007. iTunes Store.

In-text	(TVO Big Ideas Podcast)
	(Fournier) or (Fournier, "Goals and Needs")
	("BBC Question Time")
	("2057: Future of Civilization")

Personal networking site (Facebook, MySpace)	Works Cited	Fawlty, Basil. Profile at MySpace. 18 Feb. 2007. 18 Feb. 2007 ‹http://profile.myspace.com/index.cfm?fuseaction=user.viewprofile&friendid=138597116›.
		Dermott. Comment in Basil Fawlty's Friends Comments. 4 Feb. 2007, 4:41 p.m. Basil Fawlty profile at MySpace. 18 Feb. 2007 ‹http://profile.myspace.com/index.cfm?fuseaction=user.viewprofile&friendid=138597116›.
		Baroness Thatcher. Photograph and link. Basil Fawlty Friend Space. n.d. Basil Fawlty profile at MySpace. 18 Feb. 2007 ‹http://profile.myspace.com/index.cfm?fuseaction=user.viewprofile&friendid=138597116›.
	In-text	(Fawlty profile)
		(Dermott)
		(Baroness Thatcher)

E-mail, instant messages, electronic newsgroups, and listservs	Works Cited	Leis, Kathy. "Re: New Orleans family." E-mail to Karen Turkish. 3 Mar. 2008.
		Mandelbaum, Michael. E-mail to the author. 7 Feb. 2007.
		Chicago Council on Global Affairs. "Weekly Update." <u>Chicago Council Calendar</u>. E-mail to Chicago Council on Global Affairs mailing list. 6 Feb. 2007.

E-mail, instant messages, electronic newsgroups, and listservs (*continued*)	"Campus Events for Coming Week." U of Chicago e-mail to listserv. 6 Feb. 2007 ‹https://listhost.uchicago.edu/pipermail/events/2007-February/000228.html›.

▸ Include the URL if the mass e-mailing has been archived.

Lipson, Michael. Instant message to Jonathan Lipson. 9 Mar 2007.

▸ Include the time for instant messages or e-mails if they are pertinent. For example: 9 Mar. 2007, 3:15 p.m.

In-text	(Leis)
	(Mandelbaum)
	(Chicago Council) or (Chicago Council on Global Affairs)
	("Campus Events")
	(Lipson) or (Lipson, M.)

MLA uses abbreviations frequently in Works Cited. All months are shortened, for instance, except May, June, and July. Likewise, MLA abbreviates most geographic names, such as Eur., Neth., Mex., and So. Amer. Here are some other examples:

MLA: COMMON ABBREVIATIONS IN WORKS CITED

and others	et al.	figure	fig.	part	pt.
appendix	app.	library	lib.	pseudonym	pseud.
book	bk.	note	n	translator	trans.
chapter	ch. or chap.	notes	nn	verse	v.
compare	cf.	number	no.	verses	vv.
document	doc.	opus	op.	versus	vs.
edition	ed.	page	p.	volume	vol.
editor	ed.	pages	pp.		
especially	esp.	paragraph	par.		

Note: All abbreviations are lowercase, usually followed by a period. Most form their plurals by adding "s." The exceptions are note (n → nn), opus (op. → opp.), page (p. → pp.), and translator (same abbreviation).

In citing poetry, do not use abbreviations for "line" or "lines" since a lowercase "l" is easily confused with the number one. Use either the full word or if the meaning is clear, simply the number.

MLA: COMMON ABBREVIATIONS FOR PUBLISHERS

Alfred A. Knopf	Knopf
Basic Books	Basic
Cambridge University Press	Cambridge UP
Charles Scribner's Sons	Scribner's
Columbia University Press	Columbia UP
Cornell University Press	Cornell UP
D. C. Heath	Heath
Duke University Press	Duke UP
E. P. Dutton	Dutton
Farrar, Straus and Giroux	Farrar
HarperCollins	Harper
Harvard University Press	Harvard UP
Houghton Mifflin	Houghton
John Wiley and Sons	Wiley
Little, Brown	Little
McGraw-Hill	McGraw
MIT Press	MIT P
Oxford University Press	Oxford UP
Princeton University Press	Princeton UP
Random House	Random
Simon and Schuster	Simon
University of Chicago Press	U of Chicago P
University of Toronto Press	U of Toronto P
University Publications of America	U Publications of Am.
W. W. Norton	Norton
Yale University Press	Yale UP

MLA also eliminates the state for each publisher:

Full name: Hoboken, NJ: John Wiley and Sons, 2008.
MLA format: Hoboken: Wiley, 2008.

Despite all these abbreviations, MLA does not shorten the city where most publishers are headquartered:

Full name: New York: Routledge, 2008.
MLA format: New York: Routledge, 2008.

FAQS ABOUT MLA CITATIONS

How do I handle the citation when one author quotes another?
That happens frequently, as in Donald Kagan's book *The Peloponnesian War,* which often quotes Thucydides. Using MLA style, you might write:

> Kagan approvingly quotes Thucydides, who says that Athens acquired this vital site "because of the hatred they already felt toward the Spartans" (qtd. in Kagan 14).

In your Works Cited, you include Kagan but *not* Thucydides.

8

APA CITATIONS FOR THE SOCIAL SCIENCES, EDUCATION, ENGINEERING, AND BUSINESS

• • • • • • • • • • • • • •

APA citations are widely used in psychology, education, engineering, business, and the social sciences. Like MLA citations, they are in-text. They use notes only for analysis and commentary, not to cite references. Unlike MLA, however, APA emphasizes the year of publication, which comes immediately after the author's name. That's probably because as scholarship cumulates in the sciences and empirical social sciences (where APA is used), it is important to know whether the research was conducted recently and whether it came before or after other research. At least that's the rationale.

Detailed information on the APA system is available in

- *Publication Manual of the American Psychological Association,* 5th ed. (Washington, DC: American Psychological Association, 2001).

Like *The Chicago Manual of Style* and MLA style books, the APA manual should be available in your library's reference section. For more details on engineering papers, you can also consult an online guide from the American Society of Civil Engineers, available at http://www.pubs.asce.org/authors/index.html#manreq.

To get started, let's look at APA references for a journal article, a chapter in an edited book, and a book as they appear at the end of a paper. APA calls this a "Reference List." (MLA calls it "Works Cited," and Chicago calls it a "Bibliography.")

Lipson, C. (1991). Why are some international agreements informal? *International Organization, 45,* 495–538.

Lipson, C. (1994). Is the future of collective security like the past? In G. Downs (Ed.), *Collective security beyond the cold war* (pp. 105–131). Ann Arbor: University of Michigan Press.

Lipson, C. (2003). *Reliable partners: How democracies have made a separate peace.* Princeton, NJ: Princeton University Press.

This list for the distinguished author C. Lipson follows another APA rule. All entries for a single author are arranged by year of publication, beginning with the earliest. If there were two entries for a particular year, say 2008, they would be alphabetized by title and the first would be labeled (2008a), the second (2008b). A future publication would be cited as "(forthcoming)." Also note the APA's rules for capitalizing book and article titles. They are treated like sentences, with only the first words capitalized. If there's a colon in the title, the first word after the colon is also capitalized. Proper nouns are capitalized, of course, just as they are in sentences.

In these reference lists, single-author entries precede those with coauthors. So Pinker, S. (as a sole author) would precede Pinker, S., & Jones, B. In the APA system, multiple authors are joined by an ampersand "&" rather than the word "and." It is not clear why. Just accept it as a rule, like how many minutes are in a soccer game.

The authors' first names are always reduced to initials. Pagination is not included for in-text references, except for direct quotes (where the pages are preceded by "p." or "pp."). That makes it different from the other systems, as does its frequent use of commas and parentheses.

When works are cited in the text, the citation includes the author's name, for example (Wilson, 2008d), unless the author's name has already been mentioned in that sentence. If the sentence includes the author's name, the citation omits it. For instance: Nye (2008) presents considerable data to back up his claims. If you include a direct quote, then you *must* include the page number in the citation. For instance: "The policy is poorly conceived," according to Nye (2008, p. 12).

The examples in this chapter focus on the social sciences, education, engineering, and business, where APA citations are most widely used, just as the MLA examples focus on the humanities, where that style is common.

To make it easy to find the APA citations you need, I've listed them here alphabetically, along with the pages where they are described.

INDEX OF APA CITATIONS IN THIS CHAPTER

APA: REFERENCE LIST AND IN-TEXT CITATIONS

| Book, one author | Reference list | Devlin, L. (2007). *Chief of station, Congo: Fighting the Cold War in a hot zone.* New York: Public Affairs.
Naughton, B. (2007). *The Chinese economy: Transitions and growth.* Cambridge, MA: MIT Press.
Macdonald, D. (2007). *Business and environmental politics in Canada.* Peterborough, Ontario, Canada: Broadview Press. |

Book, one author (*continued*)		▸ Although U.S. states are abbreviated, Canadian provinces and territories are spelled out and the country name is included.
	In-text	(Devlin, 2007) (Naughton, 2007) (Macdonald, 2007)

Books and articles, several by same author	Reference list	Posner, R. C. (2007a). *Countering terrorism.* Lanham, MD: Rowman & Littlefield with the Hoover Institution. Posner, R. C. (2007b). *Economic analysis of law* (7th ed.). New York: Aspen Law and Business. Posner, R. C. (2007c). *The little book of plagiarism.* New York: Pantheon. Posner, R. C. (2006a). *Not a suicide pact: The Constitution in a time of national emergency.* New York: Oxford University Press. Posner, R. C. (2006b). *Uncertain shield: The U.S. intelligence system in the throes of reform.* Lanham, MD: Rowman & Littlefield with the Hoover Institution. Posner R. C., & Becker, G. S. (2006). *Suicide and risk-taking: An economic approach.* Unpublished paper, University of Chicago. ▸ Note that the author's name is repeated. APA does not use dashes for repetition. ▸ When the same author or coauthors have several publications in the same year, list them alphabetically (by the first significant word in the title). Label them as "a," "b," and "c." The last 2006 item by Posner is *not* labeled "c" because its authorship is different. ▸ Coauthored books like Posner & Becker follow a writer's single-author ones, in the alphabetical order of the second author's name.
	In-text	(Posner, 2007a, 2007b, 2007c, 2006a, 2006b; Posner & Becker, 2006)

Book, multiple authors	Reference list	Fubini, D., Price, C., & Zollo, M. (2007). *Mergers: Leadership, performance and corporate health.* New York: Palgrave Macmillan. Wells, L. T., & Ahmed, R. (2007). *Making foreign investment safe: Property rights and national sovereignty.* New York: Oxford University Press. ▸ Name the first six authors, then add "et al."
	In-text	(Fubini, Price, & Zollo, 2007) (Wells & Ahmed, 2007) ▸ For two to five authors, name all authors in the first citation. Beginning with the second reference, name only the first author, then add "et al." ▸ For six or more authors, name only the first author, then add "et al." for all citations. ▸ Use "&" within parenthetical references but not in the text itself.
Book, multiple editions	Reference list	Schweitzer, S. O. (2007). *Pharmaceutical economics and policy* (2nd ed.). New York: Oxford University Press. Strunk, W., Jr., & White, E. B. (2000). *The elements of style* (4th ed.). New York: Longman. ▸ If it says "revised edition" rather than "4th edition," use "(Rev. ed.)" in the same spot.
	In-text	(Strunk & White, 2000) ▸ To refer to a specific page for a quotation: (Strunk & White, 2000, p. 12)
Book, multiple editions, no author	Reference list	*National Partnership for Immunization reference guide* (2nd ed.). (2003). Alexandria, VA: National Partnership for Immunization. *Publication manual of the American Psychological Association* (5th ed.). (2001). Washington, DC: American Psychological Association.

Book, multiple editions, no author *(continued)*		▶ For multiple editions without authors, the form is *Title* (18th ed.). (year). City, STATE: Publisher.
	In-text	(National Partnership for Immunization [NPI], 2003) ▶ Subsequent references are (NPI, 2003) (American Psychological Association [APA], 2001) ▶ Subsequent references are (APA, 2001)
Book, edited	Reference list	Bakker, K. (Ed.). (2007). *Eau Canada: The future of Canada's water.* Vancouver, British Columbia, Canada: University of British Columbia Press. Bosworth, M., & Flavin, J. (Eds.). (2007). *Race, gender, and punishment: From colonialism to the war on terror.* New Brunswick, NJ: Rutgers University Press. Aikhenvald, A. Y., & Dixon, R. M. W. (Eds.). (2007). *Grammars in contact: A cross-linguistic typology.* Oxford, England: Oxford University Press.
	In-text	(Baker, 2007) (Bosworth & Flavin, 2007) (Aikhenvald & Dixon, 2007)
Book, online and e-books	Reference list	Reed, J. (1922). *Ten days that shook the world.* Project Gutenberg. [Etext 3076]. Retrieved February 12, 2007, from ftp://ibiblio.org/pub/docs/books/gutenberg/etext02/10daz10.txt ▶ APA does *not* put a period after the URL, making it different from most other reference styles.
	In-text	(Reed, 1922)
Multivolume work	Reference list	Johansen, B. E. (2006). *Global warming in the 21st century* (Vols. 1–3). Westport, CT: Praeger.

Pflanze, O. (1963–1990). *Bismarck and the
development of Germany* (Vols. 1–3).
Princeton, NJ: Princeton University
Press.

In-text   (Johansen, 2006)
(Pflanze, 1963–1990)

Single volume in a multivolume work	Reference list	Johansen, B. E. (2006). *Our evolving climate crisis: Vol. 1. Global warming in the 21st century.* Westport, CT: Praeger. Pflanze, O. (1990). *The period of fortification, 1880–1898: Vol. 3. Bismarck and the development of Germany.* Princeton, NJ: Princeton University Press.
	In-text	(Johansen, 2006) (Pflanze, 1990)
Reprint of earlier edition	Reference list	Smith, A. (1976). *An inquiry into the nature and causes of the wealth of nations.* E. Cannan (Ed.). Chicago: University of Chicago Press. (Original work published 1776)
	In-text	(Smith, 1776/1976)
Translated volume	Reference list	Weber, M. (1958). *The Protestant ethic and the spirit of capitalism.* T. Parsons (Trans.). New York: Charles Scribner's Sons. (Original work published 1904–1905)
	In-text	(Weber, 1904–1905/1958)
Foreign language volume	Reference list	Weber, M. (2005). *Die protestantische ethik und der Geist des Kapitalismus* [The Protestant ethic and the spirit of capitalism]. Erftstadt, Germany: Area Verlag. (Original work published 1904–1905)
	In-text	(Weber, 1904–1905/2005)

Chapter in edited book	Reference list	Cohen, B. J. (2006). The macrofoundations of monetary power. In D. M. Andrews (Ed.), *International monetary power* (pp. 31–50). Ithaca, NY: Cornell University Press.
		▸ Chapter titles are not in quotes or italics.
	In-text	(Cohen, 2006)

Journal article, one author	Reference list	Meirowitz, A. (2007). Communication and bargaining in the spatial model. *International Journal of Game Theory, 35,* 251–266.
		▸ Article titles are not in quotes or italics.
		▸ The journal's volume number is italicized, but the issue number and pages are not. The word "volume" (or "vol.") is omitted.
		▸ There's no need to name a specific issue if the journal pages are numbered continuously throughout the year. However, if each issue begins with page 1, then the issue's number or month is necessary to find the article: *45*(2), 15–30.
	In-text	(Meirowitz, 2007)

Journal article, multiple authors	Reference list	Koremenos, B., Lipson, C., & Snidal, D. (2001). The rational design of international institutions. *International Organization, 55,* 761–799.
		Tomz, M., Goldstein, J., & Rivers, D. (forthcoming). Membership has its privileges: Understanding the effects of the GATT and the WTO on world trade. *American Economic Review.*
		Guo, S., Chen, D., Zhou, D., Sun, H., Wu, G., Haile, C., et al. (2007). Association of functional catechol O-methyl transferase (COMT) Val108Met polymorphism with smoking severity and age of smoking initiation in Chinese male smokers. *Psychopharmacology, 190,* 449–456.
		▸ Name up to six authors, then add "et al."

In-text		(Koremenos, Lipson, & Snidal, 2001) for first reference. (Koremenos et al., 2001) for second reference and after.

> When a work has five authors or less, name all of them in the first textual reference. After that, use only the first author's name plus "et al."

(Guo et al., 2007)

> When a work has six authors or more, name only the first one plus "et al." For example, this would be the first mention of the Guo article: In their study of Chinese male smokers, Guo et al. (2007) find an association . . .

Journal article, online	Reference list	Garrett, L. (2007). The challenge of global health. *Foreign Affairs 86*(1), 14–38. Retrieved February 13, 2007, from http://www.foreignaffairs.org/ 20070101faessay86103/laurie-garrett/ the-challenge-of-global-health.html Baggetun, R., & Wasson, B. (2006). Self-regulated learning and open writing. *European Journal of Education 41*(3–4), 453–472. Retrieved February 12, 2007, from http://www.blackwell-synergy.com .proxy.uchicago.edu/doi/full/10.1111/ j.1465-3435.2006.00276.x Clark, M., Isaacks-Downton, G., Redlin-Frazier, S., & Wells, N. (2006). Use of preferred music to reduce emotional distress and symptom activity during radiation therapy. *Journal of Music Therapy 43*(3), 247–265. Retrieved February 12, 2007, from IIMP Full Text via ProQuest. Mitchell, T. (2002). McJihad: Islam in the U.S. global order. *Social Text, 20*(4), 1–18. Retrieved December 28, 2003, from JSTOR database: http://muse.jhu.edu/journals/ social_text/v020/20.4mitchell.html

> Your can omit the URL when citing well-known databases, such as JSTOR, ProQuest, or PsycARTICLES.

Journal article, online (*continued*)	In-text	(Garrett, 2007) (Baggetun & Wasson, 2006) (Clark, Isaacks-Downton, Redlin-Frazier, & Wells, 2006) (Mitchell, 2002)
Journal article, foreign language	Reference list	Maignan, I., & Swaen, V. (2004). La responsabilité sociale d'une organisation: Intégration des perspectives marketing et managériale. *Revue Française du Marketing, 200,* 51–66. ▸ Or Maignan, I., & Swaen, V. (2004). La responsabilité sociale d'une organisation: Intégration des perspectives marketing et managériale [The social responsibility of an organization: Integration of marketing and managerial perspectives]. *Revue Française du Marketing, 200,* 51–66.
	In-text	(Maignan & Swaen, 2004)
Newspaper or magazine article, no author	Reference list	Climate change: Heating up. (2007, February 10). *Economist,* 86. State senator's indictment details demands on staff. (2007, February 11). *New York Times* [national ed.], p. 23. ▸ Newspaper page numbers include "p." or "pp."
	In-text	(Climate change, 2007) (State senator's indictment, 2007)
Newspaper or magazine article, with author	Reference list	Kirkpatrick, D. D. (2007, February 11). *New York Times* [national ed.], p. 1.
	In-text	Kirkpatrick, 2007) or, if necessary, (Kirkpatrick, 2007, February 11)
Newspaper or magazine article, online	Reference list	Shadid, A. (2007, February 12). Across Arab world, a widening rift: Sunni-Shiite tension called region's "Most Dangerous Problem." *Washington Post* [online], p. A01. Retrieved

February 12, 2007, from http://www
.washingtonpost.com/wp-dyn/content/
article/2007/02/11/AR2007021101328.html

Pandey, S. (2007, February 11). I read the news today, oh boy. *Los Angeles Times* [online, home edition], p. M6. Retrieved February 12, 2007, from ProQuest Newspapers database.

	In-text	(Shadid, 2007) or (Shadid, 2007, February 12) (Pandey, 2007) or (Pandey, 2007, February 11)
Review	Reference list	Lane, J. H. (2006, December). [Review of the book *A kinder, gentler America: Melancholia and the mythical 1950s.*] *Perspectives on Politics, 4,* 749–750. Ferguson, N. (2007, February 4). Ameliorate, contain, coerce, destroy. [Review of *The utility of force: The art of war in the modern world*]. *New York Times Book Review,* 14–15.
	In-text	(Lane, 2006) (Ferguson, 2007)
Unpublished paper, poster session, dissertation, or thesis	Reference list	Leeds, A. (2007, February). *Interests, institutions, and foreign policy consistency.* Paper presented at the Program on International Politics, Economics, and Security, University of Chicago, pp. 1–25. ▸ Only the month and year are needed for papers. Tomz, M. (2007, January). *The effects of international agreements on foreign policy preferences.* Unpublished manuscript, Stanford University. Retrieved February 16, 2007, from http://www.stanford.edu/~tomz/working/intlagmts.pdf Noble, L. (2006). *One goal, multiple strategies: Engagement in Sino-American WTO accession negotiations.* Unpublished master's thesis, University of British Columbia.

Unpublished paper, poster session, dissertation, or thesis (*continued*)		Talmi, D. (2006). *The role of attention and organization in emotional memory enhancement.* Unpublished doctoral dissertation, University of Toronto.
	In-text	(Leeds, 2007) (Tomz, 2007) (Noble, 2006) (Talmi, 2006)
Preprint	Reference list	Hansen, M. E., & Pollack, D. (2007). Transracial adoption of black children: An economic analysis. Preprint. Retrieved February 12, 2007, from http://law.bepress.com/expresso/eps/1942 Heylighen, F. (2007). Five questions on complexity. Preprint. arXiv: nlin.AO/0702016. Retrieved February 13, 2007, from http://arxiv.org/ftp/nlin/papers/0702/0702016.pdf ▸ arXiv is a collection facility for scientific preprints. The number following "arXiv" gives the paper's classification, its subclassification, and its date of submission to the archive. ID numbers and URLs are valuable to readers who wish to follow your citation to the database itself.
	In-text	(Hansen & Pollack, 2007) (Heylighen, 2007)
Abstract	Reference list	Barahona, C., & Levy, S. (2007). The best of both worlds: Producing national statistics using participatory methods [Abstract]. *World Development, 35,* 326. ▸ Abstract obtained from original source. Use the same format to cite abstracts from published conference proceedings. Hatchard, J. (2006). Combating transnational crime in Africa: Problems and perspectives. *Journal of African Law, 50,* 145–160. Abstract obtained from *African Studies*

		Abstracts Online, 17, Abstract No. 21 (2007).
		▸ Abstract obtained from secondary source.
	In-text	(Barahona & Levy, 2007) (Hatchard, 2006/2007) ▸ If the secondary abstract source is published in a different year than the primary source, cite both dates, separated by a slash.

| Microfilm, microfiche | Reference list | U.S. House of Representatives. Records. Southern Claims Commission. (1871–1880). *First report (1871)*. Washington, DC: National Archives Microfilm Publication, P2257, Frames 0145–0165.
Conservative Party (UK). (1919). *Annual report of the executive committee to central council, March 11–November 18, 1919*. Archive of the British Conservative Party, Microfiche card 143. Woodbridge, CT: Gale/Primary Source Microfilm, 1998. (Original material located in Conservative Party Archive, Bodleian Library, Oxford, England.)
▸ You do not need to include the location of the original material, but you are welcome to. |
| | In-text | (U.S. House, 1871–1880)
(Conservative Party, 1919) |

| Encyclopedia, hard copy and online | Reference list | Balkans: History. (1987). In *Encyclopaedia Britannica* (15th ed., Vol. 14, pp. 570–588). Chicago: Encyclopaedia Britannica.
Balkans. (2003). *Encyclopaedia Britannica* [online]. Retrieved February 12, 2007, from http://search.eb.com.proxy.uchicago.edu/eb/article-9110555
Graham, G. (2005). Behaviorism. In *Stanford encyclopedia of philosophy* [online]. Retrieved February 12, 2007, from http://plato.stanford.edu/entries/behaviorism/
Emotion. (2007). *Wikipedia* [online]. Retrieved February 15, 2007, from http://en.wikipedia.org/wiki/Emotion |

Encyclopedia, hard copy and online (*continued*)	In-text	(Balkans: History, 1987) (Balkans, 2003) (Graham, 2005) (Emotion, 2007)
Reference book, hard copy and online	Reference list	Pendergast, S., & Pendergast, T. (Eds.). (2003). *Reference guide to world literature* (3rd ed., 2 vols.). Detroit, MI: St. James Press/ Thomson-Gale. Pendergast, S., & Pendergast, T. (Eds.). (2003). *Reference guide to world literature.* [E-book]. (3rd ed.). Detroit, MI: St. James Press. Colman, A. M. (2001). *A dictionary of psychology.* Oxford, England: Oxford University Press. Retrieved March 16, 2004, from http://www.oxfordreference.com/ views/BOOK_SEARCH.html?book=t87 Woods, T. (2003). The social contract (du contract social), prose by Jean-Jacques Rousseau, 1762. In Pendergast, S., & Pendergast, T. (Eds.), *Reference guide to world literature* (3rd ed., Vol. 2, pp. 1512–1513). Detroit, MI: St. James Press/ Thomson-Gale. Great Britain: Queen's speech opens Parliament. (2003, November 26). Retrieved July 10, 2007, from Facts On File database, accession no. 2003302680.
	In-text	(Pendergast & Pendergast, 2003) (Colman, 2001) (Woods, 2003) (Great Britain: Queen's speech, 2003)
Dictionary, hard copy, online, and CD-ROM	Reference list	Gerrymander. (2003). *Merriam-Webster's collegiate dictionary* (11th ed.). Springfield, MA: Merriam-Webster. Protest, *v.* (1971). *Compact edition of the Oxford English dictionary* (Vol. 2, p. 2335). Oxford, England: Oxford University Press. ▸ The word "protest" is both a noun and a verb. Here, I am citing the verb.

		Class, *n.* (2003). *Dictionary.com.* Retrieved January 4, 2004, from http://dictionary .reference.com/search?q=class
		Anxious. (2000). *American heritage dictionary of the English language* (4th ed.). [CD-ROM]. Boston: Houghton Mifflin.
	In-text	(Protest, 1971)
Bible, Qur'an (Koran)	Reference list	▸ Not needed, except to reference a particular version.
		The five books of Moses: A translation with commentary. (2004). Robert Alter (Trans. & Ed.). New York: Norton.
	In-text	Deut. 1:2 (New Revised Standard Version).
		▸ List the version you are using the first time it is mentioned in the text. After that, you omit the version.
		Genesis 1:1, 1:3–5, 2:4.
		▸ Books of the Bible can be abbreviated, such as Exod., Lev., Num., Cor., and so on.
		Qur'an 18:65–82.
Classical works	Reference list	▸ Not needed, except to reference a particular version.
		Plato. (2006). *The republic.* R. E. Allen (Trans.). New Haven, CT: Yale University Press. (Original work, approximately 360 B.C.).
		Virgil. (2006). *The Aeneid.* R. Fagles (Trans.). New York: Viking, 2006. (Original work, approximately 19–29 B.C.).
	In-text	(Plato, trans. 2006)
		(Virgil, trans. 2006).
Speech, academic talk, or course lecture	Reference list	Epstein, C. F. (2006, August 12). Presidential address at the annual meeting of the American Sociological Association. Montreal, Québec, Canada.

Speech, academic talk, or course lecture (*continued*)		Rector, N. (2007, March 6). Course lecture at the University of Toronto. Toronto, Ontario, Canada.
	In-text	(Epstein, 2006) (Rector, 2007)

Interview	Reference list	O'Connor, S. D. (2007, February 12). Justice: Bench player. Interview of retired Justice Sandra Day O'Connor by Debra Rosenberg. *Newsweek.* Retrieved February 12, 2007, from http://www.msnbc.msn.com/id/ 16960417/site/newsweek/ MacMillan, M. (2006, September 27). On her new book, *Nixon in China: The week that changed the world.* Interview by Kenneth Whyte. *Macleans.* Retrieved February 12, 2007, from http://www .macleans.ca/culture/books/article .jsp?content=20061002_133865_133865
	In-text	(O'Connor, 2007) (MacMillan, 2006) (J. M. Coetzee, personal interview, May 14, 2007) (anonymous U.S. Marine, recently returned from Iraq, interviewed by author, June 4, 2007) ▶ The reference list includes printed interviews, like O'Connor's and MacMillan's, but not personal communications such as private conversation, faxes, letters, or interviews since they cannot be accessed by other investigators. Therefore, in-text citations for personal communications, like the ones for Coetzee and the anonymous U.S. Marine, should fully describe the item, including the full date.

Personal communication	Reference list	▶ Personal communications that cannot be retrieved or examined by third parties should not be included in the reference list. They should be fully described in the text.

	In-text	(D. A. Grossberg, personal communication, May 6, 2007) (M. Yousik, instant message, 3:15 p.m., April 8, 2007) ▸ This could be an e-mail, instant message, conversation, letter, fax, phone call, memo, or smoke signal.
Television program	Reference list	Long, T. (Writer), & Moore, S. D. (Director). (2002). Bart vs. Lisa vs. 3rd grade [Television series episode]. In B. Oakley & J. Weinstein (Producers), *The Simpsons*. Fox.
	In-text	(*Simpsons,* 2002) or (Bart vs. Lisa, 2002)
Film	Reference list	Wallis, Hal B. (Producer), & Huston, J. (Director/Writer). (1941). *The Maltese falcon* [Motion picture]. Humphrey Bogart, Mary Astor, Peter Lorre, Sydney Greenstreet, Elisha Cook Jr. (Performers). Based on novel by Dashiell Hammett. Warner Studios. United States: Warner Home Video, DVD (2000). ▸ Required: You must include the title, director, studio, and year released. ▸ Optional: the actors, producers, screenwriters, editors, cinematographers, and other information. Include what you need for analysis in your paper, in order of importance to your analysis. Their names appear between the title and the distributor.
	In-text	(*Maltese falcon,* 1941) or (*Maltese falcon,* 2000)
Photograph	Reference list	Adams, A. (1927). *Monolith, the face of Half Dome, Yosemite National Park* [photograph]. Art Institute, Chicago.
	In-text	(Adams, 1927)
Photograph, online	Reference list	Adams, A. (1927). *Monolith, the face of Half Dome, Yosemite National Park* [photograph]. Art Institute, Chicago. Retrieved February

Photograph, online (*continued*)		14, 2007, from http://www.hctc.commnet .edu/artmuseum/anseladams/details/pdf/ monlith.pdf
	In-text	(Adams, 1927)

Figures: map, chart, graph, or table	Credit or explanation for figure or table	▸ Citation for a map, chart, graph, or table normally appears as a credit below the item rather than as an in-text citation.
		Note. 2006 election results, House of Representatives map. *Washington Post.* Retrieved February 18, 2007, from http:// projects.washingtonpost.com/elections/ keyraces/map/.
		Note. Retrieved February 18, 2007, from http://www-personal.umich.edu/~mejn/ election/2006/.
		Note. Topographic maps, California (2004). National Geographic Society. Retrieved February 18, 2007, from http://mapmachine .nationalgeographic.com/mapmachine/ viewandcustomize.html?task=getMap &themeId=113&size=s&state=zoomBox.
		Note. From Ken Menkhaus (2006/2007), Governance without government in Somalia: Spoilers, state building, and the politics of coping. *International Security, 31*(Winter), 79, fig. 1.
		▸ Give a descriptive title to your maps, charts, graphs, and tables. With this description, the reader should understand the item without having to refer to the text.
		Note. All figures are rounded to nearest percentile.
		▸ This is a general note explaining information in a table.
		*$p < .05$ **$p < .01$. Both are two-tailed tests.
		▸ This is a probability note for a table of statistics.
	Reference list	2006 election results, House of Representatives map. (2006). *Washington Post.* Retrieved February 18, 2007, from

http://projects.washingtonpost.com/
elections/keyraces/map/

2006 US congressional elections, House of
    Representatives. (2006). [Map]. Retrieved
    February 18, 2007, from http://www
    -personal.umich.edu/~mejn/election/
    2006/

Topographic maps, California. (2004). National
    Geographic Society. Retrieved February
    18, 2007, from http://mapmachine
    .nationalgeographic.com/mapmachine/
    viewandcustomize.html?task=getMap
    &themeId=113&size=s&state=zoomBox

Menkhaus, K. (2006/2007). Governance
    without government in Somalia: Spoilers,
    state building, and the politics of coping.
    International Security, 31(Winter), 74–106.

In-text   (2006 election results, House, 2006)
                     (2006 US congressional elections, House,
                     2006)
                     (Topographic maps, California, 2004)
                     (Menkhaus, 2006/2007)

Advertise-   Reference list   Advertisement for *Letters from Iwo Jima*
ment, hard   [Motion picture]. (2007, February 6). *New*
copy and   *York Times,* p. B4.
online   Pillarless. And, for that matter, peerless. (2007,
                                  February 12). [Advertisement for Mercedes-
                                  Benz 2007 CL-class automobiles]. *New*
                                  Yorker, 26.
                                Avis Israel Car Rentals. (2007, February 7).
                                  [Advertisement, online]. *Jerusalem Post.*
                                  Retrieved February 12, 2007, from http://
                                  www.jpost.com/, link at http://www
                                  .avis.co.il/avis/site/local/avis/english/
                                  IsraelRentals.jsp?banner=JpostHP

            In-text   (advertisement for *Letters from Iwo Jima,* 2007)
                                (Pillarless, 2007)
                                (Avis, 2007)

Government document, hard copy and online	Reference list	*A bill to promote the national security by providing for a national defense establishment: Hearings on S. 758 before the Committee on Armed Service, Senate.* 80th Cong., 1 (1947).
		▸ "80th Cong., 1" refers to page 1 (not to the first session). If the reference was to testimony by a specific individual, that would appear after the date: (1947) (testimony of Gen. George Marshall).
		▸ For documents printed by the Government Printing Office, give the full name rather than the initials "GPO."
		U.S. Census Bureau. (2008). *Statistical abstract of the U.S.* Washington, DC: U.S. Census Bureau.
		Public safety and emergency preparedness Canada (2007, January 11). The government of Canada announces $16.1 million funding for youth at risk. Retrieved February 12, 2007, from http://www.psepc.gc.ca/media/nr/2007/nr20070111-en.asp
		Federal Bureau of Investigation. (2001). *Investigation of Charles "Lucky" Luciano.* Part 1A. Retrieved February 12, 2007, from http://foia.fbi.gov/luciano/luciano1a.pdf
	In-text	(*Bill to promote national security,* 1947) (U.S. Census Bureau, 2008) (Public Safety Canada, 2007) (FBI, 2001)
Software	Reference list	▸ Standard software is not included in the reference list.
	In-text	(Dreamweaver 8, 2007) (iTunes 7.0.2, 2007) (Stata 9, 2007) (Long & Freese, 2006)
Database	Reference list	Maryland Department of Assessments and Taxation. (2007). *Real property data search*

v1.00.18. Retrieved February 12, 2007, from
http://sdatcert3.resiusa.org/rp_rewrite/
U.S. Copyright Office. (2007). *Search copyright
records: Registrations and documents*.
Retrieved February 12, 2007, from http://
www.copyright.gov/records/
Goemans, H., Gleditsch, K. S., Chiozza, G.,
& Choung, J. L. (2006). *Archigos: A
database for political leaders* (Version 2.5).
University of Rochester. Retrieved February
16, 2007, from http://mail.rochester.edu/
%7Ehgoemans/data.htm
United Nations Treaty Collection. (2007).
Access to databases. Retrieved February 12,
2007, from http://untreaty.un.org/English/
access.asp
▸ For a specific item within this database:
International convention for the protection of
all persons from enforced disappearance.
(2006). In United Nations Treaty Collection,
Access to databases (2007). Retrieved
February 16, 2007, from http://untreaty
.un.org/English/notpubl/IV_16_english.pdf

In-text
(Maryland Department of Assessments, 2007)
(U.S. Copyright Office, 2007)
(Goemans, Gleditsch, Chiozza, & Choung,
2007)
(United Nations Treaty Collection, 2007)
(International convention on enforced
disappearance, 2006)

Diagnostic
test

Reference list
Tellegen, A., Ben-Porath, Y. S., McNulty, J. L.,
Arbisi, P. A., Graham, J. R., & Kaemmer,
B. (2001). *MMPI-2 restructured clinical
(RC) scales*. Minneapolis: University of
Minnesota Press and Pearson Assessments.
Butcher, J. N., Graham, J. R., Ben-Porath,
Y. S., Tellegen, A., Dahlstrom, W. G., &
Kaemmer, B. (2001). *Minnesota multiphasic
personality inventory-2 (MMPI-2):
Manual for administration, scoring, and*

Diagnostic test (*continued*)		*interpretation* (Rev. ed.). Minneapolis: University of Minnesota Press.

▸ Manual for administering the test.

Tellegen, A., Ben-Porath, Y. S., McNulty, J. L., Arbisi, P. A., & Graham, J. R. (2003). *The MMPI-2 restructured clinical (RC) scales: Development, validation, and interpretation.* Minneapolis: University of Minnesota Press and Pearson Assessments.

▸ Interpretive manual for the test.

Microtest Q assessment system software for MMPI-2 (Version 5.07). (2003). Minneapolis: Pearson Assessments.

▸ Scoring software for the test.

In-text
(*MMPI-2 RC scales,* 2001)
(*MMPI-2 RC scales,* 2003)
(*Microtest Q,* 2003)

Diagnostic manual

Reference list
Pierangelo, R., & Giuliani, G. (2007). *The educator's diagnostic manual of disabilities and disorders.* San Francisco: Jossey-Bass.

American Psychiatric Association. (2000). *Diagnostic and statistical manual of mental disorders* (4th ed. text revision [*DSM-IV-TR*]). Washington, DC: Author.

In-text
(Pierangelo & Giuliani, 2007)
(American Psychiatric Association, *Diagnostic and statistical manual of mental disorders,* 2000) for the first use only.
(*DSM-IV-TR*) for second use and later. Title is italicized.

Web site, entire

Reference list
Digital history Web site. (2007). S. Mintz (Ed.). Retrieved February 12, 2007, from http://www.digitalhistory.uh.edu/index.cfm?
Internet public library (IPL). (2007). Retrieved February 12, 2007, from http://www.ipl.org/
Yale University, History Department home page. (2007). Retrieved February 12, 2007, from http://www.yale.edu/history/

> If a Web site or Web page does not show a date
> when it was copyrighted or updated, then list
> (n.d.) where the year normally appears.

	In-text	(*Digital history,* 2007) (*Internet public library,* 2007) or (IPL, 2007) (Yale History Department home page, 2007)
Web page, with author	Reference list	Lipson, C. (2007). "Advice on getting a great recommendation." Retrieved February 12, 2007, from http://www.charleslipson.com/courses/Getting-a-good-recommendation.htm
	In-text	(Lipson, 2007)
Web page, no author	Reference list	*The Dick Van Dyke show:* Series summary. (n.d.). *Sitcoms Online.* Retrieved February 12, 2007, from http://www.sitcomsonline.com/thedickvandykeshow.html
	In-text	(*The Dick Van Dyke show:* Series summary, n.d.)
Weblog, entry or comment	Reference list	Tobias, A. (2007, February 7). More free food [Entry post]. *Andrew Tobias: Money and other subjects* [Weblog]. Retrieved February 13, 2007, from http://www.andrewtobias.com/2007 > If this entry had no title, it would be cited as: Tobias, A. (2007, February 7). Untitled entry [Entry post]. *Andrew Tobias: Money and . . .* Kerr, O. (2007, February 12). Can Congress force the Supreme Court to televise proceedings? [Entry post]. *Volokh conspiracy* [Weblog]. Retrieved February 12, 2007, from http://volokh.com/ Crunchy Frog. (2007, February 12). Untitled comment [comment on Web post, Can Congress force the Supreme Court to televise proceedings?]. *Volokh conspiracy* [Weblog]. Retrieved February 12, 2007, from

Weblog, entry or comment (*continued*)		http://volokh.com/posts/1171256603. shtml#187745
		▸ If the wonderfully named "Crunchy Frog" had commented several times the same day and there was no link to a specific comment, then you should include the time: (2007, February 12, 12:53 a.m.).
	In-text	(Tobias, 2007) (Kerr, 2007) (Crunchy Frog, 2007)
Video clip, news video	Reference list	Archer Productions (Producer). (1951). *Duck and cover* [Video clip]. Produced for the Federal Civil Defense Administration. Retrieved February 14, 2007, from http://youtube .com/watch?v=-UVH8YRXsqo
		"High speed chase ends in shootout" (2007, February 7) [Video news clip]. *CNN .com*. Retrieved February 7, 2007, from http://dynamic.cnn.com/apps/tp/video/ us/2007/02/07/ortiz.ut.police.shootout .ktvx/video.ws.asx?NGUserID=aa5128f -31671-1169599598-1&adDEmas=R00 %26hi%26ameritech.net%2673%26usa %26602%2660601%2614%2607%26U1%
		▸ When the URL is very long and the video can be found on a searchable site, you may choose to include only the site's main page: Retrieved February 7, 2007, from www.cnn.com
	In-text	(Archer Productions, 1951) ("High speed chase," 2007)
Video blog (Vlog), video on Web site, video and text comments on other videos	Reference list	Garfield, S. (2007, January 29). Vlog soup 23 [Video post]. *Steve Garfield's video blog*. Retrieved February 7, 2007, from http://stevegarfield.blogs.com/ videoblog/2007/01/vlog_soup_23.html
		Miaarose. (2007, January 9). Mia's first vlog [Video post]. *YouTube.com*. Retrieved February 7, 2007, from http://www.youtube .com/watch?v=Hd3UC8kYCrk

Benwsp. (2007, January 10). Darragh's response to Miaarose [Video comment]. *YouTube.com*. Retrieved February 7, 2007, from http://www.youtube.com/watch?v =_-SmfbUZAxo

Lonelyinacrowd. (2007, February 6). Untitled comment [Text response to vlog]. *YouTube.com*. Retrieved February 7, 2007, from http://www.youtube.com/ watch?v=Hd3UC8kYCrk

In-text | (Garfield, 2007) or (Garfield, 2007, January 29) (Miaarose, 2007) or (Miarose, 2007, January 9) (Benwsp, 2007) or (Benwsp, 2007, January 10). (Lonelyinacrowd, 2007) or (Lonelyinacrowd, 2007, February 6)

Podcast or video podcast (vodcast)

Reference list | Fournier, M. (2007, February 3). Goals and needs [Podcast episode]. *TVO big ideas podcast*. Retrieved February 8, 2007, from iTunes Store.

BBC question time. (2007, February 1) [Video podcast episode]. BBC Web site. Retrieved February 8, 2007, from http://downloads .bbc.co.uk/rmhttp/downloadtrial/bbc1/ questiontime-videopodcast/questiontime -videopodcast_20070201-2200_40_pc.mp4
▸ Or to avoid the long URL:
BBC question time. (2007, February 1) [Video podcast episode]. BBC Web site. Retrieved February 8, 2007, from http://downloads .bbc.co.uk/

2057: Future of civilization. (n.d.) [Video podcast episode]. *Discovery channel*. Retrieved February 8, 2007, from iTunes Store.
▸ Or
Kaku, M. (Host). (n.d.). 2057: Future of civilization [Video podcast episode]. *Discovery channel*. Retrieved February 8, 2007, from iTunes Store.

In-text | (Fournier, 2007)
(BBC question time, 2007)

Podcast or video podcast (vodcast) (*continued*)		▸ Or (BBC question time, 2007, February 1) (2057: Future of civilization, n.d.) ▸ Or (Kaku, n.d.)
Personal networking site (Facebook, MySpace)	Reference list	Simpson, M. (2007) [Profile at MySpace]. Retrieved February 12, 2007, from http://profile.myspace.com/index .cfm?fuseaction=user.viewprofile&friendID =59797833 Pie, A. (2007, February 12, 3:29 p.m.). [Untitled comment]. Marge Simpson's friends' comments on MySpace. Retrieved February 12, 2007, from http://profile.myspace.com/ index.cfm?fuseaction=user.viewprofile &friendID=59797833 ▸ The time is included because Arnie Pie made several comments that day. Szyslak, M. (2007) [Photograph]. Marge Simpson profile on MySpace. Retrieved February 12, 2007, from http://profile .myspace.com/index.cfm?fuseaction=user .viewprofile&friendid=63076079
	In-text	(Simpson, 2007) (Pie, 2007) (Szyslak, 2007)
E-mail, instant messages, electronic newsgroups, and listservs	Reference list	▸ Personal e-mails, instant messages, and non-archived discussion groups are not included in the reference list because they cannot be retrieved by third parties. You should include newsgroups, listservs, and archived discussions if they can be accessed. Chicago Council on Global Affairs. (2007, February 6). *Weekly update, Chicago Council calendar* [E-mail to Chicago Council mailing list]. Campus events for coming week. (2007, February 6) [E-mail to University of Chicago listserv]. Retrieved February 12, 2007, from

https://listhost.uchicago.edu/pipermail/
events/2007-February/000228.html
- ▸ Include the URL if the mass e-mailing has
  been archived.

In-text   (Chicago Council on Global Affairs, 2007)
                        (Campus events, 2007)
                        ▸ Or
                        (Campus events, 2007, February 6).
                        ▸ Because personal e-mails and instant messages
                          are not included in the reference list, they
                          should be fully described in the text.
                        (E. Leis, e-mail message to author, 2007, May 3)
                        (M. H. Lipson, instant message to J. S. Lipson,
                        2007, March 9)
                        ▸ You may include the time of an electronic
                          message if it is important or differentiates it
                          from others. For example:
                        (M. H. Lipson, instant message to J. S. Lipson,
                        11:23 am, 2007, March 9)

APA does not permit very many abbreviations in its reference lists.
When it does, it sometimes wants them capitalized and sometimes not.
Who knows why?

APA: COMMON ABBREVIATIONS IN REFERENCE LISTS

chapter	chap.	part	Pt.
edition	ed.	revised edition	Rev. ed.
editor	Ed.	second edition	2nd ed.
no date	n.d.	supplement	Suppl.
number	No.	translated by	Trans.
page	p.	volume	Vol. (e.g., Vols. 2–5)
pages	pp.	volumes	vols. (e.g., 3 vols.)

9

AAA CITATIONS FOR ANTHROPOLOGY AND ETHNOGRAPHY

• • • • • • • • • • • • • • •

The American Anthropological Association (AAA) has designed its own citation style for the discipline. Within the text, citations use a standard author-date format, such as (Fogelson 2007) or (Comaroff and Comaroff 2008). That's the same as the familiar APA system. The difference comes at the end of the paper, in References Cited. Here, the anthropology system places the author's name on a separate line and lists all the publications below it, in a special indented form. (It's a hanging indent so the date of publication stands out.) For example:

Humphrey, Caroline
    2006 On Being Named and Not Named: Authority, Persons, and Their Names in Mongolia. *In* The Anthropology of Names and Naming. Gabriele vom Bruck, Barbara Bodenhorn, ed. Pp. 157–176. Cambridge: Cambridge University Press.

Sahlins, Marshall
    2000a Ethnographic Experience and Sentimental Pessimism: Why Culture Is Not a Disappearing Object. *In* Biographies of Scientific Objects. Lorraine Daston, ed. Pp. 158–293. Chicago: University of Chicago Press.
    2000b Waiting for Foucault. 3rd edition. Chicago: Prickly Paradigm Press.
    2004 Apologies to Thucydides: Understanding History as Culture and Vice Versa. Chicago: University of Chicago Press.

List the earliest works first. If an author has published more than one work in the same year, as Sahlins has for 2000, list them in alphabetical order and mark them "a," "b," and "c." If Sahlins has a coauthor, list that pairing on a separate line (as if they were a new author), below Sahlins as a single author.

Within the text, keep citations as simple as possible. That may be the author's name and the year of publication, such as (Silverstein 2008). If the sentence already includes the author's name, the citation can be even simpler:

Kelly (2008) offers a sophisticated argument on this point.

It is easy to include specific pages if you want to reference them. For example:

Kelly (2008:9–13) offers a sophisticated argument on this point.

You'll often want to include pages like this, and you'll need to when you quote an author.

The table below shows how to use AAA citations across a wide range of items. If you want more information, you can find it online at

- http://www.aaanet.org/pubs/style_guide.pdf

You can also find examples of citations using AAA style in the association's official journal, *American Anthropologist.*

Although AAA citations are always made with author-date references (in parentheses), your text may also include some explanatory notes. These footnotes or endnotes can be used to discuss supplementary issues; they cannot be used for citations. If you need to cite something within the note itself, simply use author-date references in parentheses, as you would elsewhere.

INDEX OF AAA CITATIONS IN THIS CHAPTER

AAA: REFERENCES CITED AND IN-TEXT CITATIONS

| Book, one author | References Cited | Silverman, Marilyn
  2005 Ethnography and Development: The Work of Richard F. Salisbury. Montreal: McGill-Queen's.
Boddy, Janice
  2007 Civilizing Women: British Crusades in Colonial Sudan. Princeton, NJ: Princeton University Press.
▸ Book titles are not italicized. |
| | In-text | (Silverman 2005)
(Boddy 2007) or, for specific pages or chapters:
(Boddy 2007:41)
(Boddy 2007:ch.4) |

Books, several by same author	References Cited	Doniger, Wendy
		   2000 The Bedtrick: Tales of Sex and
		      Masquerade. Chicago: University of
		      Chicago Press.
		   2004 Bed as Autobiography: A Visual
		      Exploration of John Ransom Phillips.
		      Chicago: Clarissa.
		   2005 The Woman Who Pretended to Be Who
		      She Was: Myths of Self-Imitation. New
		      York: Oxford University Press.
		Doniger, Wendy, and Gregory Spinner
		   1998 Misconceptions: Female Imaginations
		      and Male Fantasies in Parental
		      Imprinting. Daedalus 127(1):97–130.

> Publications from the earliest year are listed first, whether they are books or articles. When the same author or coauthors have several publications in the same year, list them alphabetically (by the first significant word in the title). Label them as "a," "b," and "c."

> Coauthored books and articles follow a writer's single-author ones, in the alphabetical order of the second author's surname.

> Books and articles are listed under an author's name only if they all have exactly the same author (or authors). Thus, the publications listed under Doniger do not include others written jointly with Gregory Spinner.

	In-text	(Doniger 2000, 2004, 2005) (Doniger and Spinner 1998)

Book, multiple authors	References Cited	Weber, Gerhard W., and Fred L. Bookstein
		   2007 Virtual Anthropology: A Guide to a
		      New Interdisciplinary Field. New York:
		      Springer.
		Norberg-Hodge, Helena, Todd Merrifield, and
		      Steven Gorelick
		   2002 Bringing the Food Economy
		      Home: Local Alternatives to Global
		      Agribusiness. London: Zed.

> AAA says to include *all* authors' names.

Book, multiple authors (*continued*)	In-text	(Weber and Bookstein 2007) (Norberg-Hodge et al. 2002) ▸ Name up to two authors. For three or more, name only the first one and then use "et al."
Book, multiple editions	References Cited	Hockings, Paul, ed. 2004 Principles of Visual Anthropology. 3rd edition. Berlin: Mouton de Gruyter. Peacock, James L. 2001 The Anthropological Lens. Rev. edition. Cambridge: Cambridge University Press. ▸ To differentiate the English and American university towns: Cambridge: Cambridge University Press. Cambridge, MA: Harvard University Press.
	In-text	(Hockings 2004) (Peacock 2001) ▸ To refer to a specific page for a quotation: (Peacock 2001:12)
Book, multiple editions, corporate author	References Cited	American Psychological Association 2001 Publication Manual of the American Psychological Association. 5th edition. Washington, DC: American Psychological Association.
	In-text	(American Psychological Association [APA] 2001) ▸ Subsequent references are (APA 2001).
Book, anonymous or no author	References Cited	Anonymous 2003 Golden Verses of the Pythagoreans. Whitefish, MT: Kessinger.
	In-text	(Anonymous 2003)
Book, edited	References Cited	Moore, Henrietta L., and Todd Sanders, eds. 2006 Anthropology in Theory: Issues in Epistemology. Malden, MA: Blackwell. Vertovec, Steven, and Robin Cohen, eds. 2002 Conceiving Cosmopolitanism: Theory,

		Context and Practice. Oxford: Oxford University Press.
	In-text	(Moore and Sanders 2006) (Vertovec and Cohen 2002)
Book, online	References Cited	Klepinger, Linda L. 2006 Fundamentals of Forensic Anthropology. Hoboken, NJ: John Wiley & Sons. Electronic document, http://www.wiley.com/WileyCDA/WileyTitle/productCd-0470007710,descCd-ebook.html, accessed February 11, 2007.
	In-text	(Klepinger 2006)
Multivolume work	References Cited	Stocking, George W., Jr., ed. 1983–1996 History of Anthropology. 8 vols. Madison: University of Wisconsin Press.
	In-text	(Stocking 1983–96)

Single volume in a multivolume work	References Cited	Peregrine, Peter N., and Melvin Ember, eds.
		   2001 Encyclopedia of Prehistory, vol. 6: North America. New York: Kluwer Academic/Plenum Publishers.
		Stocking, George W., Jr.
		   1991 History of Anthropology, vol. 7: Colonial Situations: Essays on the Contextualization of Ethnographic Knowledge. George W. Stocking Jr., ed. Madison: University of Wisconsin Press.

	In-text	(Peregrine and Ember 2001) (Stocking 1991)
Book in a series	References Cited	Whittaker, Andrea 2004 Abortion, Sin and the State in Thailand. ASAA Women in Asia Series. New York: Routledge.
	In-text	(Whittaker 2004)

Reprint of earlier edition	References Cited	Boas, Franz
		    2004[1932] Anthropology and Modern Life.
		        New Brunswick, NJ: Transaction.

	In-text	(Boas 2004) or for a specific page (Boas 2004:43) ▸ In-text citations use only the reprint date.

Translated volume	References Cited	Foucault, Michel
		    1977 Discipline and Punish: The Birth of
		        Prison. Alan Sheridan, trans. New York:
		        Pantheon.

	In-text	(Foucault 1977)

Chapter in edited book	References Cited	Silverstein, Michael
		    2000 Whorfianism and the Linguistic
		        Imagination of Nationality. *In* Regimes
		        of Language: Ideologies, Polities, and
		        Identities. Paul V. Kroskrity, ed. Pp. 85–
		        138. Santa Fe, NM: School of American
		        Research Press.
		    ▸ Chapter titles are not placed in quotes or
		        italicized.
		Deming, Alison Hawthorne
		    2007 Where Time and Place Are Lost. *In*
		        Landscapes with Figures: The Nonfiction
		        of Place. Robert Root, ed. Pp. 34–41.
		        Lincoln: Bison Books, University of
		        Nebraska.
		    ▸ Forewords, introductions, and afterwords
		        are treated the same way, with pagination
		        immediately before the place of publication.

	In-text	(Silverstein 2000) (Deming 2007)

Journal article, one author	References Cited	Fischer, Michael M. J.
		    2007 Culture and Cultural Analysis as
		        Experimental Systems. Current
		        Anthropology 22:1–65.
		    ▸ Article titles are not placed in quotes; journal
		        titles are not italicized.

> There's no need to name a specific issue if the journal pages are numbered continuously throughout the volume. However, if each issue begins with page 1, then the issue's number or month is necessary to find the article: 22(1): 1–65.

Jordt, Ingrid
   2003 From Relations of Power to Relations of Authority: Epistemic Claims, Practices and Ideology in the Production of Burma's Political Order. Theme issue, "Knowledge and Verification," Social Analysis 47(1):65–76.
Robinson, Kathryn
   2006 Islamic Influences on Indonesian Feminism. Social Analysis 50(1):171–177.

In-text (Fischer 2007)
(Jordt 2003)
(Robinson 2006)

Journal article, multiple authors

References Cited

Beck, Robin A., Jr., David G. Moore, and Christopher B. Rodning
   2006 Identifying Fort San Juan: A Sixteenth-Century Spanish Occupation at the Berry Site, North Carolina. Southeastern Archaeology 25:65–77.
> Name all authors in the References Cited.

In-text (Beck et al. 2006) for more than two authors

Journal article, online

References Cited

Conway, Paul
   2003 Truth and Reconciliation: The Road Not Taken in Namibia. Online Journal of Peace and Conflict Resolution, 5(1). Electronic document, http://www .trinstitute.org/ojpcr/5_1conway.htm, accessed December 1, 2004.
Mitchell, Timothy
   2002 McJihad: Islam in the U.S. Global Order. Social Text, 20(4):1–18. Electronic document, retrieved from JSTOR database: http://muse.jhu.edu/

Journal article, online (*continued*)		journals/social_text/v020/20.4mitchell.html, accessed December 1, 2004.
		▸ You can omit the URL when citing well-known databases, such as JSTOR or PsycARTICLES. For example:
		Mitchell, Timothy
		2002 McJihad: Islam in the U.S. Global Order. Social Text, 20(4):1–18. Electronic document, retrieved from JSTOR database, accessed December 1, 2004.
	In-text	(Conway 2003)
		(Mitchell 2002)
Newspaper or magazine article, no author	References Cited	Economist
		2007 Haiti: Building a Reluctant Nation. Economist, February 10: 35.
		New York Times
		2003 Strong Aftershocks Continue in California. New York Times, December 26: A23, national edition.
	In-text	(Economist 2007)
		▸ For multiple citations to 2007:
		(Economist 2007a)
		(New York Times 2003) or if necessary:
		(New York Times 2003a)
Newspaper or magazine article, with author	References Cited	Heffernan, Virginia
		2007 The Gangs of Los Angeles: Roots, Branches and Bloods (television review). New York Times, February 6: B8, national edition.
	In-text	(Heffernan 2007)
		▸ For multiple citations to author in 2007:
		(Heffernan 2007a)
Newspaper or magazine article, online	References Cited	Copans, Laurie
		2007 Clashes by Jerusalem Holy Site Continue. Washington Post, February 10. Electronic document, http://www

.washingtonpost.com/wp-dyn/content/
article/2007/02/10/AR2007021000544
.html, accessed February 11, 2007.

Demetriou, Danielle

2007 Inca Link Is a Bridge Too Far. Daily
Telegraph (London), February 10.
Electronic document, http://www
.telegraph.co.uk/travel/main.jhtml?xml
=/travel/2007/02/10/etddbridge110
.xml, accessed February 10, 2007.

▸ You can omit the URL when citing well-
known databases. For example:

Copans, Laurie

2007 Clashes by Jerusalem Holy Site
Continue. Washington Post, February
10. Electronic document, ProQuest
Newspapers database, accessed
February 11, 2007.

In-text	(Copans 2007) or (Copans 2007a) (Copans 2007b) (Demetriou 2007) or (Demetriou, February 10, 2007)

Review	References Cited	Banville, John 2007 *Review of* House of Meetings. New York Review of Books 54 (March 1): 38–40. Electronic document, http://www.nybooks.com.proxy.uchicago.edu/articles/19913, accessed February 11, 2007. Blackburn, Simon 2007 *Review of* Descartes: The Life and Times of a Genius. *In* New York Times Book Review, February 4.
	In-text	(Banville 2007) (Blackburn 2007)

Exhibition catalog	References Cited	Smith, Joel 2006 Saul Steinberg: Illuminations. Exhibition catalog. New Haven, CT: Yale University Press.
	In-text	(Smith 2006)
Unpublished paper, thesis, or dissertation	References Cited	Neill, Dawn 2007 Land Insecurity, Urbanization, and Educational Investment among Indo-Fijians. Paper presented at the Annual Meeting of the Society for Applied Anthropology, Tampa Bay, FL, March 28. Prough, Jennifer 2006 Reading Culture, Engendering Girls: Politics of the Everyday in the Production of Girls' Manga. Ph.D. dissertation, Department of Cultural Anthropology, Duke University. Brenneis, Donald N.d. Reforming Promise. Unpublished MS, Department of Anthropology, University of California, Santa Cruz. ▸ "MS" is in caps without a period. Marlowe, Frank W. In press Mate Preferences among Hadza Hunter-Gatherers. Human Nature. ▸ This refers to a work accepted for publication.
	In-text	(Neill 2007) (Prough 2006) (Brenneis n.d.) (Marlowe in press)
Microfilm, microfiche	References Cited	U.S. House of Representatives 1871 First Report. Southern Claims Commission. Records (1871–1880). Microfilm Publication P2257, Frames 0145-0165. Washington, DC: National Archives. Conservative Party (UK) Archive 1919 Annual Report of the Executive Committee to Central Council. March 11–

November 18. Microfiche card 143.
Woodbridge, CT: Gale/Primary Source
Microfilm, 1998. (Original material
located in Conservative Party Archive,
Bodleian Library, Oxford, UK.)

▸ You do not need to include the location of the
original material, but you are welcome to.

In-text		(U.S. House 1871)
		(Conservative Party 1919)

Archival	References	Rice Ballard Papers
materials	Cited	N.d. Southern Historical Collection. Wilson
and		Library, University of North Carolina,
manuscript		Chapel Hill.
collections,		▸ Or
hard copies		Franklin, Isaac
and online		1831 Letter to R. C. Ballard, February 28. *In*

Rice Ballard Papers, Southern Historical
Collection. Wilson Library, University of
North Carolina, Chapel Hill.

▸ In the text or explanatory notes, you may
cite directly to Isaac Franklin's letter to R. C.
Ballard and include it in your References
Cited. Or you may refer to the letter in the text
and cite to the collection (Rice Ballard Papers).

Boston YWCA Papers
N.d. Schlesinger Library, Radcliffe Institute
for Advanced Study, Harvard University.

▸ Or

Lamson, Mary Swift
1891 An Account of the Beginning of the
B.Y.W.C.A. MS [n.d.] and accompanying
letter. Boston YWCA Papers. Schlesinger
Library, Radcliffe Institute for Advanced
Study, Harvard University.

▸ If Lamson's account is the only item cited from
these papers, then it would be listed in the
References Cited.

Taft, Horatio Nelson
1861–62 Diary. Vol. 1, January 1, 1861–
April 11, 1862. Manuscript Division,

| Archival materials and manuscript collections, hard copies and online (*continued*) | In-text: | Library of Congress. Electronic document, http://memory.loc.gov/ ammem/tafthtml/tafthome.html, accessed May 30, 2004.

(Rice Ballard Papers n.d.)
(Boston YWCA Papers n.d.)
(Lamson 1891)
(Taft 1861–62) |

| Encyclopedia, hard copy and online | References Cited | Encyclopaedia Britannica
  1987 Balkans: History. 15th edition. Vol. 14. Pp. 570–588. Chicago: Encyclopaedia Britannica.
  2007 Balkans. Electronic document, http:// search.eb.com.proxy.uchicago.edu/eb/ article-9110555, accessed February 10, 2007.
Brumfiel, Elizabeth M.
  2001 States and Civilizations, Archaeology of. *In* International Encyclopedia of Social and Behavioral Sciences. N. J. Smelser and P. B. Baltes, eds. Pp. 14983–14988. Oxford: Elsevier Science.
Graham, George
  2005 Behaviorism. *In* Stanford Encyclopedia of Philosophy. Electronic document, http://plato.stanford.edu/entries/ behaviorism/, accessed February 11, 2007.
Haas, Jonathan
  2001 Kayenta Anasazi. *In* Encyclopedia of Prehistory: North America, vol. 6. Peter N. Peregrine and Melvin Ember, eds. Pp. 40–42. New York: Kluwer Academic/ Plenum Publishers. |
| | In-text | (Encyclopaedia Britannica 1987)
(Encyclopaedia Britannica 2007)
(Brumfiel 2001)
(Graham 2005)
(Haas 2001) |

Reference book, hard copy and online	References Cited	Pendergast, Sara, and Tom Pendergast, eds. 2003 Reference Guide to World Literature. 3rd edition. 2 vols. Detroit: St. James Press/Thomson-Gale. Pendergast, Sara, and Tom Pendergast, eds. 2003 Reference Guide to World Literature. 3rd edition. Detroit: St. James Press/ Thomson-Gale. E-book. Colman, Andrew M. 2001 A Dictionary of Psychology. Oxford: Oxford University Press. Electronic document, http://www.oxfordreference .com/views/BOOK_SEARCH.html?book =t87, accessed March 16, 2004. Great Britain: Queen's Speech Opens Parliament 2003 FirstSearch. Facts On File database. December 11. Accession no. 2003302680.
	In-text	(Pendergast and Pendergast 2003) ▸ For a specific page in a specific volume: (Pendergast and Pendergast 2003, vol. 2:619) (Colman 2001) (Great Britain: Queen's Speech 2003)
Dictionary, hard copy, online, and CD-ROM	References Cited	Merriam-Webster's Collegiate Dictionary 2003 Caste. 11th edition. Springfield, MA: Merriam-Webster. Compact Edition of the Oxford English Dictionary 1971 Protest, v. Oxford: Oxford University Press. Vol. 2:2335. ▸ The word "protest" is both a noun and a verb. Here, I am citing the verb. Dictionary.com 2007 Class, n. Electronic document, http://dictionary.reference.com/ search?q=class, accessed February 11, 2007. American Heritage Dictionary of the English Language

Dictionary, hard copy, online, and CD-ROM (*continued*)		2000 Folklore. 4th edition. Boston: Houghton Mifflin. CD-ROM.
		Speake, Jennifer, ed.
		    2003 Where MacGregor sits is the head of the table. *In* Oxford Dictionary of Proverbs. 4th edition. P. 161. Oxford: Oxford University Press.
		Winthrop, Robert H.
		    1991 Caste. *In* Dictionary of Concepts in Cultural Anthropology. Pp. 27–30. New York: Greenwood.

	In-text	(Merriam-Webster's Collegiate Dictionary 2003) (Compact Edition of the Oxford English Dictionary 1971) (Dictionary.com 2007) (American Heritage Dictionary 2000) (Speake 2003) (Winthrop 1991)

Speech, academic talk, or course lecture	References Cited	Bilsborough, Alan
		    2006 Species, Pattern and Adaptation in Human Evolution. Presidential address, Royal Anthropological Institute, Canterbury, Eng., November 3.
		Comaroff, John L.
		    2007 Course lecture. University of Chicago, Chicago, April 12.

	In-text	(Bilsborough 2006) (Comaroff 2007)

Interview	References Cited	Wilson, E. O.
		    2007 Personal interview regarding evolution. Cambridge, MA, February 1.
		Douglas, Mary
		    2003 Interview with John Clay. Electronic document, http://www.bhag.net/int/intdougm/intdougm_inte.html, accessed February 10, 2007.
		▶ Unpublished personal communications are often identified parenthetically in the

text, such as (John Doe, interview with author, May 1, 2008). Some authors include communications like this in References Cited; some don't. AAA seems to be of two minds. Their online style guide says to omit them, but articles in their official journals frequently include them. My suggestion: it's your choice, but be consistent and definitely include communications that can be accessed by your readers, such as items posted online.

	In-text	(Wilson 2007) (Douglas 2003)

Television program	References Cited	Moore, Steven Dean, dir.
		    2002 Bart vs. Lisa vs. 3rd Grade. The Simpsons. Fox, November 17.
		▸ To emphasize the title, a writer, or a particular actor, put that name on the top line (and include the director in the line below):
		Long, Tim, writer
		    2002 Bart vs. Lisa vs. 3rd Grade. Steven Dean Moore, dir. The Simpsons. Fox, November 17.

	In-text	(Moore 2002) (Long 2002)

Film	References Cited	Apted, Michael, dir.
		    2006 Amazing Grace. 111 min. Samuel Goldwyn Films. Hollywood.
		Asch, Timothy, and Napoleon Chagnon, creators
		    1975 The Ax Fight. 30 min. Black-and-white. National Anthropological Archives and Human Studies Film Archives, SA-81.5.1.
		▸ Or to emphasize the title rather than the creators:
		Ax Fight, The
		    1975 Timothy Asch and Napoleon Chagnon, creators. 30 min. Black-and-white.

Film (*continued*)		National Anthropological Archives and Human Studies Film Archives, SA-81.5.1. ▸ Films may be included in the References Cited or may be listed separately in a section entitled "Filmography References" or "Films Cited."
	In-text	(Apted 2006) (Asch and Chagnon 1975) or (Ax Fight 1975)

Photograph	References Cited	Adams, Ansel
		  1927 Monolith, the Face of Half Dome, Yosemite National Park. Photograph. Chicago: Art Institute.
		▸ Or if you used a photograph online:
		Adams, Ansel
		  1927 Monolith, the Face of Half Dome, Yosemite National Park. Photograph. Chicago: Art Institute. Electronic document, http://www.hctc.commnet .edu/artmuseum/anseladams/details/ pdf/monlith.pdf, accessed February 11, 2007.
		▸ Photographs are seldom included in reference lists. They are usually identified in the article itself, immediately beneath the photo. For example, a photo of rural houses might include this explanation: Typical sharecropper homes, Quitman County, Mississippi (January 2008) (Photo by Maude Schuyler Clay)

	In-text	(Adams 1927)

Figures: map, chart, graph, or table	Credit or explanation for figure or table	▸ Give a descriptive title to your maps, charts, photos, graphs, and tables. Place an identifying credit or clarifying information below the item, such as Dancing at Carnival, Rio de Janeiro (2008) (Photo by Eric Cartman) President James Knox Polk, three-quarter-length portrait (1849) (Daguerreotype by Mathew Brady) (Collection of the Library of Congress)

Ceremonial grave markers (Mohawk)
(Collection of Art Institute of Chicago)
All figures in this table are rounded to nearest
percentile.
Two-tailed significance tests: *$*p < .05$ **$*p < .01$

> ▸ You may also need to list sources for a figure,
> map, chart, graph, or table. Here, for example,
> is a title for a table, with an asterisk after the
> title to identify the sources of information on
> which it is based. These sources (Jones and
> Smith) are identified by in-text citations on a
> line below the table. Full information about
> them appears in the References Cited.

Table 4: Fertility rates of Bedouins in Israel*
*Sources: Jones (2007), Smith (2008)

Musical recording	References Cited	Johnson, Robert 　1961　Cross Road Blues. *From* Robert Johnson: King of the Delta Blues Singers. New York: Columbia Records.
	In-text	(Johnson 1961)
Sound recording	References Cited	Doniger, Wendy 　2003　The Essential Kamasutra. 5-CD set. Boulder, CO: Sounds True.
	In-text	(Doniger 2003)
Government document, hard copy and online	References Cited	U.S. Senate, Committee on Armed Services 　1947　Hearings on S. 758: A bill to promote the national security by providing for a national defense establishment. 80th Cong., 1st sess. U.S. Bureau of the Census 　2007　Statistical Abstracts of the U.S. Washington, DC: U.S. Bureau of the Census. Federal Trade Commission 　2006　How to Buy Genuine American Indian Arts and Crafts. Electronic document, http://www.doi.gov/iacb/brochures/

Government document, hard copy and online (*continued*)		indianartftc.pdf, accessed February 11, 2007. UN Development Programme 2005 Human Development Report 2005: International Cooperation at a Crossroads: Aid, Trade and Security in an Unequal World. Electronic document, http://hdr.undp.org/reports/global/2005/, accessed February 11, 2007.
	In-text	(U.S. Senate, Committee on Armed Service 1947) (U.S. Bureau of the Census 2007) (Federal Trade Commission 2006) (UN Development Programme 2005)
Database	References Cited	Anthropology Review Database N.d. ARD: Anthropology Review Database. http://wings.buffalo.edu/anthropology/ARD/, accessed February 22, 2007. National Archeological Database 2004 NADB Reports. Electronic document, http://www.cast.uark.edu/other/nps/nadb/nadb.mul.html, accessed February 19, 2007.
	In-text	(Anthropology Review Database n.d.) (National Archeological Database 2004)
Website, entire	References Cited	Digital History Website N.d. Website. Sidney Mintz, ed. http://www.digitalhistory.uh.edu/index.cfm?, accessed February 11, 2007. ▸ AAA format spells "website" as one word. Internet Public Library (IPL) 2007 Website. http://www.ipl.org/, accessed February 15, 2007. Harvard University, Department of Anthropology 2007 Website. http://www.fas.harvard.edu/~anthro/, accessed February 16, 2007. ▸ If a Website or Web page does not show a date when it was copyrighted or updated, then list "N.d." where the year normally appears.

	In-text	(Digital History n.d.) (Internet Public Library 2007) or (IPL 2007) (Harvard University, Dept. of Anthropology 2007)

Web page	References Cited	Yale University, Department of Anthropology
		    2007 Graduate Program. Web page.
		        Electronic document, http://www.yale
		        .edu/anthro/grad/graduate.html,
		        accessed February 17, 2007.

	In-text	(Yale University, Dept. of Anthropology Graduate Program 2004)

Weblog,
entry or
comment
	References Cited	Drezner, Daniel
		    2007 Is Economic Protectionism on the
		        Rise in China? Weblog posting at
		        Daniel W. Drezner. February 2. Electronic
		        document, http://www.danieldrezner
		        .com/blog/, accessed February 11, 2007.
		"Rex" (Alex Golub)
		    2007 More Anthro Classics on Google.
		        Weblog posting at Savage Minds:
		        Notes and Queries in Anthropology.
		        February 7. Electronic document, http://
		        savageminds.org/, accessed February 11,
		        2007.
		Koehler, Benedikt
		    2007 Response to More Anthro Classics
		        on Google. Weblog comment at
		        Savage Minds: Notes and Queries in
		        Anthropology. February 7. Electronic
		        document, http://savageminds
		        .org/2007/02/07/more-anthro-classics
		        -on-google/#comments, accessed
		        February 11, 2007.

	In-text	(Drezner 2007) ("Rex" 2007) (Koehler 2007)

10

CSE CITATIONS FOR THE BIOLOGICAL SCIENCES

. . . .

CSE citations, devised by the Council of Science Editors, are widely used for scientific papers, journals, and books in the life sciences. The citations are based on international principles adopted by the National Library of Medicine.

Actually, the CSE system lets you choose among three ways of citing documents:

- *Citation-sequence:* Citations are numbered (1), (2), (3), in the order they appear in the text. Full references appear at the end of the paper—in the same order. They are *not* alphabetized.
- *Citation-name:* Citations are numbered, with full references at the end of the paper—in alphabetical order. The first item cited in the text might be number 8 on the alphabetical list. It would be cited as (8), even though it appeared first—and (8) if it appears again.
- *Name-year:* Citations in the text are given as name and year, such as (McClintock 2006). Full references appear at the end of the paper in alphabetical order, just as they do in APA citations.

Whichever format you choose, use it consistently throughout the paper. Ask your instructor which one she prefers.

Citation-sequence: Cite the first reference in the text as number 1, the second as number 2, and so on. You can use brackets [1], superscripts[1], or parentheses (1). At the end of the paper, list all the items, beginning with the first one cited. The list is *not* alphabetical. If the first item you cite is by Professor Zangwill, then that's the first item in the reference list. If you cite Zangwill's paper again, it's still [1], even if it's the last citation in your paper. If you want to cite several items at once, simply include the number for each one, separated by commas, such as [1,3,9] or [1,3,9] or (1,3,9). If items have successive numbers, use hyphens: 4-6,12-18.

Citation-name: Begin by assembling an alphabetical list of references at the end of the text and numbering them. Each item in the list will have a number, which is used whenever that book or article is cited in the text. If the Zangwill article is thirty-sixth in the alphabetical list, then it is always cited with that number, even if it's the first item you cite in the paper. The next reference in the text might be [23], the one after that might be [12]. Citations can be set as superscripts, in brackets, or in parentheses. If you want to cite several items at once, include a number for each one, such as [4,15,22] or [4,15,22] or (4,15,22). Use hyphens for continuous numbers (1-3). So a citation could be (4,16-18,22).

Name-year: For in-text citations, use the (name-year) format without commas, such as (Cronin and Siegler 2007) and (Siegler et al. 2008). The reference list is alphabetical by author and includes all cited articles. If an author has several articles, list the earliest ones first. Follow the same method if an author has published several articles in the same year. List the first one as 2008a, the second as 2008b, and so on by the month of publication. To cite several articles by Susan Lindquist, then, the notation might be (Lindquist 2007d, 2008a, 2008h), referring to those three articles in the reference list.

In the same way, you can also cite articles by different authors within the same reference. Separate them by semicolons, such as (Liebman 2007; Ma and Lindquist 2008; Outeiro and Lindquist 2008).

If the author's name appears in the sentence, you do not need to repeat it in the citation. For example, "According to LaBarbera (2007), this experiment . . ."

What if LaBarbera had ten or fifteen coauthors? That's certainly possible in the sciences. Articles sometimes have dozens of authors because they include everyone involved in the experiments leading to publication. My colleague Henry Frisch, a high-energy physicist, told me that one of his articles has nearly eight hundred coauthors![1] I grew up in a town with a smaller phone book. Really.

How many of these authors should you include when you use name-year

---

1. Professor Frisch's own practice is to list himself as author only if he actually helped write the paper. His practice is unusual, but a number of scientists think he's right and that current practices are unclear and often lax. To correct the problem,

citations in the text? Don't go overboard. Just list the first seven hundred. If you do that in the first sentence, you'll reach the paper's word limit before you even have to write a second sentence. That's one easy science paper.

Actually, CSE offers clear recommendations, stopping a bit short of seven hundred authors. If there are only two authors, list them both, separated by "and." If there are three or more authors, list only the first one, followed by "et al." For example: (LaBarbera et al. 2008). Later, I'll show you how to handle coauthors in the reference list at the end of the paper.

QUICK COMPARISON OF CSE STYLES

STYLE	IN-TEXT CITATIONS	REFERENCE LIST AT END OF PAPER
Citation-sequence	(1), (2), (3), (4)	Items listed in order of their text appearance
Citation-name	(31), (2), (13), (7)	Items listed alphabetically, by author surname
Name-year	(Shapiro 2008)	Items listed alphabetically, by author surname

STYLES OF REFERENCE LISTS

All three styles require reference lists following the text. CSE emphasizes brevity and simplicity for these lists. Instead of using the authors' first names, use only their initials. Omit periods after the initials and don't put spaces between them: Stern HK.

Shorten journal names with standard abbreviations, such as those given in the *Index Medicus* system, available online at ftp://nlmpubs.nlm .nih.gov/online/journals/ljiweb.pdf. CSE doesn't use periods in shortening journal titles. So, J Biosci Bioeng (without periods) is the abbreviation for the *Journal of Bioscience and Bioengineering*.

CSE uses sentence-style capitalization for titles. Capitalize only the first word, proper nouns, and the first word after a colon. Print the titles in normal type rather than italics.

If you cite something you've read online rather than in print, cite the

some scientists are circulating proposals that would require coauthors to specify how they contributed to joint papers. For Frisch's comments on the metastasizing growth of coauthors, see his Web page, http://hep.uchicago.edu/~frisch.

electronic version. After all, the two versions may differ. To do that, CSE style requires you to add a couple of items to the citation: (1) the date you accessed the document and (2) the fact that it was an Internet document. In the citation, you should insert [Internet] in square brackets, immediately after the journal title, and the date you accessed it; then, after the article's pagination, insert the URL.

Print citation	Pugliese A, Beltramo T, Torre D. 2007. Emerging and re-emerging viral infections in Europe. Cell Biochem Funct. 25:1–13.
Internet citation	Pugliese A, Beltramo T, Torre D. 2007. Emerging and re-emerging viral infections in Europe. Cell Biochem Funct [Internet]. [cited 2007 Feb 14]; 25:1–13. Available from: http://www3.interscience.wiley.com.proxy.uchicago.edu/cgi-bin/fulltext/112775037/PDFSTART

If you wish to include a document identification number (DOI) or other database number, put it last. There is no period after the DOI.

Internet citation with URL and document ID number	Pugliese A, Beltramo T, Torre D. 2007. Emerging and re-emerging viral infections in Europe. Cell Biochem Funct [Internet]. [cited 2007 Feb 14]; 25:1–13. Available from: http://www3.interscience.wiley.com.proxy.uchicago.edu/cgi-bin/fulltext/112775037/PDFSTART. DOI: 10.1027/cbf.1342

This article, like nearly all printed articles, was not modified after it was published. But preprints are often modified and so are articles in electronic journals. You need to include that information in the citation so your readers will know which version you are citing. That information appears in the square brackets, immediately before the date you accessed the item.

Modified paper	Pugliese A, Beltramo T, Torre D. 2007. Emerging and re-emerging viral infections in Europe. Cell Biochem Funct [Internet]. [modified 2007 Mar 4; cited 2007 Mar 8]; 25:1–13. Available from: http://www3.interscience.wiley.com.proxy.uchicago.edu/cgi-bin/fulltext/112775037/PDFSTART. DOI: 10.1027/cbf.1342

Don't worry about remembering all these details. There are too many of them. I'll explain them in the tables that follow and include plenty of examples. If you use this style often, you'll gradually grow familiar with the fine points.

These tables show CSE recommendations for in-text citations and reference lists, using all three formats. Not every journal follows them exactly, so you'll see some variation as you read scientific publications. Journals differ, for example, in how many coauthors they include in the reference list. Some list only the first three authors before adding "et al." One lists the first twenty-six. (Imagine being poor coauthor number 27.) The CSE says to name up to ten and then adding "et al."

These tables are based on Council of Science Editors, *Scientific Style and Format: The CSE Manual for Authors, Editors, and Publishers,* 7th ed. (Reston, VA: Council of Science Editors, 2006).

CSE: NAME-YEAR SYSTEM

Journal article	Reference list	Zheng M, McPeek MS. 2007. Multipoint linkage-disequilibrium mapping with haplotype-block structure. Am J Hum Genet. 80(1):112–125. Wong KK, et al. 2007. A comprehensive analysis of common copy-number variations in the human genome. Am J Hum Genet. 80(1): 91–104. ▸ The Wong article has eleven authors. CSE says to list the first ten, followed by "et al." But individual journals vary in their practice. Some would include all of them in the reference list. Most would include only the first two.
	In-text	(Zheng and McPeek 2007) (Wong et al. 2007) ▸ If your list includes several publications by Wong and other authors in 2007, your in-text reference should include coauthors to clarify exactly which article you are citing. For example: (Wong, deLeeuw et al. 2007).
Journal article, online	Reference list	Alvarez-Dolado M. 2007. Cell fusion: Biological perspectives and potential for regenerative medicine. Front Biosci [Internet]. [cited 2007 Feb 12]; 12:1–2. Available from: http://www .bioscience.org ▸ This journal article is online only. Do *not* add a period at the end of the URL.
	In-text	(Alvarez-Dolado 2007)

Abstract of article	Reference list	Erkut S, Uckan S. 2006. Alveolar distraction osteogenesis and implant placement in a severely resorbed maxilla: A clinical report [Abstract]. J Prosthet Dent. 95(5):340–343.

- CSE's 7th edition of *Style and Format* does not specify a style for citing abstracts. The format shown here is consistent, however, with other citation rules in that edition.

Erkut S, Uckan S. 2006. Alveolar distraction osteogenesis and implant placement in a severely resorbed maxilla: A clinical report. J Prosthet Dent. 95(5):340–343. In: Dent Abstr. 2007;52(1):17–19.

- The upper reference is to the abstract, as published in the article itself. The lower reference is to the abstract, published in a different journal.

In-text
(Erkut and Uckan 2006)
(Erkut and Uckan 2006)

Book, one author	Reference list	Brereton RG. 2007. Applied chemometrics for scientists. Hoboken (NJ): John Wiley & Sons.

Wiggins CE. 2007. A concise guide to orthopaedic and musculoskeletal impairment ratings. Philadelphia: Lippincott Williams & Wilkins.

- If the publisher's city is well known, you may omit the state.

In-text
(Brereton 2007)
(Wiggins 2007)

- To cite the same author for works written in several years:

(Wiggins 2006, 2007a, 2007b, 2008)

- To cite works by authors with the same surname published in the same year, include the authors' initials:

(Wiggins CE 2008; Wiggins LJ 2008)

Book, multiple authors	Reference list	Villas-Boas SG, Nielsen J, Smedsgaard J, Hansen MAE, Roessner-Tunali U. 2007. Metabolome analysis: An introduction. Hoboken (NJ): John Wiley & Sons. ▸ In the reference list, name up to ten authors, then add "et al."
	In-text	(Villas-Boas et al. 2007) ▸ If there are just two authors, name them both: (Villas-Boas and Nielsen 2008)
Book, multiple editions	Reference list	Tropp BE. 2007. Molecular biology: Genes to proteins. 3rd ed. Sudbury (MA): Jones and Bartlett. Snell RS. 2007. Clinical anatomy by regions. 8th ed. Philadelphia: Lippincott Williams & Wilkins. ▸ For a revised edition, the phrase "Rev. ed." appears where "8th ed." currently does.
	In-text	(Tropp 2007) (Snell 2007)
Book, multiple editions, no author	Reference list	Publication manual of the American Psychological Association. 2001. 5th ed. Washington (DC): American Psychological Association.
	In-text	(Publication manual . . . 2001) ▸ Do not use "Anonymous" in place of the author name. Instead, use the first word or first few words of the title and an ellipsis, followed by the date.
Book, edited	Reference list	Baluka F, Mancuso S, Volkmann D, editors. 2006. Communication in plants: Neuronal aspects of plant life. Berlin: Springer-Verlag.
	In-text	(Baluka et al. 2006)
Chapter in edited book	Reference list	Kelley SO. 2007. Nanowires for biomolecular sensing. In: Vo-Dinh T, editor. Nanotechnology

in biology and medicine: Methods, devices, and applications. Boca Raton (FL): CRC Press/ Taylor & Francis. p. 95–101.

| | In-text | (Kelley 2007) |

| Preprint | Reference list | Osheroff JA et al. 2007. A roadmap for national action on clinical decision support. Preprint. J Am Med Inform Assoc [Internet]. [cited 2007 Feb 12]. Available from: http://www.jamia .org/cgi/reprint/M2334v1. PMID:17213487. doi :10.1197/jamia.M2334 |

> ▸ CSE's 7th edition of *Style and Format* does not specify a style for citing preprints. The format shown here is consistent, however, with other citations rules in that edition.

| | In-text | (Osheroff et al. 2007) |

| Government document, hard copy or online | Reference list | Marinopoulos SS, Dorman T, Ratanawongsa N, Wilson LM, Ashar BH, Magaziner JL, Miller RG, Thomas PA, Prokopowicz GP, Qayyum R, Bass EB. 2007. Effectiveness of continuing medical education. Rockville (MD): Agency for Healthcare Research and Quality. AHRQ Pub. No. 07-E006. |

[AHRQ] Agency for Healthcare Research and Quality. 2007. Testing for cytochrome P450 polymorphisms in adults with non-psychotic depression treated with selective serotonin reuptake inhibitors (SSRIs) [Structured Abstract]. Rockville (MD): AHRQ; [cited 2007 Feb 13]. AHRQ Pub. No. 07-E002. Available from: http://www.ahrq.gov/clinic/tp/cyp450tp .htm

Smith PW, Congressional Research Service. 2006. The National Institutes of Health (NIH): Organization, funding, and congressional issues. Washington (DC): Congressional Research Service, Library of Congress; [cited 2007 Feb 11]. Available from: http://www.nih

Government document, hard copy or online (*continued*)		.gov/about/director/StrategiesfortheFuture .pdf ▸ If an organization is both author and publisher, the name may be abbreviated as publisher. For example, Washington (DC): CRS.
	In-text	(Marinopoulos et al. 2007) (Smith 2006)
CD-ROM or DVD	Reference list	Complete human anatomy [DVD-ROM]. 2005. London (England): Primal Pictures.
	In-text	(Complete human anatomy 2005)
Database	Reference list	RCSB Protein Data Bank [Internet]. 2007 [cited 2007 Feb 23]. Available from: http://www.rcsb .org/pdb/home/home.do [NIH] National Institutes of Health, Office of Dietary Supplements. 2007. International Bibliographic Information on Dietary Supplements (IBIDS) Database [Internet]. [cited 2007 Feb. 23]. Available from: http://ods .od.nih.gov/Health_Information/IBIDS.aspx
	In-text	(RCSB Protein Data Bank 2007) (NIH 2007) or (NIH IBIDS Database 2007)
Web site or Web page	Reference list	[CSE] Council of Science Editors. [date unknown]. Citing the Internet: Formats for bibliographic citation [Internet]. Reston (VA): Council of Science Editors; [cited 2007 Feb 12]. Available from: http://www .councilscienceeditors.org/publications/ citing_internet.cfm ▸ Where this citation says only [Internet], yours might say [monograph on Internet] or [database on Internet]. [USDA] US Department of Agriculture, National Agriculture Library. Research and technology [Internet]. Washington (DC): USDA; 2007 [cited 2007 Feb 22]. Available from: http://lincoln

		.nal.usda.gov/index.php?mode=subject &subject=nal_science&d_subject=Research %20and%20Technology [NLM] National Library of Medicine. Recommended formats for bibliographic citation, supplement: Internet formats [Internet]. 2001 [cited 2007 Feb 12]. Available from: http:// www.nlm.nih.gov/pubs/formats/internet.pdf
	In-text	(CSE date unknown) (USDA 2007) (NLM 2001)

The next table shows CSE references using citation-sequence and citation-name formats. The main difference from the previous table is that the date appears later in the reference. I have used the same examples, in case you want to compare formats.

CSE: CITATION-SEQUENCE AND CITATION-NAME SYSTEMS		
Journal article	Reference list	Zheng M, McPeek MS. Multipoint linkage-disequilibrium mapping with haplotype-block structure. Am J Hum Genet. 2007;80(1):112–125. Wong KK, deLeeuw RJ et al. A comprehensive analysis of common copy-number variations in the human genome. Am J Hum Genet. 2007;80(1):91–104.
Journal article, online	Reference list	Alvarez-Dolado M. Cell fusion: Biological perspectives and potential for regenerative medicine. Front Biosci [Internet]. 2007 [cited 2007 Feb 12]; 12:1–2. Available from: http:// www.bioscience.org ▸ This journal article is online only.
Abstract	Reference list	▸ How you list an abstract depends on whether you are referring to: • An abstract included in the article itself • An abstract that appears in a different journal and that you are citing *without* reading the original article

Abstract (*continued*)		• An abstract that appears in a different journal and that you are citing together with the article you read ▸ Abstract only, within the article itself: Erkut S, Uckan S. 2006. Alveolar distraction osteogenesis and implant placement in a severely resorbed maxilla: A clinical report [Abstract]. J Prosthet Dent. 95(5):340–343. ▸ Abstract only, in a different journal from the article: Erkut S, Uckan S. 2006. Alveolar distraction osteogenesis and implant placement in a severely resorbed maxilla: A clinical report. J Prosthet Dent. 95(5):340–343. In: Dent Abstr. 2007;52(1):17–19.
Book, one author	Reference list	Brereton RG. Applied chemometrics for scientists. Hoboken (NJ): John Wiley & Sons; 2007. Wiggins CE. 2007. A concise guide to orthopaedic and musculoskeletal impairment ratings. Philadelphia: Lippincott Williams & Wilkins. ▸ If the publisher's city is well known, you may omit the state abbreviation, if you wish.
Book, multiple authors	Reference list	Villas-Boas SG, Nielsen J, Smedsgaard J, Hansen MAE, Roessner-Tunali U. Metabolome analysis: An introduction. Hoboken (NJ): John Wiley & Sons; 2007. ▸ In the reference list, name up to ten authors, then add "et al."
Book, multiple editions	Reference list	Tropp BE. Molecular biology: Genes to proteins. 3rd ed. Sudbury (MA): Jones and Bartlett; 2007. Snell RS. Clinical anatomy by regions. 8th ed. Philadelphia: Lippincott Williams & Wilkins; 2007. ▸ For a revised edition, use "Rev. ed." in place of "8th ed."

Book, multiple editions, no author	Reference list	Publication manual of the American Psychological Association. 5th ed. Washington (DC): American Psychological Association; 2001.
Book, edited	Reference list	Baluka F, Mancuso S, Volkmann D, editors. Communication in plants: Neuronal aspects of plant life. Berlin: Springer-Verlag; 2006.
Chapter in edited book	Reference list	Kelley SO. Nanowires for biomolecular sensing. In: Vo-Dinh T, editor. Nanotechnology in biology and medicine: Methods, devices, and applications. Boca Raton (FL): CRC Press/Taylor & Francis; 2007. p. 95–101.
Preprint	Reference list	Osheroff JA et al. A roadmap for national action on clinical decision support. Preprint. J Am Med Inform Assoc [Internet]. 2007 [cited 2007 Feb 12]. Available from: http://www.jamia.org/cgi/reprint/M2334v1. PMID:17213487. doi:10.1197/jamia.M2334
Government document	Reference list	Marinopoulos SS, Dorman T, Ratanawongsa N, Wilson LM, Ashar BH, Magaziner JL, Miller RG, Thomas PA, Prokopowicz GP, Qayyum R, Bass EB. Effectiveness of continuing medical education. Rockville (MD): Agency for Healthcare Research and Quality; 2007. AHRQ Pub. No. 07-E006. [AHRQ] Agency for Healthcare Research and Quality. Testing for cytochrome P450 polymorphisms in adults with non-psychotic depression treated with selective serotonin reuptake inhibitors (SSRIs) [Structured Abstract]. Rockville (MD): AHRQ; 2007 [cited 2007 Feb 13]. AHRQ Pub. No. 07-E002. Available from: http://www.ahrq.gov/clinic/tp/cyp45otp.htm Smith PW, Congressional Research Service. The National Institutes of Health (NIH): Organization, funding, and congressional issues. Washington (DC): Congressional

Government document (*continued*)		Research Service, Library of Congress; 2006 [cited 2007 Feb 11]. Available from: http://www.nih.gov/about/director/ StrategiesfortheFuture.pdf
CD-ROM or DVD	Reference list	Complete human anatomy [DVD-ROM]. London (England): Primal Pictures; 2005.
Database	Reference list	RCSB Protein Data Bank [Internet]. 2007 [cited 2007 Feb 23]. Available from: http://www.rcsb .org/pdb/home/home.do [NIH] National Institutes of Health, Office of Dietary Supplements. 2007. International Bibliographic Information on Dietary Supplements (IBIDS) Database [Internet]. [cited 2007 Feb. 23]. Available from: http://ods .od.nih.gov/Health_Information/IBIDS.aspx
Web site or Web page	Reference list	[USDA] US Department of Agriculture, National Agriculture Library. Research and technology [Internet]. Washington (DC): USDA; 2007 [cited 2007 Feb 22]. Available from: http://lincoln.nal.usda.gov/index.php?mode =subject&subject=nal_science&d_subject =Research%20and%20Technology [CSE] Council of Science Editors. Citing the Internet: Formats for bibliographic citation [Internet]. Reston (VA): Council of Science Editors; [date unknown]. [cited 2007 Feb 12]. Available from: http://www .councilscienceeditors.org/publications/ citing_internet.cfm [NLM] National Library of Medicine. Recommended formats for bibliographic citation, supplement: Internet formats [Internet]. 2001 [cited 2007 Feb 12]. Available from: http:// www.nlm.nih.gov/pubs/formats/internet.pdf

  ▸ Where this citation says [Internet], yours might say [monograph on Internet] or [database on Internet].

Although individual references (shown above) are the same for both the citation-sequence and citation-name systems, their full reference lists are compiled in different orders.

Order of items within reference lists:

- Citation-name system: alphabetical by author
- Citation-sequence system: order of first appearance in the text

To illustrate, let's take the opening sentence of an article and show how each style would handle the citations and reference list.

CSE: CITATION-SEQUENCE SYSTEM (ILLUSTRATION OF REFERENCE LIST ORDER)

Opening sentence	This research deals with the ABC transporter family and builds on prior studies by Thacker et al.,[1] Sheps et al.,[2] and Kerr.[3]
Reference list (in order of appearance in text)	1. Thacker C, Sheps JA, Rose AM. Caenorhabditis elegans dpy-5 is a cuticle procollagen processed by a proprotein convertase. Cell Mol Life Sci. 2006;63:1193–1204.
	2. Sheps JA, Ralph S, Zhao Z, Baillie DL, Ling V. The ABC transporter gene family of Caenorhabditis elegans has implications for the evolutionary dynamics of multidrug resistance in eukaryotes. Genome Biol. 2004;5:R15.
	3. Kerr ID. Sequence analysis of twin ATP binding cassette proteins involved in translational control, antibiotic resistance, and ribonuclease L inhibition. Biochem Biophys Res Commun. 2004;315:166–173.
	▸ Thacker's article is listed first because it is the first one mentioned in the text.

CSE: CITATION-NAME SYSTEM (ILLUSTRATION OF REFERENCE LIST ORDER)

Opening sentence	This research deals with the ABC transporter family and builds on prior studies by Thacker et al.,[3] Sheps et al.,[2] and Kerr.[1]
Reference list (alphabetical)	1. Kerr ID. Sequence analysis of twin ATP binding cassette proteins involved in translational control, antibiotic

resistance, and ribonuclease L inhibition. Biochem
Biophys Res Commun. 2004;315:166–173.

2. Sheps JA, Ralph S, Zhao Z, Baillie DL, Ling V. The ABC
transporter gene family of Caenorhabditis elegans
has implications for the evolutionary dynamics of
multidrug resistance in eukaryotes. Genome Biol.
2004;5:R15.

3. Thacker C, Sheps JA, Rose AM. Caenorhabditis
elegans dpy-5 is a cuticle procollagen processed by a
proprotein convertase. Cell Mol Life Sci. 2006;63:1193–
1204.

▸ Thacker's article is listed last because it is last
alphabetically.

The two systems, citation-sequence and citation-name, present *each
item* in the reference list the same way. What's different are (1) the *order* of
items in the reference list and (2) their *citation numbers* in the text.

There's one more item you may wish to include in your citations: the
PMID number. All medical articles have this electronic tag, which identifies them within the comprehensive PubMed database. The PMID appears as the last item in the citation and is *not* followed by a period:

Kerr ID. Sequence analysis of twin ATP binding cassette proteins involved in translational control, antibiotic resistance, and ribonuclease
L inhibition. Biochem Biophys Res Commun [Internet]. 2004 [cited
2007 Feb 12]; 315:166–73. PMID: 15013441

The PubMed database, covering more than four thousand biomedical
journals, was developed at the National Library of Medicine and is available online at www.ncbi.nlm.nih.gov/entrez.

Detailed information about CSE citations for the sciences can be
found in

• *Scientific Style and Format: The CSE Manual for Authors, Editors,
and Publishers,* 7th ed. (Reston, VA: Council of Science Editors,
2006).

AMA CITATIONS FOR THE BIOMEDICAL SCIENCES, MEDICINE, NURSING, AND DENTISTRY

. . . .

AMA citations are used in biomedical research, medicine, nursing, dentistry, and some related fields of biology. They are based on the *AMA Manual of Style: A Guide for Authors and Editors,* 10th ed. (Oxford: Oxford University Press, 2007).

Citations are numbered (1), (2), (3), in the order they appear in the text. Full references appear at the end of the paper—in the same order. For coauthored books and articles, you should list up to six authors. If there are more, list only the first three, followed by "et al." Rather than using the authors' first names, use their initials (without periods) and do not put spaces between the initials: Lipson CH. Abbreviate the title of journals. There's a standard list of abbreviations (the *Index Medicus* system) available online at ftp://nlmpubs.nlm.nih.gov/online/journals/ljiweb.pdf.

AMA CITATIONS

Journal article

Van Gijn J, Kerr RS, Rinkel GJE. Subarachnoid haemorrhage. *Lancet.* 2007;369(9558):306–318.
Sehgal S, Drazner MH. Left ventricular geometry: Does shape matter? *Am Heart J.* 2007;153(2):153–155.
Drinka PJ, Krause PF, Nest LJ, Goodman BM. Determinants of vitamin D levels in nursing home residents. *J Am Med Dir Assoc.* 2007;8(2):76–79.

▸ Name up to six authors in articles or books. If there are more, name the first three, then use "et al." This article, for example, has thirteen listed authors:

Journal article (*continued*)	Morton N, Maniatis N, Weihua Z, et al. Genome scanning by composite likelihood. *Am J Hum Genet.* 2007;80(1): 19–28. Singh AK, Szczech L, Tang KL, et al. CHOIR Investigators. Correction of anemia with epoetin alfa in chronic kidney disease. *N Engl J Med.* 2006;355(20):2085–2098. ▸ Journal titles are abbreviated without periods. (There is a period after "*Genet.*" only because it is the last word in the journal's title.) Likewise, there is a period after "et al" only because a period always follows the final author's name.
Journal article, online	Varol E, Ozaydin M, Altinbas A, Aslan SM, Dogan A, Dede O. Elevated carbohydrate antigen 125 levels in hypertrophic cardiomyopathy patients with heart failure. *Heart Vessels.* 2007;22(1):30–33. http://www.metapress .com.proxy.uchicago.edu/content/q66273161043v65v/ fulltext.pdf. Accessed February 10, 2007. Alvarez-Dolado M. Cell fusion: Biological perspectives and potential for regenerative medicine. *Front Biosci.* 2007;12:1–2. http://www.bioscience.org. Accessed February 10, 2007. ▸ This article is online only and does not have an issue number.
Abstract of article	Erkut S, Uckan S. Alveolar distraction osteogenesis and implant placement in a severely resorbed maxilla: A clinical report [abstract]. *J Prosthet Dent.* 2006;95(5):340–343. Erkut S, Uckan S. Alveolar distraction osteogenesis and implant placement in a severely resorbed maxilla: A clinical report [abstract taken from *Dent Abstr.* 2007;52(1):17–19]. *J Prosthet Dent.* 2006;95(5):340–343. ▸ The upper reference is to the abstract, as published in the article itself. The lower reference is to the abstract, published in a different journal.
Preprint or other unpublished material	Osheroff JA, Teich JM, Middleton BF, Steen EB, Wright A, Detmer DE. A roadmap for national action on clinical decision support. Preprint January 9, 2007. *J Am Med Inform Assoc.* http://www.jamia.org/cgi/reprint/

M2334v1. Accessed February 10, 2007. PMID:17213487
.doi:10.1197/jamia.M2334.
Davids T. Auditory responses to electrical stimulation.
Grand Rounds, Department of Otolaryngology, Head and
Neck Surgery, University of Toronto; January 26, 2007.

Published letter, comment, or editorial	Guazzi M, Reina G. Regarding article, Aspirin use and outcomes in a community-based cohort of 7352 patients discharged after first hospitalization for heart failure [Letter]. *Circulation.* 2007;115(4):e54. DOI: 10.1161/ CIRCULATIONAHA.106.646182. Simon DI, Pompili VJ. Far-fetched benefit of inflammation [editorial]. *Circulation.* 2007;115(5):548–549.
Book, one author	O'Grady E. *A Nurse's Guide to Caring for Cardiac Intervention Patients.* Chichester, England: John Wiley & Sons; 2007. Wiggins CE. *A Concise Guide to Orthopaedic and Musculoskeletal Impairment Ratings.* Philadelphia, PA: Lippincott Williams & Wilkins; 2007. Hands L. *Vascular Surgery.* New York, NY: Oxford; 2007. ▸ Note, also, that states are included even after well-known cities.
Book, multiple authors	Mazze R, Strock ES, Simonson GD, Bergenstal RM. *Staged Diabetes Management.* 2nd rev ed. Hoboken, NJ: John Wiley & Sons; 2007.
Book, multiple editions	Snell RS. *Clinical Anatomy by Regions.* 8th ed. Philadelphia, PA: Lippincott Williams & Wilkins; 2007. Higgins CB, de Roos A, eds. *MRI and CT of the Cardiovascular System.* 2nd ed. Philadelphia, PA: Lippincott Williams & Wilkins; 2006. ▸ The edition number appears between the book's title and the place of publication. ▸ For a revised edition, use "Rev ed." in place of the specific edition.

Book, multiple volumes	Chorghade MS, ed. *Drug Discovery and Development.* 2 vols. Hoboken, NJ: John Wiley & Sons; 2007.
	▸ To cite only the second volume:
	Chorghade MS, ed. *Drug Discovery and Development.* Vol 2. Hoboken, NJ: John Wiley & Sons; 2007.
	▸ To cite the second volume by name, begin with the author (or editor) of that volume, plus its title and publication date, followed by the editor of the entire series, the series name, and the volume within the series.
	Chorghade MS, ed. *Drug Development.* Hoboken, NJ: John Wiley & Sons; 2007. Chorghade MS, ed. *Drug Discovery and Development;* vol 2.

Book, multiple editions, no author	*Dorland's Illustrated Medical Dictionary.* 30th ed. Philadelphia, PA: Saunders; 2003.
	Nursing 2007 Drug Handbook. 27th ed. Springhouse, PA: Springhouse; 2006.

Reference book	Vandersall D. *Concise Encyclopedia of Periodontology.* Ames, IA: Blackwell; 2007.
	Lewis RJ Sr. *Hawley's Condensed Chemical Dictionary.* 15th ed. Hoboken, NJ: John Wiley & Sons; 2007.
	Federative International Committee on Anatomical Terminology (FICAT). *Terminologia Histologica: International Terms for Human Cytology and Histology.* Philadelphia, PA: Lippincott Williams & Wilkins; 2007.
	Fuster V, Alexander RW, O'Rourke RA, et al, eds. *Hurst's The Heart.* Vol 2. 11th ed. New York, NY: McGraw Hill; 2004.
	▸ "Vol" does not have a period. AMA eliminates periods after abbreviations.

Reference online and CD	*Medical Dictionary (Medline).* http://www.nlm.nih.gov/ medlineplus/mplusdictionary.html. Accessed February 10, 2007.
	Dorland's Online Dictionary. http://www.dorlands.com/ wsearch.jsp. Accessed February 10, 2007.
	Lewis RJ Sr. *Hawley's Condensed Chemical Dictionary* [CD-ROM]. 15th ed. Hoboken, NJ: John Wiley & Sons; 2007.

Book, edited	Oppenheimer SJ ed. *Neural Tube Defects.* New York, NY: Informa Healthcare USA; 2007. Gravlee GP, Davis RF, Stammers AH, Ungerleider RM, eds. *Cardiopulmonary Bypass Principles and Practice.* 3rd ed. Philadelphia, PA: Lippincott Williams & Wilkins; 2007.
Chapter in edited book	Matthias Föhn M, Bannasch H. Artificial skin. In: Hauser H, Fussenegger M, ed. *Tissue Engineering.* 2nd ed. Totowa, NJ: Humana Press; 2007:732–739. Rizk NJ. Parallel and computational approaches to evolutionary biology. In: Zomaya AY, ed. *Parallel Computing for Bioinformatics and Computational Biology: Models, Enabling Technologies, and Case Studies.* Hoboken, NJ: John Wiley & Sons; 2006:3–28.
Government document, hard copy or online	Agency for Healthcare Research and Quality (AHRQ). Testing for cytochrome P450 polymorphisms in adults with non-psychotic depression treated with selective serotonin reuptake inhibitors (SSRIs). Structured Abstract. January 2007. AHRQ, Rockville, MD. http://www.ahrq.gov/clinic/tp/cyp45otp.htm. Accessed February 12, 2007. Marinopoulos SS, Dorman T, Ratanawongsa N, et al. Effectiveness of continuing medical education. AHRQ Pub No 07-E006. Rockville, MD: Agency for Healthcare Research and Quality; 2007. Medicare Advantage cost plans and demonstrations: Landscape of plan options in Mississippi 2007. Washington, DC: US Dept of Health and Human Services, n.d. http://www.medicare.gov/medicarereform/mapdpdocs2007/MAPDLandscapeMS07.pdf. Accessed February 10, 2007. Smith PW, Congressional Research Service. The National Institutes of Health (NIH): Organization, funding, and congressional issues. Washington, DC: Congressional Research Service, Library of Congress; 2006. http://www.nih.gov/about/director/StrategiesfortheFuture.pdf. Accessed February 10, 2007.

Personal comment, untitled lecture, or informal communication	▶ Using AMA style, your reference list cannot include personal communications such as letters, e-mails, and private discussions. It cannot include lectures except for those given at conferences.
CD-ROM or DVD	National Library of Medicine. *Changing the Face of Medicine* [DVD]. Washington, DC: Friends of the National Library of Medicine; 2004. *Complete Human Anatomy* [DVD-ROM]. London, England: Primal Pictures; 2005.
Database	RCSB Protein Data Bank. http://www.rcsb.org/pdb/home/home.do. Accessed February 18, 2007. National Institutes of Health. Office of Dietary Supplements. International Bibliographic Information on Dietary Supplements (IBIDS) Database. http://ods.od.nih.gov/Health_Information/IBIDS.aspx. Accessed February 18, 2007. National Center for Health Statistics. Summary health statistics for the U.S. population: National health interview survey, 2005. *Vital Health Stat* 10 (233). DHHS Pub No 2007-1561. Hyattsville, MD: National Center for Health Statistics (US Dept of Health and Human Services); 2007.
Web site or Web page	Frequently asked questions. US Public Health Service Commissioned Corps Web site. http://www.usphs.gov/html/faqs.html. Accessed February 28, 2007. US Preventive Services Task Force. Screening for prostate cancer: Recommendations and rationale. Agency for Healthcare Research and Quality Web site. http://www.ahrq.gov/clinic/3rduspstf/prostatescr/prostaterr.htm. Accessed February 28, 2007.

To illustrate how these citations appear in the text, let's take the opening sentence of an article.

AMA (ILLUSTRATION OF REFERENCE LIST ORDER)

Opening sentence	This research deals with the ABC transporter family and builds on prior studies by Thacker et al,[1] Sheps et al,[2] and Kerr.[3]

Reference list (in order of appearance in text)	1. Thacker C, Sheps JA, Rose AM. *Caenorhabditis elegans dpy-5* is a cuticle procollagen processed by a proprotein convertase. *Cell Mol Life Sci.* 2006; 63(10):1193–1204.
	2. Sheps JA, Ralph S, Zhao Z, Baillie DL, Ling V. The ABC transporter gene family of *Caenorhabditis elegans* has implications for the evolutionary dynamics of multidrug resistance in eukaryotes. *Genome Biol.* 2004;5(3):R15.
	3. Kerr ID. Sequence analysis of twin ATP binding cassette proteins involved in translational control, antibiotic resistance, and ribonuclease L inhibition. *Biochem Biophys Res Commun.* 2004;315(1):166–173.
	▸ Thacker's article is listed first because it is the first one mentioned in the text. Notice that "et al" does not include a period when it is used in sentences, according to AMA style.

Finally, all medical articles have an electronic identification number, known as a PMID. You are not required to include it, but it often helps your readers. It will help you, too, if you need to return to the article. The PMID appears as the last item in the citation and is followed by a period:

Yeates TO. Protein structure: Evolutionary bridges to new folds. *Curr Biol.* 2007;17(2):R48–50. PMID: 17240325.

The PMID identifies the document within the PubMed database, which includes virtually all biomedical journals. This database was developed at the National Library of Medicine and it is available online at www.ncbi.nlm.nih.gov/entrez.

12

ACS CITATIONS
FOR CHEMISTRY

. . . .

The American Chemical Society (ACS) has its own style guide, which gives you a choice of citation formats:

- In-text citations with name and year, similar to APA or CSE. The reference list is alphabetized and appears at the end of the paper.
- Numbered citations, with a reference list at the end of the paper. End references are numbered in the order they appear in the text. These numbered citations, as they appear in the text itself, are either
  - superscript, such as[23], or
  - parentheses with the number in italics, such as (23).

Each format is used by scores of chemistry journals. Your lab, instructor, or journal may prefer one over the other. Whichever one you choose, use it consistently throughout each paper.

Fortunately, you collect the same information for either format. In fact, the items in the reference list are presented exactly the same way, whether the list is numbered or alphabetized.

- The author's last name appears first, followed by a comma and then initials (instead of given names), such as Fenn, J. B. Initials are followed by periods.
- Instead of "page," the reference list uses "p" and "pp" without periods.
- The reference list uses hanging indents. That is, the first line of each reference is full length; all subsequent lines are indented.

- For books
  - Include the title and italicize it. That's true for edited books, too.
  - Put the publisher's name before the location, as in CRC Press: Boca Raton, FL.
  - Include the year of publication, using normal typeface, such as Wiley-Interscience: New York, 2004.
  - Show pagination in books by using "pp"—for example: CRC Press: Boca Raton, FL, 2004; pp 507–515.
  - For edited books, you may include (or omit) the titles of specific chapters; just be consistent.
- For journals
  - Include the journal title, abbreviated and italicized, such as *J. Am. Chem. Soc.*
  - Include the year of publication in **boldface,** the volume number in italics, and the complete pagination of the article in normal type, such as *Org. Lett.* **2007,** *9,* 2609–2611.
  - Show pagination in articles *without* using "pp"—for example: *Chem. Eng. News.* **2007,** *85,* 31–34.
  - Include or omit the article's title, whichever you prefer. (Be consistent, of course.) Until recently, article titles were always omitted. Now the *ACS Style Guide* (3rd ed.) considers it "desirable" to include the title, both to indicate the subject matter and to help readers find it.

There is no explanation for these mysterious details. My guess: the chemists were overcome by fumes many years ago, and the odd results are now beloved traditions.

ACS (CHEMISTRY): REFERENCE LIST AND IN-TEXT CITATIONS

Journal article	Reference list	Luft, J.; Meleson, K.; Houk, K. Transition Structures of Diastereoselective 1,3-Dipolar Cycloadditions of Nitrile Oxides to Chiral Homoallylic Alcohols. *Org. Lett.* **2007,** *9,* 555–558.
		▸ Or
		Luft, J.; Meleson, K.; Houk, K. *Org. Lett.* **2007,** *9,* 555–558.

Journal article (*continued*)		Xing, Y.; Lin, H.; Wang, F.; Lu, P. An Efficient D-A Dyad for Solvent Polarity Sensor. *Sens. Actuators, B* **2006,** *114,* 28–31.

▸ Or

Xing, Y.; Lin, H.; Wang, F.; Lu, P. *Sens. Actuators, B* **2006,** *114,* 28–31.

▸ Article title may be included or omitted. The *ACS Style Guide* (3rd ed.) recommends inclusion. Words in the article title are capitalized, as they would be in a book title.

▸ Year of publication is in boldface; volume number is italicized.

▸ Journal titles are italicized and abbreviated according to the *Chemical Abstracts Service Source Index* (CASSI).

	In-text	(Luft et al., 2007)
		(Xing et al., 2006)

Journal article, online	Reference list	Zaki, M.; Nirdosh, I.; Sedahmed, G. *Chem. Eng. J.* [Online] **2007,** *126,* 67–77.
	In-text	(Zaki et al., 2007)

Chemical abstract	Reference list	Taneda, A.; Shimizu, T.; Kawazoe, Y. *J. Phys.: Condens. Matter* **2001,** *13* (16), L305–312 (Eng.); *Chem. Abstr.* **2001,** *134,* 372018a.

▸ This article by Taneda was published in a journal and referenced in *Chemical Abstracts.* This citation shows a reference to both the full article and the abstract. The abstract always comes second and is separated from the article by a semicolon.

Taneda, A.; Shimizu, T.; Kawazoe, Y. *Chem. Abstr.* **2001,** *134,* 372018a.

▸ Same article but shown only as mentioned in *Chemical Abstracts.* It is better to refer to the full published article than the abstract, but that requires you actually examine the full article.

Chem. Abstr. **2001,** *134,* 372018a.

▸ This is the same article, referred to solely by its *Chemical Abstract* number. That number—

134, 372018a—is the CAS accession number. The number *134* is the volume and *372018a* is the abstract number in the print version of *Chemical Abstracts.*

▸ In some earlier editions of *Chemical Abstracts,* there are several abstracts per page. Abstract f on page 1167 can be cited as 1167*f* (or 1167*f*).

▸ It is usually better to include the authors, as in the previous references to Taneda et al.

In-text	(Taneda et al., 2001) (*Chem. Abstr.*, 2001)

Book, one author	Reference list	Tilley, R. *Crystals and Crystal Structures;* John Wiley & Sons: Chichester, U.K., 2006; pp 23–42. ▸ Or: Chapter 3 instead of the pagination.
	In-text	(Tilley, 2006)

Book, multiple authors	Reference list	Williams, R. J. P.; Fraústo da Silva, J. J. R. *The Chemistry of Evolution: The Development of Our Ecosystem;* Elsevier: Amsterdam, 2006. ▸ What if there are many authors? *The ACS Style Guide* says to name them all. It also notes that some chemistry journals list only the first ten, followed by a semicolon and "et al."
	In-text	(Williams and Fraústo da Silva, 2006) ▸ Include up to two names for in-text citations. If there are three or more, use this form: (Williams et al., 2007)

Book, multiple editions	Reference list	McMurry, J.; Castellion, M. E.; Ballantine, D. S. *Fundamentals of General, Organic, and Biological Chemistry,* 5th ed.; Prentice-Hall: Upper Saddle River, NJ, 2006. ▸ For a revised edition, use "Rev. ed." instead of "5th ed."
	In-text	(McMurry et al., 2006)

Book multiple editions, no author	Reference list	*Reagent Chemicals: Specifications and Procedures,* 10th ed.; American Chemical Society: Washington, DC, 2005. *McGraw-Hill Encyclopedia of Science and Technology,* 9th ed.; McGraw-Hill: New York, 2002; 20 vols.
	In-text	(*Reagent Chemicals,* 2005). (*McGraw-Hill,* 2002) ▸ To cite a particular volume: (*McGraw-Hill,* Vol. 6, 2002)
Book, multivolume	Reference list	*The Encyclopedia of Mass Spectrometry;* Gross, M. L., Caprioli, R., Eds.; Elsevier Science: Oxford, 2007; Vol. 6. *Hyphenation Methods;* Niessen, W., Ed. Vol. 8. In *The Encyclopedia of Mass Spectrometry;* Gross, M. L., Caprioli, R., Eds.; Elsevier Science: Oxford, 2006.
	In-text	(Gross and Caprioli, Vol. 6, 2007) (Niessen, Vol. 8, 2006)
Book, edited	Reference list	*Polyketides: Biosynthesis, Biological Activity, and Genetic Engineering;* Rimando, A. M., Baerson, S. R., Eds.; American Chemical Society: Washington, DC, 2007.
	In-text	(Rimando and Baerson, 2007)
Chapter in edited book	Reference list	Lavine, B. K., et al. In *Chemometrics and Chemoinformatics;* Lavine, B. K., Ed.; American Chemical Society: Washington, DC, 2005; pp 127–143. ▸ Or Lavine, B. K.; Davidson, C. E.; Breneman, C.; Katt, W. In *Chemometrics and Chemoinformatics;* Lavine, B. K., Ed.; American Chemical Society: Washington, DC, 2005; pp 127–143. ▸ You may include or omit the chapter title; just be consistent.

▸ How many authors should you include for items on the reference list? If there are only two authors, list both: Jones and Smith. If there are three or more authors, the *ACS Style Guide* says to list them in abbreviated form: Jones et al. In practice, many chemical journals list up to nine or ten authors; for larger numbers, they list only the first author plus "et al."

	In-text	(Lavine et al., 2005)

▸ Normally use only one or two names for in-text citations. Occasionally, though, you will find top chemistry journals citing more authors, such as:
(Lavine, Davidson, Breneman, and Katt, 2005)

Conference paper	Reference list	Monti, M.; Cataletto, B. Molecular Characterization and Morphological Variability of Seven Strains of the Dinoflagellate *Prorocentrum Minimum* PO.01-07. Presented at the 12th International Conference on Harmful Algae, Copenhagen, Denmark, September 2006; Poster.
	In-text	(Monti and Cataletto, 2006)

Reference work or encyclopedia	Reference list	Vaidya, R.; Löpez, G.; Lopez, J. A. Nanotechnology (Molecular). *Van Nostrand's Encyclopedia of Chemistry* [Online]. John Wiley & Sons: Hoboken, NJ, 2005. http://www.mrw.interscience.wiley.com/vec/articles/vec1690/bibliography-fs.html (accessed July 8, 2007).
	In-text	(Vaidya et al., 2005)

Government document	Reference list	U.S. Consumer Product Safety Commission. *School Chemistry Laboratory Safety Guide (October 2006);* DHHS (NIOSH) Publication No. 2007–107; National Institute for Occupational Safety and Health: Cincinnati, OH, 2007.

Government document (*continued*)		National Emission Standards for Hazardous Air Pollutants for Source Categories from Oil and Natural Gas Production Facilities. *Fed. Regist.* **2007,** *72* (1), 26–43. ▸ The *Federal Register* is treated like a journal.
	In-text	(*School Chemistry Laboratory Safety Guide,* 2007)
Patent	Reference list	Lieber, C. M., et al. Methods of Forming Nanoscopic Wire-Based Devices and Arrays. U.S. Patent 7,172,953 B2, 2007. ▸ It is also acceptable to omit the name of the patent.
	In-text	(Lieber et al., 2007)
CD-ROM or DVD	Reference list	Luceigh, B. A. *Chem TV: Organic Chemistry* 3.0 [CD-ROM]; Jones and Bartlett: Sudbury, MA, 2004. Lewis, R. J., Sr. *Hawley's Condensed Chemical Dictionary,* 15th ed. [CD-ROM]; John Wiley & Sons: New York, 2007. Lide, D. R. *Handbook of Chemistry and Physics on CD-ROM Version 2007,* 8th ed. [CD-ROM]; CRC Press/Taylor & Francis: Boca Raton, FL, 2006.
	In-text	(Luceigh, 2004) (Lewis, 2007) (Lide, 2006)
Internet	Reference list	Biochemical Periodic Tables. http://umbbd .ahc.umn.edu/periodic/links.html (accessed Feb 12, 2007). ▸ If the page has an author, his name and initial appear before the title of the page: Oxtoby, J. Biochemical Periodic Tables. http:// . . .
	In-text	(Oxtoby, 2007)

Detailed information on ACS citations is available in

- Anne M. Coghill and Lorrin R. Garson, eds., *The ACS Style Guide: Effective Communication of Scientific Information,* 3rd ed. (Washington, DC: American Chemical Society, 2006).

13

PHYSICS, ASTROPHYSICS, AND ASTRONOMY CITATIONS

. . . .

AIP CITATIONS IN PHYSICS

Physics citations are based on the *AIP Style Manual,* 4th ed. (New York: American Institute of Physics, 1990) and the more recent *AIP Physics Desk Reference,* 3rd ed. (2003).[1] Most physics journals use numbered citations in the text and the reference list. Items appear in the numbered reference list in the order they appear in the text. The items are not indented.

The citations may be numbered either in superscript or brackets, that is, as [99] or [99]. The *AIP Style Manual* uses superscripts, as do AIP's official journals, such as *Chaos* and *Low Temperature Physics.* On the other hand, the organization's own *AIP Physics Desk Reference* uses brackets, as do journals from the American Physical Society (APS), such as *Physical Review E.* Either approach is fine. Just be sure you use the same style for the text and reference list. (A few physics journals use the author-year style instead. It has an alphabetized reference list with hanging indents.)

Whichever format is used, individual items in the reference list look the same, at least for articles and preprints (which are the way researchers communicate). References are brief: Authors' names (M. Shochet and S. Nagel), abbreviated journal title, **boldface number for the journal volume,** first page number of the article, and, finally, the year in parentheses.

---

1. E. Richard Cohen, David R. Lide, George L. Trigg, eds., *AIP Physics Desk Reference,* 3rd ed. (New York: Springer-Verlag, 2003).

AIP (PHYSICS): REFERENCE LIST

Journal article

[1] O. Budriga and V. Florescu, Euro. Phys. J. D **41,** 205 (2007).

[2] A. N. Khorramian, S. Atashbar Tehrani, and A. Mirjalili, Nucl. Phys. B **164** (Proc. Suppl.) 34 (2007).

▸ The article's title is always omitted. Journal titles are abbreviated and not italicized.

▸ The publication volume (or issue number) and series are in boldface. For example, if a reference is to an article in *Physical Letters B,* issue number 466, page 415, then it appears as Phys. Lett. B **466,** 415 (1999).

Journal article, online

[#] Ulf Leonhardt, New J. Phys. **8,** 118 (2006). ‹http://ej.iop.org/links/rIRo,rLVJ/kMLPcge42xGkINp8av5vpA/njp6_7_118.pdf›.

▸ This is an online-only journal.

▸ The citation may also include a DOI or PII after the URL. DOI is a digital object identifier. PII is a publisher item identifier. Both are ways of uniquely identifying electronic documents. For the Leonhardt article, DOI: 10.1088/1367-2630/8/7/118; PII: S1367-2630(06)25618-0.

▸ Online articles are referenced the same way as articles in print, except that they may include an electronic article number (if one is available), instead of this issue and page number. Example: Phys. Rev. B **75,** 012408 (2007).

Preprint

[#] Manu Mathur, preprint, hep-lat/0702007 (2007). ‹http://arxiv.org/PS_cache/hep-lat/pdf/0702/0702007.pdf›.

[#] N. Michel, W. Nazarewicz, and M. Ploszajczak, preprint, nucl-th/0702021 (2007). ‹http://arxiv.org/PS_cache/nucl-th/pdf/0702/0702021.pdf›. Accepted in Phys. Rev. C (figure corrected).

[#] M. Medved, preprint, hep-th/0301010J (2003). ‹http://arxiv.org/abs/hep-th/0301010›. Published in High Energy Phys. **5,** 008 (2003). ‹http://www.iop.org/EJ/abstract/1126-6708/2003/05/008/›.

▸ hep-lat = Heidelberg High Energy Physics (HEP) Preprint Service, e-prints on lattices; nucl-th = nuclear theory; hep-th = e-prints on theoretical physics.

Book, one author	[#] Robert M. White, *Quantum Theory of Magnetism: Magnetic Properties of Materials* (Springer, Berlin, 2007).
Book, multiple authors	[#] D. Gatteschi, R. Sessoli, and J. Villain, *Molecular Nanomagnets* (Oxford University Press, Oxford, 2006). ▸ The *AIP Style Manual* says to list up to three authors. If there are more authors, name only the first and add "*et al.*" in italics. Example: Gatteschi *et al., Molecular Nanomagnets* . . .
Book, multiple editions	[#] A. F. J. Levi, *Applied Quantum Mechanics,* 2nd ed. (Cambridge University Press, New York, 2006).
Book, multivolume	[#] J.-P. Françoise, G. L. Naber, and T. S. Tsun, editors, *Encyclopedia of Mathematical Physics.* 5 vols. (Academic Press/Elsevier, San Diego, CA, 2006).
Book, edited	[#] Z. Li and H. Meng, editors, *Organic Light-Emitting Materials and Devices* (CRC Press/Taylor & Francis, Boca Raton, FL, 2007).
Chapter in book	[#] Heinz Georg Schuster, in *Collective Dynamics of Nonlinear and Disordered Systems,* edited by G. Radons, W. Just, and P. Häussler (Springer, Berlin, 2005).
Database	[#] National Institutes of Standards and Technology, Physics Laboratory, Physical Reference Base. ⟨http://physics.nist.gov/PhysRefData/contents.html⟩.

CITATIONS IN ASTROPHYSICS AND ASTRONOMY

Astronomy and astrophysics don't use the AIP/physics citation style or, for that matter, any single format. But most leading journals are fairly similar. They generally use (author-year) citations in the text, followed by an alphabetical reference list. The reference list follows some fairly common rules. It generally

- uses hanging indents
- contains no bold or italics
- uses authors' initials rather than their first names
- joins coauthors' names with an ampersand "&"
- puts the publication date immediately after the authors' name (with no comma between the name and date)
- omits the titles of articles
- includes titles for books and gives publisher information
- abbreviates journal names, often reducing them to a couple of initials
- lists only the first page of an article
- ends references without a period

Because there's no published style manual for astronomy and astrophysics, citation formats vary. I've standardized them, based on the most common forms in the leading journals. Here are some illustrations, based on *Astronomy and Astrophysics* and the *Astrophysical Journal,* with a little tweaking for consistency.

ASTRONOMY AND ASTROPHYSICS REFERENCE LISTS

Journal article	Baugh, C. M. 2006, Rept. Prog. Phys. 69, 3101
	Li et al. 2007, ApJ, 655, 351
	Wang, Z., Kaplan, D. L., & Chakrabarty, D. 2007, ApJ, 655, 261
	Fechner, C., & Reimers, D. 2007, A&A, 461, 847

Journal article, several by same authors	Panaitescu, A. 2005a, MNRAS, 363, 1409
	Panaitescu, A. 2005b, MNRAS, 362, 921
	Razzaque, S., & Mészáros, P. 2006a, ApJ, 650, 998
	Razzaque, S., & Mészáros, P. 2006b, JCAP, 06, 006
	Pe'er. A., & Wijers, R. A. M. J. 2006, ApJ, 643, 1036
	Pe'er, A., & Zhang, B. 2006, ApJ, 653, 454

▸ The two articles by Panaitescu are listed as 2005a and 2005b because they have the same author.

▸ The two articles by Razzaque & Mészáros are listed as 2006a and 2006b because they have the same coauthors.
▸ The two articles by Pe'er are *not* listed as 2006a and 2006b because they do not have identical coauthors.

Journal article, online	Fechner, C., & Reimers, D. 2007, A&A 461, 847 DOI: 10.105 1/0004-6361:20065556

▸ *All* astronomy, astrophysics, and physics articles are online and available through standard scientific databases. Adding the document identifier or other search information may help your readers find them more easily.

Preprint	Curir, A., Mazzei, P., & Murante, G. 2007, A&A, in press [astro-ph/0702035] Crittenden, R., Majerotto, E., & Piazza, F. 2007, preprint [astro-ph/ 0702003]

Book, one author	Osterbrock, D. E. 2006, Astrophysics of Gaseous Nebulae and Active Galactic Nuclei (Sausalito, CA: University Science Books) Harwit, M. 2006, Astrophysical Concepts (New York: Springer Science)

Book, multiple authors	Cassen, P., Guillot, T., & Quirrenbach, A. 2006, Extrasolar Planets (New York: Springer)

Chapter in edited book	Franceschini, A. 2006, in Joint Evolution of Black Holes and Galaxies, ed. M. Colpi, V. Gorini, F. Haardt, & U. Moschella (Boca Raton, FL: CRC Press/Taylor & Francis), 63

Book in a series	Stefl, S., Owocki, S. P., & Okazaki, A. T., eds., 2006, Active Ob-Stars: Laboratories for Stellar and Circumstellar Physics (San Francisco: ASP), ASP Conf. Ser. 361

Chapter in a book in a series	Daly, P. N. 2006, in Astronomical Data Analysis Software Systems XV, ed. C. Gabriel, C. Arviset, D. Ponz, & E. Solano (San Francisco: ASP), ASP Conf. Ser. 351, 4

| Unpublished paper or dissertation | Sedrakian, A. 2007 [astro-ph/0701017], lectures available at http://theor.jinr.ru/~dm2006/talks.html
Egan, M. P., Price, S. D., Moshir, M. M., et al. 1999, Air Force Research Lab. Tech. Rep. no. AFRL-VS. T. R. 1999-1522
Fiore, F., Guainazzi, M., & Grandi, P. 1999, Cookbook for BeppoSAX NFI Spectral Analysis, available by ftp from legacy.gsfc.nasa.gov/sax/doc/software_docs/saxabc_v1.2.ps
Lee, J. 2006, Ph.D. Diss., University of Arizona |
| Internet | Skyview, the Internet Virtual Telescope ‹http://skyview.gsfc.nasa.gov› |

Researchers in the physical sciences often cite unpublished research, usually conference papers or work-in-progress that will be published later. Known as preprints (or e-prints), these papers are at the cutting edge of the field and are collected in electronic document archives. Besides collections at major research institutions, there's a huge collection at arXiv .org (http://www.arxiv.org), with mirror sites around the world. Papers are readily accessible and easy to download. What's hard—unless you are on the cutting edge of physics—is actually understanding their content!

Preprints in the arXiv collection are classified by field (physics, astrophysics, mathematics, quantitative biology, and so forth) and, within each field, by major subfields. Papers are submitted to the subfield archives and are numbered by their date of arrival. As with journal articles, the titles of preprints are omitted from citations. Here are some examples:

Amos, K., Faessler, A., Rodin, V. 2007, preprint, nucl-th/ 0702016 <http://arxiv.org/PS_cache/nucl-th/pdf/0702/0702016.pdf>
Linder, E. V. 2007, preprint, astro-ph/0702010

or

Linder, E. V. 2007, preprint (astro-ph/0702010)

The classification system is as simple as the papers are complex. Take the Linder paper. It's in astronomy and astrophysics (astro-ph), was submitted in 2007 (07), in the second month (02), and was the tenth paper submitted in its category that month (010). Hence, astro-ph/0702010.

For the Amos, Faessler, and Rodin article, I included the full URL, but that's not essential. Professionals in the field know where to find arXiv preprints, either at the main archive or mirror sites. It's sufficient to list the ID: nucl-th/0702016.

Preprints like these should be cited and included in your reference list, just like journal articles. Unpublished does not mean uncited.

14

MATHEMATICS AND COMPUTER SCIENCE CITATIONS

. . . .

Papers in mathematics and computer science use one of two citation styles. The first places an alphabetical reference list at the end of the paper. References in the text are given by bracketed numbers. The first reference might be [23], referring to the twenty-third item in the alphabetical list. The last reference in the article might be [2]. Specific pages are rarely mentioned, but if you need to, use this form: [23, p. 14]. Please use the set of positive integers.

A second system, based on the *Bulletin of the American Mathematical Society,* is often used by advanced mathematicians for publishable research. It, too, has an alphabetical reference list (a slightly different one), but what's unusual are the text references. Instead of bracketed numbers, this style uses abbreviations, based on the author's last name and date of publication. So an article by Damjanovic and Nolan, published in *Econometrica,* volume 74 (2006), would be cited in the text as something like [DaNo06] or perhaps [DN06] or maybe just [DN]. It's your choice. This abbreviation also appears in the reference list, identifying the entry for Damjanovic and Nolan's article. In the second table below, I show how to use this AMS *Bulletin* system.

Most books and articles are classified by subfield and uniquely identified in the Mathematical Reviews (MR) Database. Whichever citation system you use, you can include this MR number as the last item in each reference, after the date or page numbers. The MR Database is searchable through the American Mathematical Society's Web site at http://www .ams.org/mr-database.

If the article you are citing is available online, perhaps at the author's

Web site, mention the URL just before the MR number. If there is no MR number, the Web page appears last.

In the following tables, I show standard mathematical citation forms. Many math journals don't stick to one format. Some use numerical citations for one article and AMS *Bulletin* style for the next. To add to the fun, they'll use the same style differently in different articles. One might list the author as R. Zimmer. The very next article (using the same style) lists the author as Zimmer, R. If I kept looking, I'd probably find one that calls him Bob Zimmer. One article puts the publication date in parentheses; the next one doesn't. In one, the reference list uses italics for every article title and regular type for journal names. The next one does exactly the opposite. Some use boldface for journal numbers, and others don't. Frankly, I don't think any of this matters very much, as long as you are consistent and your professor or publisher is okay with it.

In the tables below, I've swept away these variations and idiosyncrasies. The tables use consistent rules, based on recent editions of major journals in mathematics and computer science.

Article titles and book chapters are italicized. Capitalize only the first word, the first word after a colon, and all proper nouns:

A. R. Conn and P. L. Toint, *An algorithm using quadratic interpolation for unconstrained derivative free optimization*

Book titles are capitalized normally and italicized:

Nonlinear Optimization and Applications

Journal titles are abbreviated but not italicized:

Ann. of Math.
Bull. Amer. Math. Soc.
Geom. Topol.
Trans. Amer. Math. Soc.

A full list of journal abbreviations, compiled by the American Mathematical Society, is available at http://www.ams.org/msnhtml/serials.pdf.

Publications by the same author are listed in the order of publication, beginning with the earliest. Use three em dashes to repeat an author's name, but do so only if *all* the authors are the same. For example:

[32] S. Kihara, *On the rank of the elliptic curves with a rational point of order 6*, Proc. Japan Acad. Ser. A Math. Sci. 82 (2006), pp. 81–82.

[33] ———, *On the rank of elliptic curves with a rational point of order 4, II*, Proc. Japan Acad. Ser. A Math. Sci. 80 (2004), 158–159.

[34] S. Kihara and M. Kenku, *Elliptic Curves . . .*

MATHEMATICS: NUMBERED REFERENCE LIST (ALPHABETICAL ORDER)

Journal article

[1] B. Ahrenholz, J. Tölke, and M. Krafczyk, *Lattice-Boltzmann simulations in reconstructed parametrized porous media*, Int. J. Comput. Fluid Dyn. 20 (2006), pp. 369–377.

[2] I. D. Coope and C. J. Price, *Positive bases in numerical optimization*, Comput. Optim. Appl. 21 (2003), pp. 169–175.

[3] N. P. Strickland, *Gross-Hopkins duality*, Topology 39 (2000), pp. 1021–1033.

[4] ———, *Common subbundles and intersections of divisors*, Algebr. Geom. Topol. 2 (2002) 1061–1118.

‣ Bracketed numbers go in the left margin. Articles are listed in alphabetical order, by author's name. For each author, the articles or books are listed in their order of publication, with the earliest ones first.

‣ If an author's name is repeated (and there are no new coauthors), then use three em dashes, followed by a comma. (Em dashes are simply long dashes, about the length of the letter "m." If for some reason, you can't find these em dashes, just use three hyphens.)

Journal article, online

[#] C. L. Fefferman, *Whitney's extension problem for C^m*, Ann. of Math. 164 (2006), pp. 313–359. Available at http://www.math.princeton.edu/facultypapers/Fefferman/.

[#] S. Takagi, *Formulas for multiplier ideals on singular varieties*, Amer. J. Math. 128 (2006), pp. 1345–1362. Available at http://muse.jhu.edu.proxy.uchicago.edu/journals/american_journal_of_mathematics/v128/128.6takagi.pdf.

Preprint	[#] S. Bloch, *Motives associated to graphs,* Takagi Lectures, Kyoto (2006). Available at http://www.math .uchicago.edu/~bloch/graph_rept/graph_rept061017 .pdf.

[#] A. Cheskidov, S. Friedlander, and N. Pavlović, *A dyadic model for the inviscid fluid equations: Stability of the fixed point,* preprint (2006), submitted for publication. Available at http://www.math.princeton.edu/~natasa/ publications/dburgstab2006Jun23.pdf.

[#] S. Dasgupta, *Shintani zeta-functions and Gross-Stark units for totally real fields,* preprint (2006), submitted for publication. Available at http://www.math.harvard .edu/~dasgupta/papers/shintani.pdf.

[#] J. Haglund, M. Haiman, and N. Loehr, *A combinatorial formula for non-symmetric Macdonald polynomials,* preprint (2006), to appear in Amer. J. of Math. Available at arXiv.org/abs/math.CO/0601693.

▶ In mathematics, as in physics, there's a large, easily accessible electronic archive of preprints available arXiv. The math collection is at http://www.arxiv.org/archive/ math. You can cite either the entire URL for a preprint, as the reference above for Haglund, Haiman, and Loehr does, or you can simply list the archival number and say it is available at arXiv, as the reference below for Talponen does.

[#] X. Sun, *Singular structure of harmonic maps to trees,* preprint (2001), published as *Regularity of harmonic maps to trees,* Amer. J. Math. 125 (2003), pp. 737–771. MR1993740 (2004j:58014).

[#] J. Talponen, *On weakly extremal structures in Banach spaces,* preprint (2007). Available at arXiv, math. FA/0701009.

Other unpublished papers	[#] A. Iserles and S. P. Nørsett, *From high oscillation to rapid approximation II: Expansions in polyharmonic eigenfunctions,* DAMTP Tech. Rep. 2006/NA07. Department of Applied Mathematics and Theoretical Physics, University of Cambridge, Cambridge, UK, 2006. Available at http://www.damtp.cam.ac.uk/user/ na/NA_papers/NA2006_07.pdf.

[#] L. K. Kamenova, *Hyper-Kaehler fibrations and Hilbert schemes,* Ph.D. diss., MIT, 2006.

[#] P. Rostalski, *Characterization and computation of real-radical ideals using semidefinite programming techniques,* IMA postdoc seminar, Minneapolis, MN, 2007.

Book, one author	[#] D. Eisenbud, *The Geometry of Syzygies: A Second Course in Commutative Algebra and Algebraic Geometry,* e-book, Springer, New York, 2005. [#] I. Ekeland, *The Best of All Possible Worlds: Mathematics and Destiny,* University of Chicago Press, Chicago, 2006. [#] A. Knapp, *Basic Algebra,* Birkhäuser, Boston, 2006. [#] M. A. Parthasarathy, *Practical Software Estimation: Function Point Methods for Insourced and Outsourced Projects,* Addison-Wesley Professional, Upper Saddle River, NJ, 2007.
Book, multiple authors	[#] T. Andreescu, O. Mushkarov, and L. Stoyanov, *Geometric Problems on Maxima and Minima,* Birkhäuser, Boston, 2006. ▸ If there are many authors, then name only the first and add "et al." Example: T. Andreescu et. al., *Geometric Problems . . .*
Book, multiple editions	[#] H. Fulton, *The Ruby Way: Solutions and Techniques in Ruby Programming,* 2nd ed., Addison-Wesley Professional, Upper Saddle River, NJ, 2006. [#] B. Korte and J. Vygen, *Combinatorial Optimization: Theory and Algorithms,* 3rd ed., Springer-Verlag, Berlin, 2006. MR2171734 (2006d:90001).
Book, multivolume	[#] F. Dillen and L. C. A. Verstraelen (eds.), *Handbook of Differential Geometry,* vol. 2. Elsevier, Amsterdam, 2006. [#] D. Knuth, *The Art of Computer Programming,* 3rd ed., vol. 4, fasc. 3: *Generating All Combinations and Partitions,* Addison-Wesley Professional, Upper Saddle River, NJ, 2005. MR2251472. [#] G. W. Stewart, *Matrix Algorithms.* Vol. 2: *Eigensystems,* SIAM, Philadelphia, 2001.

Book, edited	[#] P. P. Kulish, N. Manojlovic, and H. Samtleben (eds.), *Infinite Dimensional Algebras and Quantum Integrable Systems*. Progress in Mathematics 237. Birkhäuser, Boston, 2005.
Book, translated	[#] P. G. Darvas, *Symmetry,* Trans. by D. R. Evans, Springer, New York, 2007.
Chapter in edited book	[#] J. Grabowski, *Local lie algebra determines base manifold,* in *From Geometry to Quantum Mechanics: In Honor of Hideki Omori,* Progress in Math., vol. 252, Y. Maeda, P. Michor, T. Ochiai, and A. Yoshioka, eds., Birkhäuser, Boston, 2007, pp. 27–47. ▸ Notice that the chapter is capitalized like a sentence, but the book title is capitalized normally.
Chapter in multivolume edited book	[#] W. E. Hart, *A stationary point convergence theory of evolutionary algorithms,* in *Foundations of Genetic Algorithms 4,* R. K. Belew and M. D. Vose, eds., Morgan Kaufmann, San Francisco, 1997, pp. 127–134.
Software	[#] T. G. Kolda et al., *APPSPACK (Asynchronous parallel pattern search package);* ver. 5.0, 2006. Available at http://software.sandia.gov/appspack/version5.0/pageDownloads.html. [#] *Microsoft Windows Vista Enterprise 1.0.* Microsoft, Redmond, WA, 2007. Available at http:// http://www.microsoft.com/windows/products/windowsvista/buyorupgrade/default.mspx. ▸ When there is no author, as with this Microsoft program, alphabetize by its title.

Now, let's turn to the AMS *Bulletin* style. A few general points:

- To repeat an author's name, use three em dashes instead of the name. But do so only if *all* authors are the same.
- Capitalize only the first word (and proper nouns) for *article* titles. For book and journal titles, on the other hand, capitalize all important words; journal titles are also abbreviated.

- When the place of publication is contained in the publisher's name and is well known, then omit the place-name. Examples: Oxford UP, Cambridge UP, Princeton UP, and U Chicago P.
- To differentiate publications by the same author, include numbers after the initials. For example, assume you are citing one article published by J. Holt in 2002 and another in 2004. You could label them as [Ho2] and [Ho4], or as [Ho02] and [Ho04].
- To denote unpublished articles, you may add an asterisk if you wish, such as [Hop98*], but that is optional.

It may be helpful to see these AMS *Bulletin* citations used in an article text. Here are a couple of examples:

This question was posed by Pyber [Py3] and answered by Murray [Mu]. In [Bo98], uniform barriers are handled differently.

MATHEMATICS: AMS *BULLETIN* STYLE (ALPHABETICAL ORDER)

Journal article	[LePe07]	D.K. Levine and W. Pesendorfer: *The evolution of cooperation through imitation*, Games Econ. Behav. **58** (2007), 293–315.
		▸ Initials such as D.K. have no spaces between them.
		▸ Articles and chapters are capitalized in sentence style. Titles of books and journals, on the other hand, are capitalized normally. Journal titles are abbreviated and not italicized.
		▸ Volume or issue numbers are boldfaced.
	[Bo05]	I.M. Bomze: *Portfolio selection via replicator dynamics and projections of indefinite estimated covariances*, Dyn. Contin. Discrete Impuls. Syst. Ser. B Appl. Algorithms **12** (2005), 527–563. MR2167616 (**2006c:**90059)
		▸ There is no punctuation after the MR number.

Journal article, online	[Ha01]	M. Haiman: *Hilbert schemes, polygraphs, and the Macdonald positivity conjecture*, J. Amer. Math. Soc. **14** (2001), 941–1006. Available at http://www.math.berkeley.edu/~mhaiman. MR1839919 (**2002c:**14008)

Journal article, online (*continued*)	[Hoo3]	J. Holt: *Multiple bumping of components of deformation spaces of hyperbolic 3-manifolds,* Amer. J. Math. **125** (2003), 691–736. Available at http://muse.jhu.edu/journals/american _journal_of_mathematics/v125/125.4holt .pdf.
Preprint	[HHL]	J. Haglund, M. Haiman, and N. Loehr: *A combinatorial formula for non-symmetric Macdonald polynomials,* preprint (2006), to appear in Amer. J. of Math. Available at arXiv. org/abs/math.CO/0601693.
Other unpublished papers	[Hop96]	M.J. Hopkins: *Course note for elliptic cohomology,* unpublished notes (1996).
	[Hop98]	———: *K(1)-local E_∞ ring spectra,* unpublished notes (1998).
	[Ka]	L.K. Kamenova: *Hyper-Kaehler fibrations and Hilbert schemes,* Ph.D. diss. (2006), MIT.
Book, individual author	[Cro3]	R. Cressman: *Evolutionary Dynamics and Extensive Form Games,* MIT Press, Cambridge, MA, 2003. ▸ If you are citing several works by Cressman, you could name them by their year of publication, such as [Cro7], [Cro2]; or you could number them [Cr1], [Cr2].
Book, multiple authors	[HaSe88]	J.C. Harsany and R. Selten: *A General Theory of Equilibrium Selection in Games,* MIT Press, Cambridge, MA, 1988. MR **89j**:90285
Book, multiple editions	[KVo6]	B. Korte and J. Vygen: *Combinatorial Optimization: Theory and Algorithms,* 3rd ed., Springer-Verlag, Berlin, 2006. MR2171734 (**2006d**:90001)

Book, multivolume	[Kn]	D. Knuth: *The Art of Computer Programming*, 3rd ed., vol. 4, fasc. 3: *Generating All Combinations and Partitions*, Addison-Wesley Professional, Upper Saddle River, NJ, 2005. MR2251472
Chapter in multivolume book	[Py3]	L. Pyber: *Group enumeration and where it leads us*, in *European Congress of Mathematics: Budapest July 22–26, 1996*, vol. 2, Birkhäuser, Basel, 1998. MR **99i**:20037
Book, edited	[DR98] [Na02]	L.A. Dugatkin and H.K. Reeve (eds.): *Game Theory and Animal Behaviour*, Oxford UP, 1998. J. Nash: *The Essential John Nash*, H.W. Kuhn and S. Nasar (eds.), Princeton UP, 2002. MR **2002k**:01044
Chapter in edited book	[Bo98]	I.M. Bomze: *Uniform barriers and evolutionarily stable sets*. In: W. Leinfellner, E. Köhler (eds.), *Game Theory, Experience, Rationality*, Kluwer, Dordrecht, 1998, pp. 225–244. MR **2001h**:91020
Book, online	[PU1]	F. Przytycki and M. Urbański: *Fractals in the Plane—The Ergodic Theory Methods*. Available at http://www.math.unt.edu/~urbanski, to appear in Cambridge UP. ▸ Some authors add an asterisk to denote unpublished works, for example: [PU1*]. The number 1 indicates that there are other cited books by the same coauthors, such as PU2.

TEXT STYLE IN MATHEMATICS

Finally, all math papers (regardless of their citation format) have special rules governing the way to present standard terms such as theorems and proofs, as well as the way to present the text following these terms.

MATHEMATICAL TERM	PROPER FORMAT FOR THIS TERM		TEXT AFTER THE TERM
THEOREM	THEOREM	or **Theorem**	*Italicized*
LEMMA	LEMMA	or **Lemma**	*Italicized*
COROLLARY	COROLLARY	or **Corollary**	*Italicized*
PROOF	*Proof*		Standard, no italics
DEFINITION	*Definition*		Standard, no italics
NOTE	*Note*		Standard, no italics
REMARK	*Remark*		Standard, no italics
OBSERVATION	*Observation*		Standard, no italics
EXAMPLE	*Example*		Standard, no italics

For more details, see Ellen Swanson, *Mathematics into Type,* updated by Arlene O'Sean and Antoinette Schleyer (Providence, RI: American Mathematical Society, 1999). *The Chicago Manual of Style,* chapter 14, provides an alternative guide to formatting. Either is fine as long as you are consistent.

COMPUTER SCIENCE: CITING SOURCE CODE IN PROGRAMMING

Besides citing articles and texts, you should cite others' computer code and algorithms whenever you incorporate them in your own programs. Follow the same principles you do in papers: openly acknowledge the work of others and tell your readers where they can find it. That can be done easily in the comment section. Say who wrote the code segment you are using, the version or date it was written, where to find it, and the date you incorporated it. Be clear about where the borrowed material begins and ends, and explain what changes, if any, you made to it.

There is one exception to this citation requirement. If an algorithm is common knowledge, you don't have to cite it.

15

FAQS ABOUT *ALL* REFERENCE STYLES

. . . .

WHAT SHOULD YOU CITE?

Do I need to cite everything I use in the paper?
Pretty much. Cite anything you rely on for data or authoritative opinions. Cite both quotes and paraphrases. Cite personal communications such as e-mails, interviews, or conversations with professors if you rely on them for your paper. If you rely heavily on any single source, make that clear, either with multiple citations or with somewhat fewer citations plus a clear statement that you are relying on a particular source for a particular topic.

There is one exception. Don't cite sources for facts that are well-known to your audience. It's overkill to cite any authorities for the signing of the Declaration of Independence on July 4, 1776. There will be time enough to footnote them when you start discussing the politics of the Continental Congress.

How many citations does a paper have, anyway?
It varies and there is no exact number, but a couple per page is common in well-researched papers. More is fine. If there are no citations for several pages in a row, something's probably wrong. Most likely, you just forgot to include them. You need to go back and fix the problem.

How many different sources should I use?
That depends on how complicated your subject is, how intensively you've studied it, and how long your paper is. If it is a complex subject or one that is debated intensely, you'll need to reflect that with multiple sources—some to present facts, some to cover different sides of the issue. On the other hand, if it's a short paper on a straightforward topic, you might need only a couple of sources. If you are unsure, ask what your professor ex-

pects for your topic. While you're talking, you might also ask about the best sources to use.

In any case, don't base longer, more complex papers on two or three sources, even if they are very good ones. Your paper should be more than a gloss on others' work (unless it is specifically an analysis of that scholar's work). It should be an original work that stands on its own. Use a variety of sources and make sure they include a range of opinions on any controversial topic.

You certainly don't need to agree with all sides. You are not made of rubber. But, at least for longer papers and hotly debated topics, you need to show that you have read different views, wrestled with varied ideas, and responded to the most important points.

By the way, your notes can be negative citations, as well as positive. You are welcome to disagree openly with a source, or you can simply say, "For an alternative view, see . . ."

WHAT GOES IN A CITATION?

Can I include discussion or analysis in notes?
Yes, for most styles, *except in the sciences.* Footnotes or endnotes are fine spots to add brief insights that bear on your paper topic but would distract from your narrative if they were included in the text. Just remember you still need to edit these discursive notes, just as you do the rest of your writing. And don't let them become a major focus of your writing effort. The text is the main event.

If you use in-text citations such as (Tarcov 2006) and want to add some explanatory notes, you'll have to add them as a special set of citations. They are usually marked with a superscript number.

If you are writing in the sciences and already using superscripts for the citation-sequence system, you're better off avoiding explanatory notes entirely. If you really need to include one or two, mark them with an asterisk or other symbol. In this system, you cannot use numbered citations for anything except references.

I sometimes use articles from *Time* or *Newsweek*. Should they be cited like journal articles or newspaper articles?
That depends on how long and how significant the articles are. Short pieces in newsweeklies are usually treated like newspaper articles. You can

include the author, but you don't have to. Either way, short articles are not usually included in the bibliography. Major articles with author bylines are treated more like journal articles and are included in the bibliography.

Some styles, notably Chicago-style references, use shortened citations after the first citation for an item. What's the best way to shorten a title? There are some standard ways. One is to use only the author's last name: Strunk and White instead of William Strunk Jr. and E. B. White. You also drop the initial article in the title and any other needless words. *The Elements of Style* becomes *Elements of Style.* Drop the edition number and all publishing information, such as the publisher's name. For articles, drop the journal title and volume. So:

Long form	⁹⁹ William Strunk Jr. and E. B. White, *The Elements of Style,* 4th ed. (New York: Longman, 2000), 12.
	¹⁰⁰ Stefan Elbe, "HIV/AIDS and the Changing Landscape of War in Africa," *International Security* 27 (Fall 2002): 159–77.
Short form	¹⁹⁹ Strunk and White, *Elements of Style,* 12.
	²⁰⁰ Elbe, "HIV/AIDS," 162.

The shortened title for Elbe's work might be confusing if your paper dealt mainly with HIV/AIDS and was filled with similar citations. For clarity, you might decide on an alternative short title such as "Landscape of War."

If the title has two parts, put on your surgical gloves and remove the colon.

Long form	⁹⁹ Robert A. Kaster, *Guardians of Language: The Grammarian and Society in Late Antiquity* (Berkeley: University of California Press, 1988).
	¹⁰⁰ Kenneth Shultz and Barry Weingast, "The Democratic Advantage: Institutional Foundations of Financial Power in International Competition," *International Organization* 57 (Winter 2003): 3–42.
Short form	¹⁹⁹ Kaster, *Guardians of Language.*
	²⁰⁰ Shultz and Weingast, "Democratic Advantage."

You might need to shorten a title by identifying a few key words. Take Francis Robinson, ed., *Cambridge Illustrated History of the Islamic World.* There is no single right way to shorten this, but the best title is probably: Robinson, *History of Islamic World.* (Note that Robinson is simply listed as the author; his title as editor is dropped.)

In the first full note, you can also tell readers how you will shorten a title. After giving the full title for Senate Banking Committee hearings on terrorist money laundering, for instance, you might say: (subsequently called "2004 Senate hearings").

What about citing a work I've found in someone else's notes? Do I need to cite the place where I discovered the work?

This issue comes up all the time because it's one of the most important ways we learn about other works and other ideas. Reading a book by E. L. Jones, for example, you find an interesting citation to Adam Smith. As it turns out, you are more interested in Smith's point than in Jones's commentary, so you decide to cite Smith. That's fine—you can certainly cite Smith—but how should you handle it?

There's a choice. One way is to follow the paper trail from Jones's note to Adam Smith's text, read the relevant part, and simply cite it, with no reference at all to Jones. That's completely legitimate for books like Smith's that are well known in their field. You are likely to come across such works in your normal research, and you don't need to cite Jones as the guide who sent you there. To do that honestly, though, you have to go to Smith and read the relevant parts.

The rule is simple: *Cite only texts you have actually used and would have found in the normal course of your research,* not obscure texts used by someone else or works you know about only secondhand. You don't have to read several hundred pages of Adam Smith. You do have to read the relevant pages in Smith—the ones you cite. Remember the basic principle: *When you say you did the work yourself, you actually did it.*

Alternatively, if you don't have time to read Smith yourself (or if the work is written in a language you cannot read), you can cite the text this way: "Smith, *Wealth of Nations*, 123, as discussed in Jones, *The European Miracle*." Normally, you don't need to cite the page in Jones, but you can if you wish. An in-text citation would look different but accomplish the same thing: (Smith 123, qtd. in Jones).

This alternative is completely honest, too. You are referencing Smith's point but saying you found it in Jones. This follows another equally important principle: *When you rely on someone else's work, you cite it.* In this case, you are relying on Jones, not Smith himself, as your source for Smith's point.

Follow the same rule if Jones leads you to a work that is unusual or obscure *to you,* a work you discovered only because Jones did the detailed research, found it, and told you about it. For example, one of Jones's citations is to a 1668 book by Paul Rycaut, entitled *The Present State of the Ottoman Empire.* I'm not an expert on the Ottoman Empire and certainly would not have discovered that book myself. Frankly, I'd never even heard of it until Jones mentioned it. So I'd cite it as (Rycaut 54, cited in Jones). I can do that without going to the Rycaut book. On the other hand, if I were a student of Ottoman history and Jones had simply reminded me of Rycaut's work, I could cite it directly. To do that honestly, however, I would need to go to the Rycaut volume and read the relevant passage.

Some scholars, unfortunately, sneak around this practice. They don't give credit where credit is due. They simply cite Rycaut, even if they've never heard of him before, or they cite Smith, even if they haven't read the passage. One result (and it really happens!) could be that Jones made a mistake in his citation and the next scholar repeated the error. It's really a twofold blunder: an incorrect footnote and a false assertion that the writer used Smith as a source.

The specific rules here are less important than the basic concepts:

- Cite only texts you found in the normal course of your research and have actually used.
- Cite all your sources openly and honestly.

Follow these and you'll do just fine.

BIBLIOGRAPHY

Do I need to have a bibliography?

Yes, for all styles *except* complete Chicago notes. If you use complete Chicago citations, not the short versions, the first note for each item gives readers complete information, including the title and publisher, so you don't need a bibliography. (You are welcome to include a bibliography if you use Chicago style, but you don't have to, unless your professor requires it.)

All other styles require a bibliography for a simple reason. The notes themselves are too brief to describe the sources fully.

Should my bibliography include the general background reading I did for the paper?

The answer depends on how much you relied on a particular reading and which reference style you use. MLA, APA, and science bibliographies include only the works you have actually cited. Chicago-style bibliographies are more flexible and can include works you haven't cited in a note.

My advice is this: If a work was really useful to you, then check to make sure you have acknowledged that debt somewhere with a citation. After you've cited it once, the work will appear in your bibliography, regardless of which style you use. If a particular background reading wasn't important in your research, don't worry about citing it.

Does the bibliography raise any questions about my work?
Yes, readers will scan your bibliography to see what kinds of sources you used and whether they are the best ones. There are five problems to watch out for:

- Old, out-of-date works
- Bias in the overall bibliography
- Omission of major works in your subject
- Reliance on poor or weak sources
- Excessive reliance on one or two sources

These are not really problems with the bibliography, as such. They are problems with the text that become apparent by looking at the bibliography.

Old sources are great for some purposes but antiquated for others. Many consider Gibbon's *Decline and Fall of the Roman Empire* the greatest historical work ever written. But no one today would use it as a major secondary source on Rome or Byzantium. Too much impressive research has been completed in the two centuries since Gibbon wrote. So, if you were writing about current views of Byzantium or ancient Rome, *Decline and Fall* would be out-of-date. Relying on it would cast a shadow on your research. On the other hand, if you were writing about great historical works, eighteenth-century perspectives, or changing views about Byzantium, using Gibbon would be perfectly appropriate, perhaps essential.

"Old" means different things in different fields. A work published ten or fifteen years ago might be reasonably current in history, literature, and some areas of mathematics, depending on how fast those fields are changing. For a discipline moving at warp speed like genetics, an article might be out-of-date within a year. A paper in molecular genetics filled with citations from 1994 or even 2004 would cast serious doubt on the entire project. Whatever your field, you should rely on the best works and make sure they have not been superseded by newer, better research.

Bias, omission of key works, and overreliance on a few sources reveal other problems.[1] Bias means you have looked at only one side of a multi-faceted issue. Your bibliography might indicate bias if it lists readings on only one side of a contested issue. Omitting an authoritative work not only impoverishes your work; it leaves readers wondering if you studied the topic carefully.

The remedy for all these problems is the same. For longer, more complex papers, at least, you need to read a variety of major works in your subject and indicate that with citations.

However long (or short!) your paper, make sure your sources are considered solid and reliable. Your professors and teaching assistants can really help here. They know the literature and should be valuable guides.

QUOTATIONS

I am using a quotation that contains a second quote within it. How do I handle the citation?

Let's say your paper includes the following sentence:

> According to David M. Kennedy, Roosevelt began his new presidency "by reassuring his countrymen that 'this great nation will endure as it has endured, will revive and will prosper. . . . The only thing we have to fear . . . is fear itself.'"

Of course, you'll cite Kennedy, but do you need to cite *his* source for the Roosevelt quote? No. It's not required. In some cases, however, your readers will benefit from a little extra information about the quote within a quote. You can easily do that in your footnote or endnote:

[99] Kennedy, *Freedom from Fear,* 134. The Roosevelt quote comes from his 1933 inaugural address.

I am quoting from some Spanish and French books and doing the translations myself. How should I handle the citations?

Just include the words "my translation" immediately after the quote or in the citation. You don't need to do this each time. After the first quotation,

---

1. Ralph Berry, *The Research Project: How to Write It* (London: Routledge, 2000), 108–9.

you can tell your readers that you are translating all quotes yourself. Then cite the foreign-language text you are using.

In some papers, you might want to include quotes in both the original and translation. That's fine. Either the translation or the original can come first; the other follows in parentheses or brackets. For instance:

> In Madame Pompadour's famous phrase, "Après nous, le déluge." (After us, the flood.) As it turned out, she was right.

ELECTRONIC MATERIALS AND MICROFILM

Some citations list "microfilm." Others list "microform" or "microfiche." What's the difference? Do I need to mention any of them in my citations?

They are all tiny photographic images, read with magnifying tools. Libraries use these formats to save money and storage space for large document collections. *All* these images are called *microforms,* no matter what material they are stored on. When they are stored on reels of film, they're called *microfilm.* When they are stored on plastic sheets or cards, they're called *microfiche.*

When you use materials that have been photographically reduced like this, you should say so in the citation, just as you do for Web sites or electronic information. (If the microforms simply reproduce printed material exactly, some citation styles allow you to cite the printed material directly. But you are always safe if you mention that you read it on microfilm or microfiche. The same is true for citing print items that are reproduced electronically.)

The URL I'm citing is long and needs to go on two lines. How do I handle the line break?

Here's the technical answer. If the URL takes up more than one line, break *after* a

- slash
- double slash

break *before* a

- period
- comma

- question mark
- tilde (~)
- ampersand (&)
- hyphen
- underline
- number sign

Here are some examples:

Full URL	http://www.charleslipson.com/index.htm
Break after slash	http://www. charleslipson.com/ index.htm
Break before other *punctuation*	http://www.charleslipson .com/index.htm

These "break rules" apply to all citation styles.

There's a rationale for these rules. If periods, commas, or hyphens come at the end of a line, they might be mistaken for punctuation marks. By contrast, when they come at the beginning of a line, they are clearly part of the URL. To avoid confusion, don't add hyphens to break long words in the URL.

You can produce such breaks in two ways. One is to insert a line break by pressing the shift-enter keys simultaneously, at least on Windows-based systems. Alternatively, you can insert a space in the URL so your

Tips on citing Web pages: As you take notes, write down the

- URL for the Web site or Web page
- Name or description of the page or site
- Date you accessed it

Writing the name or description of a Web site is useful because if the URL changes (as they sometimes do), you still can find it by searching.

As for the access date, some citation styles, such as APA and MLA, require it. Others, such as *The Chicago Manual of Style,* make it optional. They tell you to include it only when it's relevant, such as for time-sensitive data.

If sites are particularly useful, add them to your "favorites" list. If you add several sites for a paper, create a new category (or folder) named for the paper and drop the URLs into that. A folder will gather the sites in a single location and keep them from getting lost in your long list of favorites.

word-processing program automatically wraps the URL onto two lines. (Without such a space, the word processor would force the entire URL onto one line.)

Even though you are technically allowed to break URLs before periods, commas, and hyphens, I try to avoid such breaks because these punctuation marks are easy to overlook and confuse readers. Instead, I try to break only after a slash or double slash, and then only when I am printing the final version of the paper. When I'm sending it electronically, I try to avoid breaks altogether. That way, the recipient will have "live" hyperlinks to click on.

SCIENCE CITATIONS

In the sciences, some citations include terms like DOI, PII, and PMID. What are they? Do I need to include them in my citations?
They identify articles within large electronic databases. Just like other parts of your citations, they help readers locate articles and data you have used. In fact, you may use them yourself to return to an article for more research.

Not every scientific journal includes them in citations or lists them for its own articles. Some do; some don't. My advice: When you do research, write the numbers down and consider including them in your own citations. They appear at the very end of each citation, right after the pagination and URL.

What do the various letters mean? DOI stands for digital object identifier. It's an international system for identifying and exchanging digital intellectual property. Like a URL, it can be used to locate an item. Unlike a URL, it remains the same, even if the item is moved to a new location.

PII stands for publisher item identifier. It, too, identifies the article and can be used for search and retrieval.

PMID appears in many medical and biological journals. It stands for PubMed identification. The PubMed database includes virtually all biomedical journals plus some preprints. It is available online at www.ncbi .nlm.nih.gov/entrez and has a tutorial for new users. This invaluable database was developed by the National Center for Biotechnology Information at the National Library of Medicine.

Other specialized fields have their own electronic identifiers. MR, for example, refers to articles in the Mathematical Reviews database. Physics has identifying numbers for preprints (prepublication articles), which classifies them by subfield.

You are not required to list any of these electronic identifiers in your citations, but doing so may help you and your readers.

In the sciences, I'm supposed to abbreviate journal titles. Where do I find these abbreviations?
The easiest way is to look at the first page of the article you are citing. It usually includes the abbreviation and often the full citation for the article. You can also go to various Web sites assembled by reference librarians, listing journal abbreviations in many fields. One useful site is "All That JAS: Journal Abbreviation Sources," compiled and maintained by Gerry McKiernan, Science and Technology Librarian and Bibliographer at Iowa State, http://www.public.iastate.edu/~CYBERSTACKS/JAS.htm.

THANKS

. . . .

Since this book covers citations and academic honesty across the university, it was essential to speak with specialists from different fields. I was fortunate to receive advice on science labs from Tom Christianson, Nancy Schwartz, and Paul Streileman (biological sciences), Vera Dragisich (chemistry), and Stuart Gazes (physics). All of them head lab programs at the University of Chicago. Diane Herrmann, who heads the undergraduate major in mathematics, offered a number of valuable comments about study groups. So did biologist Michael LaBarbera, who reviewed the chapter on academic honesty. For language learning, I spoke with Vincent Bertolini, Helma Dik, and Peter White, all at Chicago, and Robert Kaster at Princeton. For honor codes, I spoke with Susan Pratt Rosato and Keir Lieber, both of Notre Dame. William S. Strong, who handles copyright law for the University of Chicago Press, and Perry Cartwright, who handles contractual rights for the Press, offered wise counsel on the complex issues of plagiarism. Gerald Rosenberg, my colleague at Chicago and an expert in both law and politics, told me which legal citations would be most useful to students. James Marquardt, of Lake Forest College, offered thoughtful ideas about class participation. Physicist Thomas Rosenbaum, the University of Chicago's provost, gave helpful comments on several chapters. George Gavrilis, of the University of Texas at Austin, made the helpful suggestion that the second edition include a chapter on taking notes.

On all these issues, I spoke with students. I'd particularly like to thank Erik Cameron, an undergraduate at Reed College, and John Schuessler, a graduate of Notre Dame, for their thoughts on honor codes; Jonathan Grossberg, a graduate of Cornell and now a student at its law school, for his suggestions about effective study groups; and Jennifer London, a graduate student at Chicago, for her ideas about learning languages.

I checked all citation materials with experts, beginning with editors at *The Chicago Manual of Style*. I particularly wish to thank Linda Halvorson, who improved every aspect of this work and offered encouragement at every turn. Christopher Rhodes of the University of Chicago Press worked closely with me through the entire process. So did Mary Laur, who also produced the index. Jenni Fry offered very useful, detailed comments on several citation issues. For science citations, I was assisted by editors who supervise style manuals for two professional associations: Janet Dodd (chemistry) and Karen J. Patrias and Peggy Robinson (biological sciences). For astrophysics and astronomy, I received help from Sharon Jennings. Peggy Perkins, one of the key editors for the *Chicago Manual,* offered numerous ideas to improve the text and read the citation chapters with special care. The manuscript editor, Erin DeWitt, went through the entire volume with meticulous attention. Finally, my thanks to editor Paul Schellinger, who oversaw all aspects of the second edition with exemplary professionalism.

On general issues of academic honesty, I spoke with advisers, counselors, and deans who handle these issues every day. Special thanks go to Susan Art, the University of Chicago's dean of students, and Jean Treese, associate dean of students and longtime head of the college's Orientation Program.

In their different jobs, they all promote genuine learning and honest accomplishments, the heart of a college education. Their generous help made this book possible.

INDEX

. . . .